To General Polyakov
And to the others
Who were executed or imprisoned
And to their families

CIRCLE
OF
TREASON

CIRCLE
OF
TREASON

A CIA ACCOUNT OF
TRAITOR ALDRICH AMES
AND THE MEN HE BETRAYED

SANDRA GRIMES AND **JEANNE VERTEFEUILLE**

NAVAL INSTITUTE PRESS
Annapolis, Maryland

Naval Institute Press
291 Wood Road
Annapolis, MD 21402

First Naval Institute Press paperback edition published in 2013.
ISBN: 978-1-59114-396-3 (paperback)
ISBN: 978-1-61251-305-8 (eBook)

Library of Congress Cataloging-in-Publication Data
Grimes, Sandra.
  Circle of treason : a CIA account of traitor Aldrich Ames and the men
he betrayed / Sandra Grimes and Jeanne Vertefeuille.
     p. cm.
  Includes bibliographical references and index.
  ISBN 978-1-59114-334-5 (hardcover : alk. paper) 1. Ames, Aldrich Hazen,
1941– 2. United States. Central Intelligence Agency. 3. United States. Federal
Bureau of Investigation. 4. Intelligence officers—United States—Biography.
5. Espionage—United States. 6. Intelligence service—United States.
I. Vertefeuille, Jeanne. II. Title.
  JK468.I6G76 2012
  364.1'31—dc23
                          2012024310

♾ This paper meets the requirements of ANSI/NISO z39.48-1992
(Permanence of Paper).

Printed in the United States of America.

21 20 19 18 17 16   9 8 7 6

CONTENTS

PREFACE

MANY BOOKS HAVE BEEN WRITTEN about Cold War espionage in general, or about particular aspects, cases, or periods. The great majority of these books suffer from the same deficiency—they are written by outsiders with an imperfect knowledge of the main organizations, methods of operation, and personalities involved in this struggle. Other books, whether written by outsiders or insiders, also suffer from being written by persons with an axe to grind, or who are besotted by a pet theory, or are simply more interested in producing a marketable commodity than in searching for truth and accuracy.

This book attempts to avoid these pitfalls. It is written by insiders. The authors can speak with authority and in detail about the CIA's operations against the Soviet—and to a lesser degree, the East European—target. We were there, starting at the bottom but working up into increasingly responsible positions. Also, we were at the center of what became the Ames mole hunt. The book mainly covers the period 1961–94, the years of our greatest personal involvement.

The reader may wonder why we have chosen to air material previously considered classified. We wish to emphasize that we are not "leakers." All of our contacts with the media stem from a project conceived by the Agency to tell its side of the Ames story. After Ames was arrested in February 1994, the FBI, as is customary for that organization, launched a campaign to let the public know of their success. In the Agency's view, the decisive CIA contribution to this roll-up was getting lost. Therefore, it was decided that five of us—Sandy, Jeanne, Paul Redmond, Dan Payne, and Diana Worthen—would be tasked to participate in media interviews on the subject of the CIA's operations against the Soviet target, the devastation wrought by Ames, and our investigative efforts, which resulted in his identification as a Soviet mole. All of our early contacts took place on Agency premises and were monitored by an Agency official. Some were taped. Initially this project made us quite uneasy because we are of the old school and had been indoctrinated with the dictum that one was to avoid the media at all costs. Later we became more comfortable with the idea and continued to cooperate in selected interviews, but all of our media contacts were approved in advance.

The reader may also wonder why we have chosen certain KGB and GRU operations for extended treatment, while providing only a cursory summary for others. Throughout we have tried to adhere to one criterion: Is the information we are including already known to the KGB and its successors because of the treason of Ames, Hanssen, Howard, and the others? When this holds true, we have seen no reason to withhold it from the general reader. On the other hand, when it comes to information we believe the opposition does not know or that could prove harmful to certain individuals, we have suppressed it in our book even though sometimes it would add useful background to our story.

With this limitation in mind, we generally chose those cases that were the most significant in terms of intelligence and counterintelligence production, those in which we had the most personal engagement, those that were intrinsically the most interesting, and those where the Soviet participant paid for his involvement with his life. We regret that, with the exception of Tolkachev, we have not been able to give more coverage to the great majority of those cases that did not involve intelligence officers. While some of them were significant in the Agency's overall Cold War effort, we in the counterintelligence world often did not focus on them. We also have omitted East European cases, though some of them were of major importance and some of their stories would make fascinating reading, again because we did not focus on them on a continuing basis.

On the reverse side, our discussion of the U.S. intelligence officers who volunteered to the KGB is limited to Ames, Hanssen, and—to a lesser degree—Howard. We have not covered Richard Miller and Earl Pitts of the FBI or Harold ("Jim") Nicholson of the CIA, despite the fact that all of them have served prison time for their espionage activities. While they certainly did cause damage, compared to Ames and Hanssen they are minor players.

The authors make no pretense of neutrality. We have our opinions, and have expressed them as warranted. However, we have tried to be scrupulous about separating fact from opinion and have made every effort to concentrate on the former. Also, we have attempted to avoid writing a book overly concerned with exposing or "getting back" at those whose beliefs and actions have, in our minds, taken the CIA down the wrong track in its Soviet operations, sometimes with tragic consequences. This material does appear when it is pertinent, but for the most part it has not been given undue emphasis. Our purpose has been to give a balanced, in-depth depiction of our operations with as much accuracy as we can command. We believe that we have a story well worth telling.

As might be expected, the two authors do not agree on every point. Where the differences are significant, they have been included.

A few definitions are in order at the outset. "Counterintelligence" and "counterespionage" have been defined and redefined to the point of exhaustion over the past decades. Nonetheless, sometimes they are employed interchangeably. This book will generally use the term counterintelligence or CI. In our context CI includes all the efforts, both defensive and offensive, used to counter the attempts by foreign governments and their intelligence services to penetrate our government or to neutralize the clandestine activities of our government.

The offensive aspect of CI is exemplified by CIA and FBI recruitment of foreign intelligence officers, thus becoming privy to their services' operations. The defensive aspect includes such mundane practices as security clearances and need-to-know compartmentation, but focuses most strongly on organized attempts to uncover the moles among us.

Two other necessary definitions: This book examines at length our activities vis-à-vis the two Soviet intelligence services. These services are the KGB and the GRU. The KGB has had many names since the 1917 Bolshevik revolution: Cheka, OGPU, NKVD, and so on. Its function has been to preserve the security of the Soviet state and it has interpreted its mandate in the broadest sense. In 1954 it took the name KGB, from the initials for the Russians words for Committee of State Security, and retained that title during most of the period covered in this book. In 1991, the KGB was broken into several distinct organizations. The foreign operations component of the KGB became the SVR, from the Russian initials for Foreign Intelligence Service, while the main internal counterintelligence component became the FSB, or Federal Security Service. For simplicity's sake, however, we will use "KGB" throughout our text.

The GRU's name is derived from the Russian words for Main Intelligence Directorate and it is a component of the General Staff of the Ministry of Defense. It has changed little in form or function since the end of World War II, its mission being now as always the collection of strategic intelligence. It does not have a CI role, and does not target foreign intelligence services, but it has run a number of very successful operations against the U.S. government over the years, obtaining valuable information, primarily in the military and scientific/technical fields.

A note about transliteration: The majority of the Russian names have been translated from the Cyrillic using the National Geographic Board on Geographic Names. This was the standard used by the CIA's Directorate of Operations during the period under discussion. However, in a few instances where the individual has carved out an identity in the West we have used the transliteration preferred by this individual. Therefore, we use Gordievsky, not Gordiyevskiy and Andrei, not Andrey, Poleshchuk.

The CIA's Publications Review Board (PRB) is responsible for clearing any texts written by former CIA officers. They require the following disclaimer: All statements of fact, opinion, or analysis expressed are those of the authors and do not reflect the official positions or views of the CIA or any other U.S. government agency. Nothing in the contents should be construed as asserting or implying U.S. government authentication of information or Agency endorsement of the author's views. This material has been reviewed by the CIA to prevent the disclosure of classified information.

In general our experience with the PRB has been a frustrating one. Although more than 90 percent of the disputed issues were eventually resolved in our favor, and the book below reads essentially as it was originally conceived, it took us more than three long years to come to terms. Some of the requests for deletions were valid and we made them without quibbling, but, in our view, others stemmed from flaws in the process itself.

Finally, we could not have written this book without some help from our former colleagues. We consulted Dick C, Myrna Fitzgerald, Bob Fulton, Burton Gerber, Walt Lomac, Len and Faith McCoy, Dan Payne, Jack Platt, Andrei and Svetlana Poleshchuk, Paul Redmond, Dick Stolz, Diana Worthen, and some others who prefer to remain anonymous. This includes those who graciously provided access to their personal archives. All of them have our gratitude. We owe a special vote of thanks to Gary Grimes, who plowed through our numerous drafts and offered balanced commentary.

CHAPTER 1

JEANNE'S STORY

OCTOBER 1954. THE KOREAN WAR WAS OVER, and we had not yet become embroiled in Vietnam. I had graduated from the University of Connecticut in the spring. The job fair representatives who visited the campus during my senior year included one from the CIA. He spoke very vaguely about what the Agency did, but indicated that there would be possibilities for travel. This was what I wanted to hear. A typical product of the 1950s, I thought only in passing about equal rights for women and had no overriding visions of a rewarding professional career. My major goal was to work and live abroad, preferably in Europe.

The representative told me that the only openings he had for women were clerical, and he urged me to acquire secretarial skills. Thus after graduation I went to business school and learned how to type and take shorthand while awaiting the call from the CIA to tell me if I had been accepted.

When that call came, I took the train to Washington. My first assignment was in the unclassified typing pool, where a group of newly hired young women typed 3×5 cards listing North Korean scientists, as their names appeared in professional journals. Probably we got a lot of the names wrong, but it didn't seem to matter. We were marking time until we were called for our polygraphs and, if we passed, given a real assignment. I did pass, after having a philosophical argument about whether

Chiang Kai-shek was a boon to China, and whether one could characterize the Communists as agrarian reformers. My answers must have been
reasonably orthodox; in any event I had studied Far Eastern history in
college, and knew more about the subject than my examiner.

As part of the assignment process, I was asked if I would be interested
in serving overseas and, if so, where. "Europe" was my first answer, but the
personnel officer successfully got me to add that I would not rule out a
posting in some other part of the world. Shortly thereafter, my assignment came through: the Near East and African Division.

After I had worked there for a short time, the personnel officer offered
me a position as an administrative assistant in an outpost in French West
Africa. I did not know where it was, and neither did the personnel officer,
but we hunted it down on a map. And, after mulling it over for a day or
two, I said I would go.

In those days, a woman's educational background and linguistic
accomplishments meant nothing. I minored in German in college, with
six years of that language under my belt. I also had two years of French,
but my command of it was pretty shaky. However, the only criterion was
the ability to type, and that I could certainly do.

Fortunately, there was a hitch in the assignment, so I got to spend
almost a year in Washington before heading overseas. My friends and I
were all short of money, but managed to do our share of sightseeing and
partying. In those days the CIA was located in World War II temporary
barracks downtown, along the reflecting pool between Constitution and
Independence Avenues, so we were right in the thick of things. I traveled
by bus to work and, in those more innocent days, while waiting at the bus
stop on Constitution to go home, I would sometimes see President
Eisenhower on the golf green behind the White House practicing his putting. Among my most pleasant memories is taking my ice skates to work
in the winter, and skating on the reflecting pool during my lunch hour.

Two agreeable years in West Africa followed. I had an excellent Chief
of Station, John Edwards. A Harvard-educated gentleman of the old
school and a veteran of World War I and World War II, he had spent the
interwar years in France or Francophone countries in Africa and spoke
polished French. Under his tutelage my French became reasonably fluent.
He was an indulgent boss and let me do a lot of traveling around West
Africa. My longest and most adventurous trip was by train to Bamako,

Mali, and then by boat around the northern bend of the Niger River, with stops at exotic places like Mopti, Djenne, and Timbuktu.

The West African tour also gave me a different perspective on life. For the first time, being white put me in the minority. This struck me when I first got off the plane and it took a while before I became comfortable with the concept.

However, once I settled in I enjoyed Africa so much that I asked for a second assignment there. This time East Africa was my destination.

The East African post had its pleasant aspects. At an altitude of more than seven thousand feet, the climate was excellent and flowers bloomed year-round. Also, we were above the zone of malaria-carrying mosquitoes, poisonous snakes, and similar tropical health hazards. Sometimes we took a weekend break, going down the edge of the Great Rift Valley to the Red Sea to swim and snorkel. It was a hazardous two-hour journey, over a narrow road with more than one hundred hairpin turns, but the views were magnificent. Often we encountered baboons and dik-diks (a tiny gazelle), on the way and giant manta rays were a common sight once we reached the sea.

The only downside to this tour was that I did not get on with my boss, and there were only the two of us. Anyway, despite the after-hours and weekend adventures, I was beginning to have enough of working in Africa. As my tour wound to its end, I was offered a job in yet another African post. The duties would be the same clerical and administrative ones that I had been carrying out for years, only this time I would also be expected to be the Chief of Station's interpreter because the designated officer did not speak French!

By now I had developed some rudimentary career goals, and this did not sound like it would be a satisfying assignment. Furthermore, it was the African component's policy (freely expressed in those days) not to promote women above GS-07. I had attained that grade long ago. Looking for advancement, I sought a job outside of Africa, and found one—in Helsinki, Finland. Not only would this give me the opportunity to see a different part of the world, the job was rated as GS-09, one of the few such slots available to women then, although the situation was beginning to change.

Operationally, Finland was much more active than the African posts where I had served. Because the country bordered the USSR, the CIA in

Helsinki concentrated all its efforts on the Soviet target—a target on which I now began to gain some expertise. My routine duties included keeping the REDCAP notebook—a comprehensive listing of all the Soviet officials in the country—up to date. I developed some familiarity with Russian names, organizations, career patterns, indications of intelligence affiliation, and like details. Moreover, I became personally involved in a controversial and fascinating case, which was a hallmark of the Angletonian era. (James Jesus Angleton, of whom much will be said below, was Chief of the CIA's counterintelligence staff from 1954 until 1974.) In December 1961, KGB counterintelligence officer Anatoliy Mikhaylovich Golitsyn, with his wife and small daughter, appeared on the doorstep of CIA Station Chief Frank Friberg and announced his unalterable intention to defect. Friberg, an intelligent and decisive officer, immediately contacted Steve W and me.

Friberg gave us our marching orders. Steve was to take the passports of the Golitsyn family to the Embassy and issue them U.S. visas. Luckily, Steve was able to do this without raising any immediate questions. I was told to go to the office and get cash for the travel of Frank and the Golitsyn family. Responsibility for office funds was part of my normal administrative duties, and therefore I could get into the strongbox where we kept our money.

I immediately drove to the office, opened the strongbox, pulled out wads of currency without counting, and then proceeded as fast as I could to the airport where Frank had told Steve and me to meet him. Because this was December, snow was piled up along the streets. I recall driving up and over a cement tram stop in my Volkswagen beetle in my haste. Luckily no policeman was around to observe this illegal and bone-jarring maneuver.

Steve drove up to the departure terminal with the Golitsyn passports, and I arrived with money for their tickets and other expenses. Friberg and the Golitsyns then emplaned for Stockholm, on their way to Frankfurt and then the United States. Needless to say, my accountings did not balance that month, but Headquarters wrote off the rather large discrepancy without a murmur.

We will return to the Golitsyn story in later chapters. For now it suffices to mention that, at first, Golitsyn was debriefed by the Soviet Bloc Division at Headquarters but soon came into the hands of the CI staff.

We in Helsinki became more and more frustrated because Golitsyn had served for over a year in Helsinki and could tell us a great deal about KGB activities in Finland, yet this did not seem to be a major thrust of the debriefings and the debriefers seemed to know little about things Finnish. Eventually, much later, we got one long debriefing report that contained answers to some of the questions we had asked, but significant gaps remained.[1] Two items of information provided by Golitsyn allowed me to assess my budding skills as a counterintelligence analyst. I won one and lost one. In the first case, one of the Embassy components had wanted to hire a young woman as a secretary. She had a Russian émigré background. Further, she seemed overskilled for the position she was to fill. I advised against hiring her, and while there was some heartburn she was not brought on board. According to Golitsyn, she had indeed been sent by the KGB to penetrate the Embassy.

In the second case, we had learned that one of the Finnish employees of the U.S. embassy had made an unreported trip to Leningrad. He would have needed a Russian visa and Golitsyn, who was under consular cover, was the logical person to have issued it. We then learned that Golitsyn had traveled to Leningrad at the same time as our employee. Putting two and two together, and getting five, we called in the employee, questioned him about his trip, and eventually saw to it that he was fired. Now we learned from Golitsyn that the employee had been loyal while employed. Golitsyn had tried to recruit him in Leningrad, but had been turned down. Unfortunately, after we fired him, he changed his mind, recontacted Golitsyn, and told the KGB officer everything he could about what he had learned during his Embassy employment.

I spent more than four years in Helsinki. Late in my tour, it became obvious that professional career possibilities for women were opening up. Women were permitted to apply for the Career Training course, the gateway to officer status. There were limitations, however. In the Directorate of Operations (DO), women were accepted for only two career tracks— analyst or reports officer. We were not allowed to take the long course that teaches one to become an operations officer, and we were barred from paramilitary training. And there was no parity in numbers. We were seven women out of a total class of sixty-six.

Nonetheless, it was a rewarding and broadening experience. Given my interest in the Soviet target, perhaps the highlight of my training was the three-hour spellbinding lecture given by George Kisevalter concerning his participation in the Popov case. (Petr Semenovich Popov was a GRU officer who volunteered to us in Vienna in 1953. Kisevalter, a fluent Russian speaker and a legend throughout his career, was one of his handlers.)[2]

After successfully finishing the Career Training course, I headed back overseas, this time to the Benelux area. Arriving in the summer of 1966, I spent more than four years in a relaxed environment, working as an analyst against the Soviet target and spending as much time as possible in travels around Europe. Toward the end of this tour, I realized that I needed to spend some time at headquarters. In close to twenty years I had never had a headquarters assignment. Furthermore, my parents were aging. I had not been able to see much of them in recent years and this was an omission I wished to correct.

My first headquarters assignment was as Chief of the Biographics Branch in what was then the Soviet Bloc (SB), but soon to become the Soviet and East European (SE), Division. This was the largest branch in the Division, but among the least prestigious because it was not directly involved in operations. Our mission was to process thousands of trace replies on Soviet and East European officials for our Stations abroad and for friendly liaison services. Unfortunately for branch morale, if our initial research turned up data indicating that a particular individual was of special interest, the trace reply was taken out of our hands and we never heard what happened next.

During this period, for personal enrichment and to add to my professional skills, I began to study Russian. I took a Directorate of Intelligence course, which was geared to enabling analysts to read Russian in their areas of specialization. The years that I spent in this endeavor eventually paid off, because I was able to translate or edit some of the documents provided by GRU general Dmitriy Polyakov, by KGB defector Anatoliy Bogatyy, and by the French source Vladimir Vetrov, known as FAREWELL.

After more than three years as Chief of the Biographics Branch, I was eager for a change. I applied for a job as night and weekend duty officer for the Directorate of Operations, and was only the second woman ever approved for this position. It was tiring work, because we changed shifts from week to week, but since we reviewed priority operational traffic from around the world I developed a broader view of the Agency's responsibilities. As it happened, my service covered the period of the fall of Vietnam.

The DO duty officer stint only lasted six months. By then I was looking for a normal day job. When I was offered a position in the Counterintelligence Group of SE Division, I couldn't have been happier. The slot was that of Deputy Chief of the Research Branch, under Joseph F, a seasoned officer with a compendious knowledge of the KGB. My specific task was to write a study on the GRU. It took about eighteen months to complete this study, which was eventually published for DO consumption in November 1976 under the title The GRU Today.

While writing this study I first became privy to the Polyakov case and the fount of information he had provided. Luckily in the early 1970s we had three junior officer defectors from the GRU. While what they told us was of some interest, their production could not compare with that of Polyakov. They provided "cover," however, in that the average reader of The GRU Today would be inclined to believe that these three defectors were the source of much of the material presented. In reality, of course, Polyakov's information formed the backbone of the study. It was during the writing of this study that I first began my professional association with Sandy, who was the Agency's expert when it came to Polyakov.

By now it was the late 1970s. The Division had become aware that the U.S. intelligence community had a need for counterintelligence information, but most of what was available to us was not being disseminated outside the DO, except perhaps to the FBI. To correct this shortcoming, two new branches were established in the Counterintelligence Group. One, headed by Faith McCoy, disseminated CI reporting from Soviet sources. The other, to which I was named Chief, did the same for East European sources. This arrangement lasted for about one year. Faith then left for an overseas position, the two CI production branches were melded into one, and I became chief of CI production for all of the Division's stable of sources.

This was a responsible and rewarding job. Some of our disseminations went to the White House. The only drawback was the looming presence of Director Casey and his preconceived ideas, and his attempts to influence operations and analysis to fit these ideas.

Two Directorate of Intelligence projects closely involved the Production Branch. The first was the investigation into the possibility that the

Soviet Union had masterminded the 1981 assassination attempt on the Pope. Despite the fact that all our clandestine reporting pointed to the conclusion that the Soviets were not involved, and despite the fact that the scenario did not jibe in the least with what we knew of KGB methods of operation, there was an attempt to make the facts fit the theory so we could use the possibility of Soviet involvement as a club with which to beat the KGB.

I felt extremely frustrated when one of the officers in our branch wrote a long cable in response to a field inquiry. The cable pointed out what we did and did not know, and what conclusions it might be possible to draw. The cable got as far as the office of the then–Deputy Director for Operations (DDO) John Stein, where it was substantially altered so as to advise the field to use the unsupported theory against the KGB, whether we believed it or not. (I often argued, usually unsuccessfully, that the KGB had done a great many unsavory things, and that we should do our best to publicize these, instead of using information we knew or suspected was false, thereby lowering ourselves to their level.)

The second investigation involved the extent of Soviet support for terrorism. To hear some tell it, behind every terrorist around the world with a bomb in his hand was a KGB officer whispering "Go!" The Soviets had dug themselves somewhat into a hole on this subject, because it was indisputable that they had supported Yasir Arafat in the period when he was masterminding terrorist acts. Arafat was regarded as a "freedom fighter" and could be seen on the Kremlin stand with Brezhnev and others on special occasions. The Soviets also supported some third-world groups, again regarding them as freedom fighters against rightist governments. All this was extrapolated into an overarching conspiracy theory by CIA fundamentalists, in great part influenced by Casey and his good friend Claire Sterling's highly inaccurate *The Terrorist Network*.

Once again, I was disheartened by what I saw as attempts to skew the facts. Finally, I felt I had to get away. I applied for an overseas job, any job. John Stein saw to it that I was assigned as Chief in Libreville, Gabon, although Africa Division was not happy to have me and never provided any support during my two years on post. I enjoyed being back in Africa, but Libreville was a drowsy town in a country of little strategic interest. There were few real targets, and those that existed had been extensively worked over by my predecessor. Getting up in the morning, I would often admit to myself that nothing that I was going to do that day was of any substantial interest to the U.S. government. (The CIA eventually closed the post.)

There were some highlights, however. I thoroughly enjoyed visiting Peace Corps personnel in the various villages. In many people's opinion, including my own, the Peace Corps was the most valuable export that the United States could make to Africa.

One of the most memorable events of this tour was a safari to northern Cameroon. It was the dry season and there were few watering holes. Those that existed were magnets for large numbers of animals. At one watering hole we saw elephants far and near stretched across the horizon, some standing guard while others drank and bathed, and then changing places. It was a healthy herd, or group of herds, ranging from large old animals to toddling babies. This is one of my most vivid and treasured recollections, and for years photographs from this safari decorated my office walls.

In the summer of 1986, as my assignment in Libreville was coming to an end, I received a cable from Gus Hathaway, who had become Chief of the CI Staff. I admired Hathaway, whom I had first known when he was Chief of Station in Moscow in the late 1970s. He then became Chief of SE Division, and in effect my ultimate boss for some years. Gus' cable was vague, but he asked me to come to the staff to look into a CI problem. I accepted with alacrity. The rest of my story is entwined with what became the Ames mole hunt, and is discussed in detail in later chapters.

Overall, despite a few down periods, I had a successful and rewarding career in the CIA, and would do it all again. I entered on duty as a GS-4, never skipped a grade, and retired as a Senior Intelligence Officer, level three. Promotions do not tell the whole story, however. Along the way, I was associated with some first-class colleagues, whose expertise and work ethic enabled us to meet our goals, and with some bosses who gave me the opportunity to spread my wings. I think of them all with affection and respect.

Since my 1992 retirement, I have received a great deal of ego gratification in public acknowledgment of the success our group had in uncovering Ames as a Soviet mole. While this appreciation is undoubtedly pleasant, the approbation of trusted colleagues is far more important to me.

SANDY'S STORY

I WAS A CERTIFIED PRODUCT OF THE COLD WAR—born in August 1945, and the daughter of parents who met and married in Oak Ridge, Tennessee, while employed on the Manhattan Project. My formal schooling began in Los Alamos, the home of the atomic bomb in the Sandia Mountains of New Mexico, followed by a subsequent move to a suburb of Denver, Colorado, where I attended public schools until leaving for college in 1963.

It was there during high school that I made a decision that, unknown to me at the time, set the direction of my personal and professional future. That decision was to substitute a Russian language course for the dreaded junior year of physics, having recognized that physics was beyond my abilities in spite of the family genes. Taught by a stern taskmaster, Dr. Libor Brom, I enjoyed the class, the challenge of the language, and in 1961 the oddity of being a female in such a course. Due to Dr. Brom's encouragement and my lack of any other plan, two years later I selected Russian as my college major and the University of Washington in Seattle as my school of choice given its Slavic languages department.

The circumstances of my joining the CIA four years later were purely serendipitous. It was not out of a patriotic duty to serve my country, a desire to travel, or to join friends or acquaintances. Rather, one afternoon in October 1966 I encountered a boyfriend of several years past who mentioned that the CIA recruiter was on campus and in the former date's opinion, "You would make a perfect spy." I reluctantly agreed to pursue the suggestion to look into CIA employment, although I had never considered it and had no idea of the requirements to become a spy, noting only that student protests against the CIA were currently taking place on campus.

Motivated by the necessity to find a job before graduation, the following week I found myself in front of a CIA recruiter after crossing my first picket line. The interview lasted no more than ten minutes and consisted of the recruiter asking whether I had any additional foreign languages; my signing a secrecy agreement; and his instructing me to report for an all-day examination given to candidates for professional positions in the Agency. Following completion of the test and review by the CIA I would be notified if they had continued interest in me.

Several months later a letter arrived, containing a brief statement that the CIA was processing me for a position as a GS-06 Intelligence Assistant, contingent upon successful completion of medical and security clearances. Finally, my future had clarity—I was graduating from college; had a job regardless of what it entailed; and was going to the nation's capital, single, young, and truly on my own.

In July 1967, I reported to a CIA facility in Rosslyn, Virginia, ironically enough known as the Ames Building. There I joined six other like-titled, female intelligence assistants and 100-plus new hire Agency secretarial employees to await our polygraph, typing, or shorthand tests. Those in charge had no idea why our group of six had been pooled with typists and stenographers, because we had no such skills. They segregated us in a small room, where for the next month we socialized and, on rare occasions, did busy work such as cutting and pasting unclassified maps. It was during this period we learned that college degrees, foreign languages, and professional testing aside, we were clerical employees of the Directorate of Operations. The coveted designation of "professional" and the career opportunities it afforded did not come for several years and some in our group resigned from the Agency before that occurred.

Eventually, I was summoned to headquarters for the long-awaited polygraph. My polygrapher was a stern Marine drill instructor type who kept walking out of the examination room, leaving me to ponder my responses. After about three hours, he announced completion of the test. I immediately told him that, upon reflection, I had not been completely truthful concerning my relationship with a foreign national. I had not intended to mislead him about this contact, but it never occurred to me that my friend, a Canadian citizen, was a foreign national. They were not foreigners like Russians, French, or others. They were Canadians. Convinced that I had failed my polygraph, I returned to the Ames Building to await the bad news—no job. Two days later I was ordered to headquarters where, to my disbelief, I was not met by security officers but by a representative of the Soviet Bloc Division of the Directorate of Operations. I had passed the polygraph.

My initial assignment was to a branch in SB Division that provided guidance to the components in the Division that were targeting GRU officers worldwide. A little over a month out of college and certainly not steeped in the world of spying, I had never heard of the GRU. In retrospect, I do not believe I knew of the KGB either. Upon my arrival, Branch Chief Walter Lomac briefed me on our mission. My job was straightforward—familiarize myself with the Soviet intelligence services by reading numerous publications on their organizations and methods of operation, and by attending the basic required division training courses.

While one has to start at the bottom, the first several months of my CIA career were less than exciting. That was soon to change. One afternoon Lomac told me that the branch's overt mission of providing guidance to division components on their GRU operations was simply cover for one case—that of Colonel Dmitriy Fedorovich Polyakov, then–Soviet military attaché in Rangoon, Burma. I must note that Lomac did not use Polyakov's true name. It is used here for consistency. Within the Directorate of Operations we referred to our assets only by their cryptonym or code name. With a case of the importance of Polyakov, few people within the division would have known his true name.

Everyone in the branch was supporting the operation. As the new kid on the block, I was given the most menial tasks—filing, making copies, cataloging Polyakov's counterintelligence and positive intelligence information, and extracting his reporting on agents and other personalities onto 3x5 cards. My daily routine remained unchanged until the fall of 1968, when my new supervisor, Richards Heuer, who had assumed temporary responsibility for the branch following Lomac's reassignment, informed me that I would be attending a month-long operational training course at "The Farm," the CIA's primary training facility. I wondered why

I was being sent, but did not question the decision. At a minimum, a month out of the office sounded like a nice change.

The training was invaluable, but more memorable was my meeting SE Division legend Dick Kovich, master Soviet recruiter and agent handler. I was aware from the officers in my branch that there was a controversy of a security nature surrounding Kovich and his assignment to "The Farm" was viewed as banishment from mainstream operational activity. However, to these same individuals Kovich was a wronged folk hero who someday would be vindicated. He was a gifted instructor who spoke clearly and enthusiastically about operational philosophy and tradecraft, peppering his lectures with war stories of the glamorous and difficult world of operations against the Soviet target.

Some time later I learned that Kovich's problem was not minor. Angleton believed he was a Soviet mole, an accusation that was totally false yet took Kovich more than ten years to dispel and to restore his good reputation. Ironically, I and many others were ever thankful to Angleton for exiling Kovich to "The Farm" to train a future generation of case officers and operational support personnel in his image.

For Polyakov and me, 1969 was a year of change. He was reassigned to Moscow from Rangoon and I married Gary, beginning a marriage now more than forty years strong. At work I continued to process Polyakov's thousands of pages of production. On the surface my paper-processing tasks appeared boring and insignificant, but in reality I had struck gold. Polyakov had become my first teacher on the Soviet Union and its intelligence services; therefore, I was learning about the enemy from one of its senior officers. Gradually I was given more responsibility, such as writing reports disseminating Polyakov's counterintelligence reporting to various DO components and eventually replacing a senior intelligence analyst in the Branch.

In 1970 I was told that the division was sponsoring me for conversion to professional status, a process that required psychological testing and an interview with a senior DO officer on the review board. While thankful for the division's recognition and support, I silently thought that it was about time a wrong was corrected.

The process went smoothly until the interview. The senior officer noted that I had recently married a non-Agency employee. He then asked when I planned to get pregnant, explaining that motherhood would end my career since I would be required to stay at home and raise the children. Taken aback by the inappropriateness of such a question, I responded by inquiring as to his plans for additional children. The interview ended without further comment by either of us, along with any hope I might have had for professionalization. Fortunately for me and certainly to my amazement, several days later the division notified me that the directorate had granted me professional status. I was officially a home-based SE Division officer. I never found out who within the division pulled the strings after my disastrous interview, but was then and forever remain grateful.

For the next eleven years I stayed in the Counterintelligence Group of SE Division, holding various positions and titles. This was a conscious decision on my part despite attempts by well-meaning personnel officers for me to pursue other "career-enhancing" assignments in the directorate. In the view of many in the Agency, the field of Soviet counterintelligence was arcane. It offered few opportunities to broaden one's knowledge, and limited exposure to those who could assist with career advancement.

That assessment could not have been further from the truth. One by one I was brought into the cases of many Soviet assets and assigned various operational support tasks. As with Polyakov, each source became a teacher. I was not only able to expand my knowledge of the GRU, but also to learn about the KGB. These assets included, but were not limited to, a number of KGB political, scientific and technical, counterintelligence, and communications officers as well as GRU officers worldwide serving under both civilian and military cover.

Such schooling also afforded me the opportunity for official travel abroad and selection to several counterintelligence special projects: a four-month stint at FBI headquarters to review material on their source Aleksey Isidorovich Kulak in support of the official CIA position that he was a bona fide penetration of the KGB; an analysis of sensitive source leads on possible penetrations of the CIA; and five weeks in Kathmandu to assist in the handling of CIA source KGB officer Leonid Georgiyevich Poleshchuk. Professionally, my world was exciting, fast-paced, and challenging. The home front was equally rewarding as during this period we had two daughters, Kelly in 1972 and Tracy in 1976. Thankfully I did not listen to those who encouraged me to leave Soviet CI operations.

In the late 1970s there was an organizational change in the CI Group that brought me into direct and daily contact with Jeanne, thus establishing a friendship and professional relationship that thirteen years later culminated in the Ames mole hunt. Specifically, in 1977 George Kalaris, then–Chief of SE Division, ordered Faith McCoy, a division expert on Soviet positive intelligence reports and requirements, and me to review and recommend a change in the division's handling of counterintelligence reporting from its Soviet and East European sources. There was now an expanded audience in the U.S. intelligence community for this information, which previously had been disseminated primarily only to outside CI customers such as the FBI. Our proposal, which Kalaris adopted, was the formation of two branches in the CI Group—one to handle Soviet CI production and dissemination and one East European CI production and dissemination. Faith headed the new Soviet Branch and I became her deputy. Jeanne was named chief of the new East European branch. After a short period the two branches merged, with Jeanne as the chief. I became her Soviet section chief.

The mid-1970s to 1980 were busy times for everyone in the Soviet CI Group. (The following are some highlights of selected operations only. Details on these and other cases appear in separate chapters.) Vacations were put on hold during the summer of 1976 as we readied Polyakov's internal communications plan for his return from New Delhi to Moscow. KGB officers Piguzov and Yuzhin and GRU officers Filatov and Bokhan were abroad and productive. Gus Hathaway met with FBI source Kulak in New York to prepare him for turnover to, and internal contact with, the CIA in Moscow. As with Polyakov, Kulak provided high-level intelligence upon his return to the Soviet Union. Viktor Sheymov, a communications specialist of the KGB's Eighth Chief Directorate, volunteered while on an official trip to Warsaw. There was the successful exfiltration of Sheymov and his family from Moscow and the attempted exfiltration of Kulak from Moscow.

In 1981 after fourteen years in Soviet CI operations I left on a two-year rotation to the Directorate's Career Management Staff (CMS). While a number of interesting cases remained, the excitement was gone for me. We had lost contact with Polyakov. A year earlier, he left New Delhi on what we and he assumed would be a short trip to Moscow. He did not return. I waited for a year, hoping he would reappear in the West or re-establish contact with us in Moscow, but there was silence. The final impetus for my departure occurred during my participation in a debriefing of a junior-level GRU defector. Thanks to Polyakov I knew more about the defector's organization and modus operandi than he. Time to move on.

I was as ill prepared for my new position in the CMS as head of the secretarial/clerical panel as I had been for my initial job in SE Division. However, the change was good for me and what a change it was from the world of Soviet spies and intrigue to secretarial-clerical personnel management. The responsibilities of the new position were to balance the needs and interests of the employee with those of the operating divisions and the directorate. Expectedly, conflict was inevitable and gray areas abounded, although a satisfactory resolution was usually possible. Days were filled with career counseling, promotion panels, irate division chiefs, directorate politics, and egos galore. Despite the times of discord it was one of the most rewarding jobs I ever held.

In early 1983 my rotational assignment to the CMS was coming to an end. I preferred to return to SE Division—however, not to the CI Group as the division strongly suggested. I wanted a managerial position in SE external operations. This was the front line of CIA operational activity against the Soviet and East European target, and with few exceptions, the closest a person at headquarters could get to field operations. These jobs were staffed by experienced case officers who had served several tours abroad.

SE Division management reacted negatively to my request. I was an analyst, not a case officer, and had spent only five weeks overseas in a support role. I had neither the knowledge nor the credibility to advise field case officers on how to run their Soviet and East European cases.

Part of management's assessment was correct. I would have to establish my credibility. Part was not. During most of my thirteen years in SE CI, the group handled all recruited Soviet intelligence officers abroad, directing the field station on every aspect of its case. That work drew some of the Division's top case officers between their field assignments. Just as I had learned about the KGB and GRU from many of its senior officers, my CIA instructors in field operations were some of the best—Paul D, Ben Pepper, Don Vogel, Burton Gerber, Gus Hathaway, Walter Lomac, Ruth Ellen Thomas, Cynthia Hausmann, Dick Stolz, Serge Karpovich, and many more. It was time to put that imparted knowledge to work. After some back and forth division management agreed to give me a chance. My new assignment was as deputy chief of external operations in Africa.

Africa was fertile ground for Soviet and East European operations, with many field stations primarily staffed with enthusiastic and active Africa Division case officers. My first year in the branch was a baptism by fire. At times I wondered if I should have taken division leadership's recommendation to avoid such a position. Two weeks after my arrival the branch chief announced he would be serving on a promotion panel for the next month and a half. I was on my own. Two months later he announced that he was resigning from the Agency. I was still on my own. I remained deputy chief and was named acting chief, a dubious title I held for the next year. In late 1984 Burton Gerber, then SE Division chief replacing Dave Forden, officially named me chief of SE External Operations for Africa. His approval of my work was reward enough.

In early 1985 a friend from the past appeared. It was Poleshchuk, the first-tour KGB political intelligence officer whose operation I had participated in while on an official trip to Kathmandu in 1974. He was now in Lagos, Nigeria and had switched his specialty to counterintelligence collection and operations.

The pace of an already busy branch became frenetic. Large numbers of immediate action cables were transmitted to and from the field on meeting locations, arrangements, and agendas; requirements; compensation issues; emergency recontact plans; and so forth. The operation proceeded smoothly until 2 October 1985. On that date I was notified by the Division front office that Poleshchuk had been arrested. He was gone.

In January 1986 Gerber called me to his office, where I listened in stunned silence as he recounted loss after loss of the division's Soviet assets. Poleshchuk had not been the only one. Gerber's monologue ended with the introduction of the reason for my presence. We had a new source, and I would be part of the Gerber/Paul Redmond plan to keep him alive. Redmond was chief of the division's Counterintelligence Group and Gerber's co-crusader in the effort to stop the hemorrhaging. Because we did not know who or what had caused our losses, we would operate on the assumption that our problem still existed. This was the genesis of what was later dubbed the "back room," an implementation of security procedures never previously envisioned or required in directorate history.

For the next year I continued my duties as chief (and deputy chief) of the Africa Branch along with the new deep cover role. However, after the first two weeks of multiple assignments I was overloaded and overwhelmed. Recalling Gerber's order that I reported only to him, I related my need and asked for the assistance of Diana Worthen, an analyst in the SE CI Group. She and I had been friends and co-workers for many years on the Polyakov and other cases. Gerber quickly agreed to the request, noting only that he first had to clear it with Clair (Clair George, the DDO at the time). No one would be given access to information on the new operation without his approval. Quickly, Worthen and I were once again a team.

These were stressful and demanding times. Not long after the appearance of our GRU source, I was brought into another new operation involving an anonymous write-in to a CIA officer in Bonn. The volunteer, named by us Mister X, dropped a bombshell. Our Soviet sources had been compromised due to a penetration of CIA communications. In exchange for this information and the promise of more, the author demanded that we place $50,000 in a cache or dead drop in East Berlin. The two cases progressed through the summer along with my travel to West Berlin to deliver the second of three packages for Mister X.

Seven months later in March 1987 Gerber and Redmond summarily removed me from my position in the Africa Branch and put me in charge of the Moscow Task Force. The newly formed group was necessitated by the confession of Moscow Embassy Marine Guard Arnold Bracy that he and fellow guard Clayton Lonetree had allowed the KGB entry to the secure areas of the U.S. embassy. Having no choice but to assume that the KGB had accessed Moscow Station records and/or communications gear, the charter of the task force was twofold. We were to determine the nature and extent of Moscow Station holdings during the period in question and inform all affected U.S. government agencies of the potential compromise of their plans, programs, and personnel. The material collected and reviewed numbered in the tens of thousands of pages and the project took one year to complete.

After my task force duty I found myself formally back in the SE CI Group as chief of the Soviet and East European Production Branch, the job Jeanne held in the late 1970s and early 1980s. The most important change I made during my tenure was to formalize the "back room," naming Worthen as chief of the Special Projects Section. New sources continued to arrive and each continued to survive. Additionally, we began an exhaustive and long-term project to computerize thirty-plus years of counterintelligence information.

In 1989 I stepped down as chief of the Production Branch, requesting and receiving a part-time position in the Special Projects Section. This was strictly a personal decision. My family had made sacrifices for me and my career over the years. It was time I repaid them by spending more hours on the home front.

By early 1991 I had concluded that it was time for me to resign from the CIA. Redmond had left the division and accepted a position as deputy chief of CIC. Milton Bearden, the chief of SE, and I had completed a running battle about the handling of GTPROLOGUE, a KGB operation designed to mislead us about our losses. Polyakov's execution still bothered me. Frustration had set in and my enthusiasm for the work was waning. I told Redmond of my plans. Two days later he asked me if I would stay for one more assignment. Would I help Jeanne investigate the 1985 losses? Without hesitation I replied that he made me the only offer I could have never refused. Our dead sources deserved advocates and so began my participation in what later became known as the Ames mole hunt.

OVERVIEW OF SE OPERATIONS

F ROM THE MID-1960s until the end of the Cold War, operations against the Soviet and East European target were carried out under the same general organizational structure. The biggest change came in 1966, when the East European Division merged with the Soviet Russian Division, creating what was called the Soviet Bloc Division. From then on, the structure changed only in minor ways. There was a component targeting Soviets and East Europeans around the world, and another component responsible for our stations and their operations in the Soviet Union and the East European countries. Additionally, there was a centralized reports and requirements component, an operational support component, and a counterintelligence component. This last-named group was responsible for running those operations that involved KGB and GRU officers, although in the late 1970s the division's geographic targeting components assumed responsibility for a number of these cases. Additionally, it provided CI guidance, reviewed selected cases, and produced studies and research papers for various audiences. This is the component in which the authors spent much of their careers.

In December 1961, an event took place that was to have a profound and deleterious effect on operations against the Soviet target. Major Anatoliy Mikhaylovich Golitsyn (KGB) defected to the CIA in Helsinki. He was a CI officer who, before his posting to Finland, had served at KGB headquarters in a component that worked against the NATO target.

Golitsyn predicted that following his defection to the Americans the Soviets would send false defectors or in-place sources from both the KGB and the GRU to discredit him and his reporting. Further and of more significance, Golitsyn said that the KGB had designed these operations to deflect any U.S. investigations of a high-level penetration of the CIA. Golitsyn had no knowledge of any false defectors in the wings, but he did have the ear of the chief of the CI staff, James Angleton.

Within the CIA a maze of double- and triple-think developed toward all operational activity against the Soviet Union. It was later dubbed the "Monster Plot" and its subscribers were known as the "Black Hats." According to the Black Hat theory, every CIA or FBI success against the Soviet target was really a KGB success, with the KGB controlling the operations from beginning to end—misleading, confusing, and deceiving the naive Americans.[1] This cabal was headed by Angleton and his senior staff, the leadership of SE Division, the leadership of SE Division's CI Group, and the Illegals/Investigations Branch in the SE CI Group managed by Joe Evans and Peter Kapusta.

The Angletonian Monster Plot mind-set centered around the purported existence of false Soviet defectors—KGB or GRU officers who pretend to be disaffected and who wish to lead a new life in the West. Many defectors have been so accused, most recently (as far as the authors know) Vitaliy Sergeyevich Yurchenko, the KGB CI officer who defected to the CIA in Rome at the beginning of August 1985. Sandy and Jeanne are of the firm opinion that the phony defector is an urban myth that has not existed since at least the end of World War II. The reason is simple and can be summed up in one word—trust. The Soviet leadership could not and would not trust any citizen with knowledge of its "State secrets" enough to have him come totally under our control for more than an exceedingly brief period. Soviet intelligence officers of any rank fell into this category. As we have seen in KGB double agent operations, such "sources" were made available to us only under very limited conditions, and the "source" would describe himself as having only peripheral or infrequent access, despite his KGB connection. In one case the "source" had a duty station outside Moscow and only visited his headquarters on rare occasions. In another case, the "source" was retired and his access was limited to chance conversations with his former colleagues. In a third case, the "source" would make himself available to us for extremely short periods, claiming that he could only skip out on his colleagues for a few minutes at a time. Understandably from the Soviet viewpoint, the risks inherent in a phony defector operation are enormous. Exposure for whatever reason negates the value of the ruse. At a minimum, failure results in highly valuable grist for U.S. intelligence and counterintelligence, not to mention a propaganda coup.[2]

Despite the pressures, a few in SE Division did not march to the Angleton drummer. While the division bears the responsibility for its participation in the horrendous treatment of KGB defector Yuriy Ivanovich Nosenko, and other unforgivable activities, there was one officer who risked his professional future by speaking out against the perceived theory that Nosenko was a false defector. That man was Leonard McCoy, a brilliant division reports officer, who in 1966 not only put his contrary views in writing but also took a career-hazarding stand when he later sent his analysis of Nosenko's bona fides to Helms. He decided on such action despite his division chief's promise that he would be fired if he ever mentioned even the existence of his writings. Thanks to McCoy alone a chain of events was set in motion that eventually led to the vindication of Nosenko and his release from CIA imprisonment. In addition to McCoy, Walter Lomac, Sandy's first branch chief, whose story is told in a subsequent chapter, put principle over career. Each deserves great credit for standing up for justice and common sense regardless of the consequences, which ranged from ridicule to expulsion from the division and a future without promotions.

At the same time, in what is a classic example of doublethink, the message from the SE front office was that the business of the division was to recruit Soviet and East European officials. Case officers were told to concentrate their efforts accordingly. While many in Division management may have swallowed the idea that every contact between our officers or our agents was orchestrated by the KGB and therefore, at best, a waste of time, guidance to the rank and file did not reflect this belief. And, over the years, the Monster Plot theory gradually eroded as it bore less and less connection to reality.

Soviet Bloc operations in the 1960s may have been unduly complicated, involving indirect contacts via an intermediary, known as an "access agent," or a "transplant," a CIA officer who showed up in some foreign location in an alias identity to contrive a meeting with a Soviet or East

European target. Audio operations, the insertion of a "bug" in a target's residence, were also in vogue in the early days. Moreover, cold approaches, where we made a recruitment pitch to someone with whom we had no personal relationship, took place from time to time. They were unanimously unsuccessful, and sometimes resulted in physical altercations.

We had always had volunteers and defectors—individuals who approached us. By the mid-1970s, however, we were actively searching for a Soviet or East European official who was disaffected for one reason or another. And instead of cold approaches, we were developing personal relationships with individuals in whom we were interested.

While Moscow Station had opened in the 1960s, and had supported the Popov and Polyakov cases, it did not reach a significant level of operational activity until the next decade. One of the catalysts was Gus Hathaway, who served as chief of station from June 1977 to January 1980. He was followed in this position by Burton Gerber, who held the job until September 1982. Both subsequently became chiefs of SE Division.

At its simplest, the role of Moscow Station was to accept all internal volunteers when they made their initial approach and then separate the wheat from the chaff. What the station had to determine was which volunteers had at least some grasp on sanity, which ones had access to information of importance to the U.S. government, and which ones were "dangles" or "provocations," false volunteers orchestrated by the KGB and intended to give us some specific piece of disinformation or to tie up our slender resources. The KGB knew that we had had some genuine internal volunteers who were privy to important secrets. The most famous of these was Colonel Oleg Penkovskiy (GRU), who made repeated attempts to approach us in Moscow starting in the summer of 1960. Another internal volunteer of potential importance was Aleksandr Nikolayevich Cherepanov, a KGB officer who provided fifty pages of KGB documents via an intermediary in November 1963. Unfortunately for him, the U.S. embassy in Moscow did not believe his approach was genuine. They turned the documents over to the KGB, although the Station was able to make copies before that happened. Cherepanov tried to flee the Soviet Union but was arrested near the border and later executed.[3] Perhaps the most important internal volunteer was Adolf Tolkachev, a scientist with valuable information on Soviet secret research and development projects, who approached us in 1977.

As part of the process of vetting volunteers, in 1971 Burton Gerber, then a young case officer, reviewed all the approaches that had occurred during the previous ten years. His study was published in July of that year and Burton followed it with briefings to various audiences. This study resulted in a more positive attitude toward volunteers because the research revealed that a number of cases thought to be provocations at the time were in fact legitimate. An additional point made was that there were no intelligence officer dangles. (Subsequently there were at least two attempts using intelligence officer dangles to deceive us about Ames' activities. However, in each case the person described himself as not having unfettered access to his organization's secrets.)

Another influential study in the same time frame was written by Ruth Ellen Thomas. It reviewed all the Illegals cases known up to that time, and provided a profile of just what constituted an Illegal. It showed that the classic Illegal, a KGB or GRU staff officer under a false non-Bloc identity, was being phased out in favor of the Illegal Agent, generally a true citizen of a third country. A big part of the new definition was that these "agents" were handled by impersonal means such as enciphered radio messages rather than by direct contact with KGB or GRU personnel. It was this handling method that differentiated them from ordinary agents.

The study also pointed out that Illegals operations were expensive and dangerous, and were generally only undertaken against priority targets. There were no hordes of Illegals around the world. These well-documented conclusions provoked numerous discussions and had a major impact.

A third study followed a short time later. It focused on KGB residencies abroad and clearly showed that SE did not consider KGB officers to be invincible superior beings. This study, written by Tom Blackshear and based on reporting from sensitive KGB sources, demonstrated that KGB residencies abroad were sometimes poorly managed, that they exaggerated their operational successes in reporting to Moscow, often based their reporting on overt press articles instead of clandestinely obtained intelligence, and made their share of mistakes in running operations.

Jeanne's study on the GRU made some of the same points. While GRU officers had many of the attributes of conventional military officers, and were dogged in their pursuit of human-source intelligence, they were also narrowly educated and had little understanding of the world outside the Soviet Union. Further, because the GRU had no responsibility for counterintelligence, GRU officers often were not aware of the capabilities of Western services and the pitfalls that a Soviet intelligence officer could encounter in the course of his operations.

In 1973 or 1974, while John Horton was chief and Dick Stolz his deputy, the Soviet Bloc Division was renamed the Soviet and East European Division. This was a recognition that Albania and Yugoslavia and, to a lesser degree, Romania, could no longer be considered "Bloc" countries. What is interesting is that the change took place while Angleton was still in power and pushing the theory that any Yugoslav and Chinese breaks with Moscow were merely a sham. To a great extent, SE Division by this time simply ignored the Angletonian interpretation of world events. To many he had become a joke, a sick joke certainly, but a joke nevertheless.

CHAPTER
4

THE POLYAKOV CASE—
THE BEGINNINGS

D MITRIY FEDOROVICH POLYAKOV, a Soviet military intelligence officer, was the highest-ranking spy ever run against the Soviet Union during the Cold War. In 1961, during his second tour of duty with the Soviet military mission to the United Nations in New York, he sought contact with the U.S. government. Working for a brief period with the FBI and then with the CIA, Polyakov spied for the United States for nearly twenty years—in New York, Rangoon, and New Delhi, and while assigned to GRU headquarters in Moscow. During that time, he rose in rank from lieutenant colonel to one-star general.[1]

Polyakov's clandestine contact with us ended in 1980, when he took an official trip to Moscow from his post in New Delhi, and never returned. While we became ever more concerned and anxious over this turn of events, we had tremendous confidence in his ability as a professional intelligence officer to handle any possible security or political problems he might be facing in Moscow.

Many years later we learned that our faith in his ability was justified. It was not he who erred. Polyakov's path had crossed with two American traitors who volunteered to the Soviets—FBI special agent Robert Hanssen and CIA officer Aldrich Ames. Hanssen's 1979 reporting probably resulted in Polyakov's return to Moscow in 1980. Ames' treachery undoubtedly resulted in Polyakov's 1986 arrest and 1988 execution. Had it not been for these two men, Polyakov would have been one of the most successful spies of all time, his identity and accomplishments known only to a privileged few. Regrettably, he did not live to see the end of the Cold War, to which he had made a major contribution.

According to official FBI memoranda provided to the CIA in 1965, Lieutenant Colonel Polyakov approached General Edward O'Neil, commanding officer of the First Army headquartered in New York in November 1961 and asked to be put in touch with "American intelligence." Shortly thereafter O'Neil facilitated the introduction of Polyakov to FBI Special Agent John Mabey at a reception to which Polyakov and others had been invited.[2] During a brief exchange Polyakov told Mabey that he had changed his mind and wanted no further contact. Mabey refused to accept Polyakov's rebuff and continued his pursuit, occasionally appearing unexpectedly in Polyakov's path during his daily routine. In January 1962 Mabey's persistence paid off. Polyakov agreed to enter into a clandestine relationship with the U.S. government and in the authors' opinion this special agent deserves the credit for the subsequent decades of the Polyakov, FBI, and CIA cooperation. Meetings between the two professionals continued for the next five-plus months both in New York and in the *Queen Elizabeth* as Polyakov and his family sailed to Europe en route to Moscow and his reassignment to GRU headquarters.

Polyakov's counterintelligence production throughout the New York phase of the operation was noteworthy. In addition to the identification of GRU and KGB officers in the United States, he provided the names of GRU Illegals who had been dispatched to the United States and leads to the following four American servicemen who were spying for the GRU, each providing varying levels of classified information as their assignments would indicate: Jack Dunlap, a U.S. Army sergeant assigned to the National Security Agency; Herbert Boeckenhaupt, a U.S. Air Force staff sergeant and communications technician; William Whalen, a U.S. Army officer working for the Joint Chiefs of Staff; and Nelson Drummond, a U.S. Navy enlisted man who served tours of duty abroad and in the United States.

The FBI did not officially inform the CIA of Polyakov's recruitment until June 1962, when they needed CIA assistance. Polyakov was scheduled for reassignment to Moscow in several months and agreed to maintain communications through ads placed in the *New York Times* as well as dead drops and signal sites that only the CIA's Moscow Station could provide and service. Admittedly, it would not be surprising to learn that Angleton was unofficially told of Polyakov's recruitment either in January 1962 or in the course of the next several months, given his close relationship with several high-level FBI officers.

Moscow Station provided the FBI with the requested sites, some of which Polyakov accepted and some of which he rejected, as became his pattern throughout our years of cooperation. However, despite repeated attempts by the FBI to initiate recontact in Moscow through *New York Times* ads, Polyakov remained silent until early 1965, when Moscow Station personnel observed a marked signal site and unloaded a dead drop from Polyakov. The drop included a message in which he said he was well and would probably soon be reassigned abroad.

Polyakov arrived in Rangoon in November 1965 as Soviet military attaché and GRU resident. Initially, the FBI met with Polyakov in Burma. This arrangement was groundbreaking—the CIA ceding its authority to the FBI for the handling of a Soviet intelligence officer abroad. In reality the CIA had no alternative, because the FBI recruited Polyakov and it made operational sense for them to re-establish the contact.

To document the agreement, the two organizations adopted a Memorandum of Understanding, which detailed the responsibilities of each in the operation. In brief, the CIA said it would provide any and all field support Mabey required, including communications with his headquarters.

Mabey re-established contact with Polyakov in January 1966; however, after four and a half months it became clear that this arrangement could not continue. A simple but basic problem had developed—a communications barrier. Mabey did not speak Russian. He conducted his meetings with Polyakov in English, but Polyakov's English had deteriorated since departing the United States in 1962. While the language problem did not affect all portions of the debriefings, it did not allow for accurate and thorough discussions on specialized topics such as Soviet military weaponry and other priority collection requirements of the time. The FBI, therefore, decided to turn the operation over to the CIA.

The CIA selected Jim F, an SE Division case officer with a superb command of Russian, to replace Mabey in Rangoon. Jim was a tall, thin man who wore thick glasses and, with the exception of a neatly pressed white shirt with frayed cuffs, always dressed in black—shoes, suit, and tie. He usually held a non-filtered cigarette in his hand, continually dropping ashes and embers that resulted in scorched fabric and numerous holes in his clothes.

Jim was a man of tremendous intellectual capacity, a graduate of Yale who was well read and knowledgeable in a myriad of fields, particularly the Soviet intelligence services. He did not suffer fools kindly, often looking over his coke bottle–thick lenses to lecture any officer in the vicinity on how to conduct operations against the KGB and GRU. He came across as an opinionated professor who insisted on complete control in his classroom—which consisted of his co-workers and, on occasion, his superiors. While he was usually correct in his pronouncements, this approach did not win him many friends or admirers.

Unknown to Polyakov as he awaited contact with a new case officer, his greatest enemy at the time was not the KGB and not a mole in the CIA or FBI, but a group of people within the organization to which he had entrusted his secrets and his life. Before Polyakov had met or exchanged a word with any CIA representative, these individuals had concluded that he was under the control of the KGB and was not a legitimate penetration of the GRU. Rather, he was an enemy to be feared and certainly not to be trusted. Jim F shared these views. The group even believed it possible that the KGB might try to kidnap him, and he was authorized a firearm for protection. In the minds of these CIA officers, it followed logically that Polyakov's personal security was meaningless and that he was expendable.

How and why did the CIA conclude that a source who had already provided American intelligence with valuable information was a fraud? The answer is not simple and has been the subject of several books that have detailed its history and effect on U.S. intelligence collection against the Soviet Union in general and the personnel of the CIA and FBI in particular. We will not recount this history at length here, but only address how Polyakov fell into this dark hole. The story of other sources will follow.

Unfortunately for Polyakov, he volunteered to the FBI within a year of Golitsyn's 1961 defection. In the eyes of some, Golitsyn's prediction of false defectors had become reality and Polyakov's approach was proof of the KGB plot. First Angleton and then many others forgot, did not want to believe, or did not have the courage to point out that there was no factual basis for Golitsyn's predictions and that they could be nothing more than the ramblings of a paranoid and egotistical defector. Thus, when the

CIA sent Jim F to Rangoon, he had orders to prove that Polyakov was a KGB plant.

One cannot imagine two more different personalities: Polyakov, a military man meticulous in his dress and appearance; Jim F, a civilian with nicotine-stained fingers and teeth, and, in his own words, only owning three suits in his professional career; Polyakov, an accomplished sportsman, with a passion for hunting, fishing, and other outdoor activities; Jim, more comfortable with books and an audience of like-minded dilettantes; Polyakov, an occasional social drinker; Jim, a martini man who enjoyed his silver bullets; Polyakov, an expert in the nuts and bolts world of spy gear and internal communications techniques; and Jim, the big-picture thinker who enjoyed the search for answers to "what if" questions. We can only guess at Polyakov's personal reaction to Jim and to a lesser extent Jim's reaction to Polyakov. Jim was always closemouthed on any discussion of Polyakov the man, and even years later would simply comment that he found Polyakov to be a cold person with beady eyes.

In sum, Jim viewed the operation as an adversarial relationship. To Polyakov it was a business partnership. He provided information the U.S. government needed and it, in turn, fulfilled his requests for career assistance and remuneration. He understood his role and recognized more than anyone the great risk he had taken when he volunteered to the U.S. government in New York in 1961. He was the agent who just happened to be a Soviet intelligence officer and Jim was his case officer. Jim asked the questions and he answered them. Totally unaware of the controversy surrounding him, the only hint of frustration Polyakov displayed during his two years with Jim was with Jim's preoccupation with requirements on GRU Illegals operations of the 1950s.

From 1956 to 1959 Polyakov had been the GRU headquarters desk officer responsible for GRU Illegals sent to the United States, and in this position he knew their true names, false identities, and operational objectives. He even participated in their mission training. John Mabey had debriefed Polyakov on these cases in 1961–62 in New York and again during their recontact in Burma in 1966, but Jim covered the same ground in greater detail and in meeting after meeting. For Polyakov this was history, perhaps intellectually interesting but certainly not of critical or strategic importance to the United States. Some of the cases went back ten years, and none was active. The GRU Illegal in question had either returned to

Moscow or was under FBI control. Polyakov felt that valuable time was being wasted; he had knowledge of many items of more importance to provide the Americans—Soviet military and economic assistance to the North Vietnamese, Soviet-Chinese relations, GRU agent operations in Southeast Asia, GRU collection requirements against the United States, identities of GRU officers worldwide, and an array of other subjects.

The Black Hats viewed the questions about the old GRU Illegals cases quite differently. Polyakov's responses would serve as evidence that he was under KGB control, because they had independent reporting on Polyakov's role in the Illegals cases from Petr Semenovich Popov, a lieutenant colonel in the GRU who volunteered to the CIA in Vienna in 1952. In 1957 Popov was assigned to East Berlin, where he handled Polyakov's GRU Illegals as they transited East Berlin en route to the West. If any portion of Polyakov's reporting on these cases differed from Popov's, it was proof that Polyakov was lying. If Polyakov's information corroborated Popov's, the Black Hats' lecture was always the same: "The KGB has to provide us with some good information to guarantee that we will continue to handle the operation." With such circular reasoning, no source could establish his bona fides. Polyakov's lighthearted impatience on the topic of Illegals was seen as a further sign of KGB control of the contact, intended only to mask the "truth."

Fortunately for Polyakov, there were some brave souls who did not accept the Monster Plot theory. The SE Division component that provided day-to-day support to the Polyakov operation was headed at the time by Walter Lomac. Lomac was a gentle bear of a man with an infectious laugh who took a straightforward approach to the case. To him, there were two simple questions that needed to be asked, and the answers to these questions would determine whether Polyakov was what he claimed—a GRU staff officer who was committing continuous treason against the USSR. First, was Polyakov providing the U.S. government with secrets he should have access to as a colonel in the GRU, as the Soviet military attaché in the Soviet embassy in Rangoon, and as head of the GRU contingent in Burma? Second, did the members of the U.S. intelligence community to whom this information was disseminated judge it to be accurate and valuable? If the answers to these two questions were yes and remained yes after each debriefing, Polyakov's bona fides were established to Lomac's satisfaction and the Black Hats were wrong.

Under Lomac's oversight, the branch's duties were the same as those of any DO headquarters component responsible for managing an agent from a hostile intelligence service. Lomac insisted that the focus remain on those duties.

The branch had a small number of employees at the time, and a typical day would find officers and secretaries in their cramped quarters writing and typing cables, dispatches, and memoranda; transcribing and translating Russian language material; and collating and filing the mounds of paper generated by the operation. The branch had infrequent contact with Joe Evans, Peter Kapusta, and other Black Hats in SE CI's Investigations Branch. They viewed the GRU component as enemy territory, an attitude Lomac did not discourage, and appeared only briefly to deliver follow-up questions about the GRU Illegals of the 1950s, with instructions to send them to the field in time for the next meeting.

Angleton himself did not personally visit the branch, but during Polyakov's tour in Burma all correspondence to the field had to be coordinated with him. If he objected to something, the cable was changed or not sent. Simply stated, Angleton had veto rights in the management of the case and used them as he saw fit. This was contrary to accepted DO policy and practice because such authority belonged to the operating division. Yet this was the daily routine in the Polyakov case until his departure from Rangoon.

Lomac's stance was not without personal risk. Frequently summoned to the division's front office, berated for his position on the case, and ordered to see the light, he never wavered in his two-question, two-answer approach to the operation and by extension to Polyakov himself. He protected his branch, but his belief in Polyakov eventually cost him his career.

In early 1968 William Colby, then–chief of the Far East Division, was scheduled to take over the Soviet Division from David Murphy. Colby had apparently heard rumors as to discord within the division on the Polyakov case, and asked to be briefed by Lomac. Lomac was instructed to present the case to Colby along management's line that Polyakov was a suspected provocation agent. Lomac flatly refused, claiming that his views regarding management's theory about the Monster Plot and the Polyakov case were well known to management and he was not about to reverse his opinion or perjure himself to the incoming division chief.

During his briefing Lomac presented Colby with two written reports summarizing Polyakov's production in both the counterintelligence and positive intelligence areas. Colby seemed impressed with the reports and asked for Murphy's opinion on the contents of the reports. Lomac had not sought Murphy's approval of their content before passing them, knowing that such approval would not be forthcoming. Indeed he had not even told Murphy of their existence because they had been prepared specifically for Colby's briefing. (Colby's assignment to the Soviet Division never took place as he was chosen to head the Phoenix Program in Vietnam instead. Rolfe Kingsley, a European Division officer, was selected as Murphy's replacement in lieu of Colby.)

Not surprisingly, Murphy was enraged. He called Lomac into his office the next day and gave him a "directed assignment" abroad, which in DO parlance meant you packed your bags and went where ordered. You did not argue and you did not complain. Should you choose not to comply, the consequences were understood. The next "directed assignment" would lead out the door.

Lomac returned to his office immediately after his meeting with Murphy, called the branch together, and announced that he had been assigned to Africa. Several officers gasped. For an SE Division officer who was responsible for a major operation, an assignment to Africa was banishment—the equivalent of an FBI officer being sent to Idaho. Lomac, however, chuckled and said: "Thank God Murphy doesn't know his geography. I'm going to Nairobi!" Laughter erupted from those in the know. Africa may have been exile, but Nairobi at the time was a jewel of a location—wonderful climate, beautiful and spacious housing, Western amenities and conveniences, and a fertile environment for operations against Soviet and East European targets. Lomac would have rewarding work and his family would be comfortable, but he also understood that he no longer would be considered part of SE Division's pool of candidates for advancement.

While Lomac did subsequently have a long and productive career, his assessment was correct in terms of advancement—a GS-14 in 1968, he retired as a GS-15 in 1979, awarded one promotion in twelve years. But Lomac's story did not end there. The CIA finally acknowledged his sacrifices and in 1979 publicly recognized his stand in the Polyakov case during a medal ceremony in the director's conference room, where he was awarded the Intelligence Medal of Merit. Lomac had put Polyakov's security and the viability of the operation above career and personal ambition and in direct opposition to every man in his chain of command. He had lived by his principles of intellectual honesty and personal integrity during a difficult and unfortunate time and he richly deserved the belated recognition.

In 1968 there were major changes in the Polyakov operation. At headquarters Lomac's duties were assumed by caretaker Richards Heuer, deputy chief of the SE CI Group and a Black Hat hard-liner. In the field Jim F was replaced as Polyakov's case officer by another Russian speaker, Al K. Al was a devotee of the Angleton/Golitsyn Monster Plot theory and in essence reflected division management's continued belief in the KGB-controlled-source saga.

Al K was a plodding case officer and his operational skills did not impress the full colonel in the GRU. Nevertheless, during their year together they developed a collegial relationship that had been nonexistent with Jim F. Al, like Polyakov, was of Ukrainian descent. He had a jovial personality and, again unlike Jim, masked his feelings that the colonel was under KGB control. Moreover and of probably equal significance was that Al was not saddled with asking Polyakov endless follow-up questions on the extinct GRU Illegals cases. Instead, meaningful and critical requirements on the priority issues of the times streamed to the field. Polyakov was pleased and the quality and quantity of his production continued to soar.

Meetings began with a brief discussion of what we called housekeeping items, to include a review of the details of the next scheduled contact and the passage of requested gifts or monies. Then it was time for business. Polyakov handed over rolls of undeveloped 35-mm film that contained the contents of the GRU pouch from Moscow and the return pouch from Rangoon. He briefly described the items, highlighting those dispatches of priority interest so that once the film was developed and printed the most important or time-critical information could be pulled for immediate translation. Next he detailed the cables his residency had received from Moscow since the last meeting. Rarely did he photograph this material because GRU security regulations required that cable traffic be read in the presence of the GRU code clerk and then returned for destruction. Even as the local GRU chief, Polyakov was only permitted to take brief notes on cable contents. The remainder of a contact with Polyakov was devoted to coverage of CIA counterintelligence and positive intelligence requirements. Meetings generally lasted no more than an hour, and ended with polite good-byes.

To appreciate fully the significance of the information Polyakov provided in Rangoon, and subsequently in New Delhi, one must understand how the Soviet system worked. First, as a Soviet military officer and member of the General Staff Polyakov had access to documents on Soviet military plans and philosophy. Second, as a Soviet intelligence officer he had access to documents on, and knowledge of, GRU operations, agents, spy gear, modus operandi, and the identities of GRU staff officers worldwide. Third, as a senior member of a Soviet Embassy abroad and as a Communist Party activist he had access to classified Soviet Ministry of Foreign Affairs material and Party directives. Fourth, his rank of Colonel and of greater import General afforded him access to strategic information denied to the vast majority of lower-ranking GRU officers. Lastly, Polyakov was an insider—a member of the "old boy" network based on his wartime record, his many years of service in the GRU, and his innate character and personality. This took him into his organization's most inner circle, which gave him access to state secrets that he otherwise would have been denied solely by his rank and position title.

Polyakov was not a passive asset, simply content to pass documents that Moscow center decided to send to his residency. Conversely, he was not reckless, requesting material that raised the eyebrows of KGB security monitors within GRU headquarters. He took a measured approach, asking for additional information only when a situation presented itself. This was exemplified with his documentary production on spy equipment and began when an asset of the Rangoon residency was scheduled for training on a long-range agent communications device. Polyakov saw and seized the opportunity. Unknown to us, he asked GRU headquarters to send the top secret, 100-plus-page design manual for the equipment along with the standard training brochures. Moscow reasoned the manual was of use only to the engineers at headquarters and denied Polyakov's request. Undeterred, he asked for reconsideration, citing the possible need for equipment repair given the hot, humid climate in Burma and his recognized technical expertise in the agent communications field. Moscow acceded and headquarters approved his request. He successfully made the same argument for other items issued to residency assets, such as document copying devices, miniature recorders, rollover cameras, and the latest in short-range and long-range communications equipment.

Polyakov took special delight in providing this information. Over time he had developed a distrust of CIA spy gear, opining that it was neither user-friendly nor reliable. He preferred the Soviet-made equipment that was of simple design and rugged construction, was easy to use for case officer and agent alike, and was dependable. Polyakov believed that CIA engineers could benefit from the technical documents he provided. Unfortunately, to our chagrin, on one occasion we learned that possession of the GRU manuals did not rectify all the technical difficulties we encountered with the Polyakov operation, as outlined in the paragraph below.

During Polyakov's first assignment to New Delhi, his communicator notified him of the receipt of an urgent cable from Moscow that was classified "Top Secret of Special Importance" and that contained instructions that it be passed to the Soviet Deputy Minister of Foreign Affairs, Mikhail Kapitsa, who was in New Delhi as part of a tour of Southeast Asian capitals. Later dubbed the "Kapitsa Document" by U.S. intelligence, the cable was a detailed, straightforward commentary on Soviet foreign policy plans and objectives for every major country in the world. Immediately recognizing the significance and importance of the information and that this was a one-time bonanza, Polyakov decided to violate GRU regulations. He took the document to a curtained-off area of the residency and photographed it using a newly developed CIA rollover camera that was based in part on the GRU rollover manual he had provided years earlier. Still distrustful of the reliability of our devices Polyakov also took pictures of the cable with his trusty 35-mm camera, even though he realized that the clicks of each frame snapped might be heard by his code clerk who was only feet away.

Polyakov's misgivings about our state-of-the-art camera were well founded. Only one image was readable; the remaining frames were blank. Thankfully, the 35-mm copies were perfect and the U.S. government had the worldwide blueprints of Soviet foreign policy for years to come.

THE POLYAKOV CASE—
THE MIDDLE

POLYAKOV RETURNED TO MOSCOW in August 1969, where he became Chief of the China Direction, responsible for GRU operations against the People's Republic of China. At CIA headquarters Sandy's branch turned over day-to-day responsibility for the case to the branch that supported Moscow Station activities. Before departing Rangoon, Polyakov was issued the standard internal communications plan: dead drop and signal sites, one-time cipher pads, secret writing, prewritten cover letters, instructions for a one-way voice link for radio communications from our headquarters, and accommodation addresses. Although he was issued a two-way plan, he simply chose to ignore any CIA-initiated communication, which he considered too dangerous given the omnipotence of the local KGB and, by extension, the CIA's inability to operate securely in that environment. As practiced by Polyakov, our communication link was one way: from him to us.

In 1971 David Blee became chief of SE Division and from his first day on the job began a shake-up that affected everyone from headquarters and field personnel to potential targets and recruited sources. A career Near East Division officer with little Soviet operational experience, Blee continued the removal of many of the division's Black Hat officers begun by Rolfe Kingsley and told the rest of the division that the years of a cautious and methodical approach to the Soviet target were over. Aggressiveness and risk taking would be the norm. No longer would the security of an operation determine its pace, whether that operation was abroad or inside the Soviet Union. Polyakov became the centerpiece of Blee's dictum.

As of early 1972, Polyakov had been silent for about a year—no dead drops with photographed documents or messages. Blee demanded to know his status and our future plans. He ordered that personal contact be established with Polyakov in Moscow. To many involved in the case such a move was reckless endangerment of the agent. The KGB might not be ten feet tall as the Angletonians believed, but the Soviet Union was its turf with tens of thousands of officers and agents available, and the laws in its favor. If we were unsuccessful, we had placed Polyakov's life in grave danger for what some judged to be simply a curiosity-driven operation. Even if we were successful, Polyakov, who refused to participate in two-way impersonal contact with the CIA in Moscow, let alone a one-on-one meeting, might choose to sever all subsequent operational ties with the United States.

To dissuade Blee from this course of action, a brief analysis was prepared estimating the timing and location of Polyakov's reappearance in the West. Based on our knowledge of available GRU overseas positions, assignment policies and practices, and Polyakov's career path, the paper concluded that the Colonel would likely show up in New Delhi, India within the next several years as GRU resident and Soviet military attaché. Blee dismissed the finding as "witchcraft." The show would go on.

Blee left the development of the recontact plan to the division desk officers who were responsible for the Polyakov operation but reminded them that he would not wait months for its implementation. The officers involved worked feverishly, rejecting numerous proposals for security reasons until they agreed to one that was ingenious in its simplicity and, most important, limited risk of compromise to Polyakov.

The primary actors were a CIA case officer and a U.S. diplomatic acquaintance of Polyakov's from Rangoon. The operational scenario called for the latter, along with his wife, to visit diplomatic friends in Moscow during a round-the-world post-retirement trip. The U.S. embassy there arranged a cocktail reception in the retiree's honor. The invitees would include Polyakov and the CIA case officer, thus providing the opportunity for a brief exchange between the two.

At first glance such a scenario appeared to guarantee that Polyakov would receive the unwanted attention of KGB security personnel—an unsolicited invitation to a GRU officer from a retired U.S. diplomat visiting Moscow. However, there was a twist in the operational plan that gave Polyakov cover. During his tour in Burma, Polyakov had falsely characterized his now-retired U.S. diplomatic acquaintance as a developmental contact to GRU headquarters, regularly reporting their get-togethers as required by his regulations. With a complete record of the meetings in GRU files, we felt that the KGB could find nothing nefarious about the invitation. Polyakov was a Soviet intelligence officer who had pursued a legitimate target with the blessing of his superiors.

Unfortunately we later learned to our chagrin that the best-laid plans can go awry for the most mundane reasons. Polyakov informed us upon his subsequent arrival in New Delhi in 1974 that GRU headquarters could not find the files that documented his contact with the U.S. diplomatic colleague. They had either been destroyed or simply misplaced. As a consequence, the KGB questioned him at length. Who was this American? What was his interest in you? Backed by his co-workers at GRU headquarters, the KGB eventually accepted Polyakov's story that the U.S. diplomat was one of his developmental contacts in Rangoon and that the relationship was officially sanctioned and properly reported. As a result, the KGB allowed Polyakov to accept the invitation.

In June 1972 the CIA officer and Polyakov met briefly at the reception. The Colonel displayed no outward surprise or anger. He informed our officer that all was well, that he was scheduled for assignment to North Vietnam as the Soviet military attaché in late 1973 or early 1974, and that in preparation for this tour of duty he would travel to Hanoi in the fall as a member of the delegation of Air Marshal Batitskiy.

CIA headquarters greeted this news with a sigh of relief, shouts of joy, and the realization that we faced a daunting task. Polyakov was alive and well. We not only would have a source in the enemy camp, but he would also have high-level and direct access to the critical collection requirement of the decade—North Vietnam's military program, plans, and operations targeted against the U.S. soldier. However, there was the stark reality that we had to find a way to communicate with him in Hanoi. Direct contact appeared to be a nonstarter since the United States did not have diplomatic relations with North Vietnam. The CIA had no miniature long-range, two-way, short-burst communications device that would encode and decode transmitted messages. Some said our situation was bleak, given our lack of viable options. Others opined that it was far worse, as we awaited confirmation of Polyakov's travel with the Batitskiy delegation.

About six months later, Batitskiy and his group arrived in North Vietnam. Polyakov was not among them. The obvious questions were asked over and over again with no satisfactory answers. What happened? Was his upcoming assignment canceled or changed? If so, why? Did something occur at the cocktail reception that caught the attention of the known KGB watchdogs who were present? Had he been compromised for this, or some other reason? Would he appear elsewhere abroad? If so, when and where? Now what? Thankfully for all intimately involved in the case at CIA headquarters, no serious consideration was given to another attempt to establish personal contact with Polyakov in Moscow. It possibly had worked once, but a second try would be irresponsible. The only viable option was to wait and trust Polyakov to make the decision as to when, where, and how to re-establish contact.

After an extended period, word came from Moscow Station that Polyakov had marked one of his signal sites. This indicated he was ready to put down a dead drop. A station officer unloaded the drop, which contained a short message that he was being processed for assignment to New Delhi as Soviet military attaché. In a roundabout way, and with thanks to the Soviet bureaucracy as Polyakov later told us, the analytical "witchcraft" paper presented earlier to Blee was correct. The June 1972 meeting in Moscow had been a waste of time and money and had unnecessarily risked the life of an important and productive agent. As Polyakov so bluntly told us at our first meeting in New Delhi, "Don't ever do that again."

Polyakov's two-year assignment in New Delhi was the pinnacle of our long and productive association. He achieved one of his personal GRU goals when he was promoted to one-star general shortly after his arrival.[1] The CIA at last erased the remnants of the Angleton era, and officially accepted Polyakov for what he had been throughout our thirteen years of contact—a legitimate penetration of the GRU. Our relationship had come full circle, evolving from adversarial to a collaborative partnership with a bond of mutual respect and admiration between professional intelligence officers from opposite sides of the Cold War. The CIA had finally gotten it right.

Polyakov's new case officer was Paul D, one of our finest. He was not selected for the assignment just because of the quality of his Russian language; of more import were his operational skills and human qualities. Paul greeted every task with enthusiasm, integrity, and balance whether it was a minor question with a simple answer or an impending disaster with no apparent solution. He was a devout Catholic and when he was out of earshot his subordinates respectfully and affectionately called him Father Paul. He never demanded the respect and loyalty of those he led; he unknowingly commanded it with his wit, charm, and unassuming way.

Earlier in his career Paul managed to avoid scrutiny by the Black Hats in the division by packing up his expanding family and accepting overseas assignments far from their crosshairs. Luckily for him, by the time he returned to headquarters in about 1971, division management had regained a modicum of control over its operational and personnel assignments from Angleton. Paul was given a supervisory position in the Counterintelligence Group, where he remained until his selection as Polyakov's new field confidant in 1974.

Vowing to assemble the best field team possible, division management did not stop with Paul. Diana Worthen, who later played an instrumental role in the Ames investigation, was tapped to be the Soviet analyst for our office in New Delhi, with primary responsibility for Paul and Polyakov, or as analysts often described their function, "the care and feeding of those I support."

A graduate of the University of New Mexico, Worthen joined the Agency in November 1970 as a secretary-stenographer. After several assignments, including an overseas tour, she returned to headquarters and a secretarial position in the counterintelligence component, where she was converted to professional status as an analyst and discovered her calling in Soviet operations. Worthen was a no-nonsense officer who set high standards for herself and expected the same from others, on occasion advising them of their shortcomings. Conversely, she was a private person whose devotion to her job and to her carefully selected friends was paramount in her life. Little did she know before leaving for New Delhi that her commitment to Polyakov would later collide with a valued friendship, when Ames betrayed both in 1985.

The final member of the triumvirate was the prototypical DO operations officer whose command of the Russian language and knowledge of the Soviet system was legendary. We will call him "Mr. K." He traveled as an ordinary American businessman and his occasional presence at debriefing sessions demonstrated to Polyakov the importance we attached to him and his work on our behalf. To add a layer of security to the contact, Polyakov reported his contact with an "American businessman" target to GRU headquarters, with a fictional description of their nature and content. This earned him points with his unsuspecting management for his supposed work against the Main Enemy.

Paul D and Polyakov were the perfect match. The GRU General came to understand that he had a trustworthy co-conspirator in Paul and it was time to discard his belief that he was merely an agent whose only value was the information he provided. Polyakov was also a human being for whom we had assumed a personal responsibility when he volunteered his services. Under these circumstances, Polyakov found sanctuary in his meetings with Paul and not unexpectedly began to provide glimpses into his rationale for volunteering to American intelligence. It would be inaccurate to characterize his comments on motivation as an emotional catharsis. Polyakov was and remained a circumspect individual whose character and military training never would have permitted such a display. Nevertheless, his specific comments on and oblique references to the subject provided a framework from which we could further extrapolate with some certainty.

Polyakov's motivation probably went back to his service and experiences during World War II. As an artillery officer in the Soviet Army who was awarded decorations for bravery, Polyakov witnessed the courage and sacrifice of the Russian soldier despite unbearable conditions and unspeakable horrors. After the war he attended the Frunze Military Academy, from which he was recruited by the GRU. It is believed that sometime during this period Polyakov began to view the Soviet leaders as corrupt thugs who subjugated the common man for personal power and to line their pockets and those of their sycophants. To him these select few were mocking the sacrifices of the Russian people and he only saw a future of continued corruption and thirst for power expanding throughout the world. The Russian people were slaves of their leaders, helpless and alone in the world. Of equal significance, the Western world in general and the United States in particular were not a counterbalance to Soviet power. As viewed by Polyakov, our military was weak, our leaders lacked fortitude and, of greater consequence, were bound by civilized rules of behavior. His were bound by none and Polyakov concluded that the Soviet Union would win the Cold War.

In early 1968 during a meeting in Rangoon, Polyakov lectured Al K on the cowardice of the commander of the USS *Pueblo* who allowed North Korean gunboats to capture his vessel without firing a shot. In a paraphrase of Polyakov's words, a Soviet naval commander would have fought to the death before surrendering his ship to the enemy. However long the process or the twists and turns in his reasoning, Polyakov eventually came to view himself as an individual who just might be able to make a difference in the struggle between East and West. At a minimum he could level the playing field or, in a best-case scenario, tilt it in favor of the United States. Events such as the *Pueblo* only strengthened his position that without his assistance we were doomed to live under the hammer and sickle of Soviet domination.

On a more practical level, Polyakov wanted to guarantee a future for his sons in the Soviet system, but to accomplish this he had to curry favor from the powerful within his organization. The Americans were the means by which he could succeed in this ambition, providing him with gifts that allowed him to buy influence. As he rose within the GRU organization, doors opened for his sons and they were afforded the benefits of higher education and employment opportunities commensurate with their father's rank and position.

Polyakov never championed our causes of freedom, justice, and democracy. Quite the contrary; these were lofty ideals that did not matter to him and his daily life. On the few occasions when we raised the possibility of defection to the West, he quietly but forcefully ended the conversation. Polyakov was born a Russian and would die a Russian.

Christmas came early and often for everyone involved in the Polyakov operation during the New Delhi phase, and we waited anxiously for the highlights cable from Paul D after each meeting. What was Polyakov sending us this time? Over the years we had come to expect everything on GRU operations and personnel to which he had access, but it was his positive intelligence that had consumers in the U.S. government talking. Was it the "secret" version of *Military Thought*, a monthly publication of the Soviet general staff on military doctrine and strategy? While dry prose to many of us in operations, analysts throughout the intelligence community found it invaluable to understanding the Soviet military threat and came to expect the monthly disseminations as if they were a subscription to a favorite magazine. Was it the top secret Soviet embassy annual report that was a comprehensive statement of Soviet embassy relations with its host country and included contributions from the GRU and KGB chiefs? Was it the famous "Top Secret of Special Importance" Kapitsa document detailed earlier in Chapter 4? Was it the hundreds of pages of the top secret Military Industrial Commission's collection requirements on Western military technology, staggering in their reflection of Soviet knowledge of highly classified U.S. military plans and programs, and a bombshell according to many in the intelligence community? (The Military Industrial Commission [VPK] of the USSR Council of Ministers coordinated and controlled all research, design, development, testing, and production of Soviet military equipment and systems. An integral part of the VPK's responsibility was the issuance of collection requirements on military matters for all Soviet government agencies from the KGB and GRU to the Ministry of Foreign Affairs and the Ministry of Foreign Trade.)

The gifts and other remuneration we furnished Polyakov were trinkets compared to those he provided us. Of greater significance, most items he requested were not for his personal use. They were earmarked for his superiors whose influence he courted or others in the GRU whose daily support he needed—for example his desk and personnel officers. Accordingly, our shopping sprees always took place one or two months before Polyakov's return to Moscow on vacation or on permanent assignment. These handouts ranged from wristwatches and crystal glassware to inexpensive ballpoint pens, depending on the rank or position of the intended recipient.

Oddly, during one period Polyakov began to ask for large numbers of these pens, which brought quizzical looks and out-loud questioning in the CIA as to his need for such quantities. Much to our embarrassment, we found the answer in a safe containing his production and the answer was doubly embarrassing. Polyakov had earlier given us a copy of a GRU headquarters collection requirement that tasked its residencies quarterly to acquire a specific brand of ballpoint pen for use as GRU concealment devices. Seeing an easy way to fulfill his headquarters request, Polyakov enlisted our support, thinking we were aware of its genesis because he had given us a copy of the requirement. The CIA was now providing concealment devices for potential use by GRU agents worldwide. However, once we sheepishly and belatedly understood what the pens were to be used for, we disseminated the GRU collection requirement to the appropriate agencies in the intelligence community.

Throughout the years of our contact with Polyakov, he asked for and we paid him the paltry sum of less than one thousand dollars a year. The items he requested for personal use were, for the most part, inexpensive things he could not purchase in Moscow and were related to his passion for hunting, fishing, and woodworking. They included fishhooks, sinkers, fly rods, shotguns, ammunition, bow and arrows, wading boots, hand warmers, drills, and sandpaper. The only luxury item he ever wanted was a strand of pearls for his wife, Nina, which we later had to replace as he had given the original to a high-ranking Soviet official visiting his embassy.

While the Polyakov operation was running smoothly in the field, a mini-revolution was about to begin at headquarters that would have a lasting and profound effect on the case and on the handling of future generations of sensitive sources. The man at the center of the upheaval was Richard (Dick) Stolz, a career Soviet operations officer and newly appointed deputy chief of SE Division. A kind, thoughtful man with impeccable operational skills, Stolz was the model for the adage that good men can and do succeed in bureaucracies. He had become intimately involved in the Polyakov operation in the early 1970s, when he was chief of the division's Counterintelligence Group. Accordingly he was well aware of our June 1972 one-on-one contact with Polyakov in Moscow and our subsequent realization that we had severely limited options to communicate with him during his scheduled assignment to Hanoi. To Stolz this was unacceptable and, as the consummate professional, he quietly vowed that if he ever found himself in a position to rectify this shortcoming he would take on the challenge. That opportunity presented itself several years later when he returned to the division following his tour of duty as chief in Belgrade.

Stolz's request to the technical support component responsible for supporting agent operations was specific. Provide our source with a short-range, high-speed, two-way communications device that encrypted the transmitted information, was small in size to allow for concealment, was portable, and would function for years. Stolz's explanation as to the importance of his request was equally direct. We were currently handling the highest ranking Soviet intelligence officer in the history of the U.S.

government and he would be returning to Moscow in about two years from what could be his last overseas assignment. Time-critical intelligence would be available to this source and we were obligated to provide him with the most secure, current, and reliable means possible to report that information. It would be a dereliction of duty if we were forced to rely only on a cumbersome and dangerous series of dead drops and signal sites to communicate with a source of such stature and access.

The engineers' response to Stolz's request was equally straightforward. Sorry, but it could not be accomplished. We have neither the funds nor the expertise and we do not believe the latter exists elsewhere. Not to be deterred, Stolz broadened his efforts, taking his problem to an Agency group that did not routinely support DO efforts but that researched and developed cutting-edge technologies, on occasion in concert with private industry. Perhaps eager to enter the world of clandestine operations or perhaps simply to be part of a new and exciting scientific adventure, they offered to broker contact with an external company they believed could develop and deliver the requested equipment within the required time frame.

The Division eagerly accepted the offer with one proviso. A division case officer had to be directly and intimately involved in the project from the beginning. Accepted by the specialized Agency group, Dick C, a division officer with Moscow experience, met with the contractor's engineers and designers and, among other things, negotiated the system requirements and designs, and developed the testing and operational scenarios.

Two years later and just before Polyakov's reassignment to Moscow in 1976, the cooperation between a private contractor and SE Division resulted in the completion of Polyakov's handheld, two-way, encrypted communications device. Appropriately code-named Unique, but known as Buster in the CIA's technical support group, it was the first of its kind in U.S. spy equipment annals. Although built only for Polyakov on an accelerated basis, many of the lessons learned from its development were incorporated in successor systems.

Unique was a two-way system that was agent-initiated and consisted of three primary components: two portable base stations and one agent unit. The base station received Polyakov's message and then transmitted acknowledgment of receipt to Polyakov's agent unit along with any other required brief message. The cryptography in the equipment was revolutionary in that it synchronized automatically between the base station and the agent unit. Plans called for one of the base stations to be located in the CIA premises inside the U.S. embassy in Moscow and one to be taken to a CIA officer's apartment or used on the street for prescheduled opportunities, thus affording Polyakov additional transmission sites. Before a scheduled exchange Polyakov typed his comments on a small keyboard built into his agent unit, placed it in his pocket, and boarded public transportation that took him past the U.S. embassy. Approaching the embassy he activated the unit, which transmitted the information to the base station in a 2.6-second burst. Polyakov's tram continued on its way and he read our message in the privacy of his apartment.

In early 1976 the Polyakov operation was running on autopilot, with a satisfied asset and satisfied intelligence community customers who received his production. Difficulty and impending tragedy then struck. A cable arrived from New Delhi with the news that Paul was sick—potentially very sick. He eventually was evacuated to Georgetown University Hospital, where he was diagnosed with a rare and terminal lung disease. Within the corridors of headquarters our first concern was for Paul's well-being and that of his family. Nevertheless, we also had to focus on our friend in the field. We had meetings to conduct, intelligence to process, and, of critical importance, an asset to ready for internal handling on untested state-of-the-art communications equipment.

The last meeting between Paul and Polyakov was bittersweet. Business as always came first and then it was time for the final good-bye. Neither discussed the future difficulties each might face, although each understood that Paul's had more clarity than Polyakov's. The atmosphere and banter was simply that of two old friends relaxing and enjoying one another's company. As a token of the personal and secret bond they had forged, Polyakov presented Paul with a bottle of his Ukrainian homeland's Three Stars cognac, the first gift he had given to one of his CIA handlers. The meeting ended with a handshake and this chapter in the operation was closed. Paul would lose his personal battle after a four-year struggle.

THE POLYAKOV CASE—
THE END

THE SENIOR CIA OFFICER KNOWN for this book's purposes as "Mr. K" assumed the role of Polyakov's case officer following Paul's departure from India. By design, his participation in the operation had always been important. Now his role was crucial. In the past he appeared for debriefing sessions infrequently; however, now his travel and meetings with Polyakov became more recurrent and lengthy. Moreover, he assumed complete responsibility for the successful implementation of an internal communications plan with equipment that neither he nor Polyakov had seen. Those at headquarters in charge of assembling the required volume of material and equipment were mindful that Mr. K knew the intelligence business far better than they and that he would not tolerate mistakes or omissions. Accordingly, frantic days were the rule during July and early August of 1976, as we anxiously awaited the arrival of the final components of the system from the contractor as well as the completion of the concealment device Stolz had requested from the DO engineers. We met our deadline for transmittal to the field with only a few days to spare. It was time to cross our fingers and pray that everything would work and that the two principals would be pleased.

Polyakov was stunned by Unique. Always a harsh critic of CIA spy equipment, he had not expected a system that was so technically advanced, tested perfectly, and was agent-friendly. Needless to say, Mr. K did not tell Polyakov that the CIA had not developed Unique, and remained silent when Polyakov complimented "the boys from the center" for their success. This was a phrase he previously had used only when irritated with our handling of a particular matter, noting that any shortcoming in the operation was never the fault of field personnel but always those at the center. Over the years we had made minor mistakes such as selecting the incorrect size of fishhook or other miscellaneous hunting accessories he had requested. However, he was right and we gladly accepted such observations as "Can't they tell the difference between a brook trout and a sturgeon?"

Polyakov left New Delhi in August 1976 confident that our mutual commitment and cooperation would continue uninterrupted until his retirement from the GRU regardless of whether that occurred before or after another overseas tour. He had Unique and was headed for a senior position as Chief of the Second Faculty at the GRU's Military-Diplomatic Academy (MDA). The MDA was the GRU's training facility for new officers as well as providing course instruction to military intelligence officers from allied socialist countries such as East Germany and Bulgaria.

Our first scheduled contact with Polyakov following his return to Moscow was planned for early December via Unique. We were confident that there would be a successful exchange, but as professionals we recognized there were many variables that could lead to failure. Anything could go wrong—from a technical malfunction to a snowstorm forcing tram route closures. At this point all we could do was wait. A cable finally arrived from Moscow Station with the news that the first Unique exchange had taken place on schedule and without mishap. The Stolz-inspired and Stolz-led mini-revolution had achieved success. At headquarters we opened the bottle of Three Stars cognac. With a collective sigh of relief and thanks, the privileged few aware of the achievement toasted Polyakov, whose sacrifices required that we perform beyond what we imagined possible.[1]

The next three years in the operation were more productive than anyone could have envisioned. It was long recognized that Polyakov's access in Moscow would be far greater than when he was abroad, but the breadth and depth of that access as a general at the MDA was unexpected. The quality and number of documents he photographed and passed via dead drop was staggering even to the most knowledgeable headquarters officer. On the counterintelligence side highlights included hundreds of pages of the complete GRU training manual, which was immediately dubbed the "GRU Bible." It was a comprehensive statement of GRU operational philosophy, modus operandi, and rules and regulations governing espionage activities outside the Soviet Union. Polyakov also provided the identities, biographic information, and training results of three-plus years of GRU graduating classes slated for assignment abroad, in effect eradicating their cover and that of their replacements for years. And, in his usual subtle and personal way, Polyakov surprised us by requisitioning GRU-fabricated concealment devices to pass his photographed material. This was the first time he had not handcrafted the device he used to pass us materials, and it was viewed by many at headquarters as a statement from the old soldier. "I've given you the gold mine and, just for the fun of it, here's another gift for the technical boys at the center." Our technical personnel were amazed at the simplicity, craftsmanship, and obvious long-term durability of the GRU spy gear.

On the positive intelligence side he passed copies of a highly restricted top secret version of *Military Thought*, top secret Communist Party publications never before acquired, and more of the Military-Industrial Commission collection requirements mentioned earlier. The translation load at headquarters was enormous, but no one complained.

Our exchanges via Unique continued uninterrupted, with the exception of an extended period beginning in September 1977, when then–Director of the CIA Stansfield Turner ordered Moscow Station to cease all operational activity until further notice. (The genesis and consequences of this stand-down are covered in Chapter 7 on the Kulak case.) The following year Polyakov advised us that he would be returning to New Delhi on what would surely be his last tour in the West. Once again it was time to gear up for handling abroad.

Headquarters received news of Polyakov's impending assignment with mixed reactions. On the positive side, we would be able to sit down with our trusted and respected comrade and work toward our common goals. However, that he was being posted to New Delhi again was selfishly greeted with less enthusiasm. We already had a wealth of information on GRU operations and Soviet plans and intentions in India that he had supplied during his previous tour. What could have changed in the three years since that could not be covered in several meetings? Despite our preference for an assignment to Tokyo or Beijing, where Polyakov would have been in a position to satisfy critical collection requirements about technology transfer and Chinese military capabilities and weapons development, the same energy and thought that went into the planning of the first New Delhi tour went into the "Delhi Two" operational phase.

Scotty S, another Russian-speaking SE Division employee, was tapped to serve as Polyakov's primary handler. A likable, well-regarded officer in his late thirties, Scotty had established a reputation as a hardworking, dependable professional who would ensure that there would be no mistakes in the operation. The only potential problem he and headquarters had to address was Polyakov's reaction to the almost eighteen years difference in their ages. As a Soviet military man, Polyakov tended to equate age with rank and, by extension, his importance in our eyes. To assuage his possible misgivings, Mr. K continued his participation in the operation. It was he who traveled to New Delhi to re-establish contact with Polyakov, conduct initial debriefings, and lay the groundwork for the introduction of Scotty. Our concerns were unfounded. Polyakov had no reservations about Scotty's relative youth, and together they established a productive and personal relationship.

In May 1980 Polyakov informed us that GRU headquarters had requested that he return to Moscow to attend a meeting on military attaché matters. Unexpected news or events always occurred in operations, but they were never welcomed, particularly with an asset of Polyakov's stature and importance. Was this a security problem or a legitimate request from GRU headquarters? There was no consensus. While we had no history or current knowledge of such a conference, there were no looming security issues in the Polyakov operation. Accordingly, the guidance to Scotty for the last meeting before Polyakov's departure was basic and clear-cut. Review the internal communications plans and the timing of his anticipated return to New Delhi.

Polyakov was strangely calm during our final contact. He reassured Scotty and by extension CIA headquarters that our contact would not be severed. In the unforeseen circumstance that he should not return, he had Unique and would be in touch. "I will survive. Do not worry about me." Toward the end of the meeting, Scotty nervously commented that he looked forward to the day when he and Polyakov could enjoy drinks and a meal together in the United States. Polyakov's response was the same as on several previous occasions, but more relaxed and matter-of-fact. He was born, had lived, and would die a Russian. When asked what would happen if our cooperation were discovered, he quietly replied, "a common, unmarked grave." There were no good-byes, but simply a handshake and a "see you upon your return."

Polyakov failed to reappear in New Delhi, and there was no communication from Moscow. Months passed and then several years. Endless discussions took place at headquarters about his status with no satisfactory answers. Unfortunately, due to an inexcusable error we were unaware that shortly after Polyakov's return he began writing articles for the monthly Soviet hunting and sporting magazine *Okhota*, a publication to which he had been a contributing author between overseas assignments. Personnel in the division's component responsible for acquiring the issues each month did not initiate the collection requirement until asked for a status report of their review of the material. Back issues were immediately obtained and scanned for mention of D. F. Polyakov. While our inattention to operational detail was indefensible, it was ameliorated by the news that Polyakov had been a frequent contributor to *Okhota* since his arrival in Moscow.

A collective sigh of relief and a thank God could be heard among those working on the case. Polyakov was alive, and apparently well, given the appearance of his articles. He had not been compromised, but what had happened? The possibilities were as numerous as the meetings on the matter. They ranged from medical problems that forced his retirement to his continued GRU employment but having an inoperable Unique. Nevertheless, the previously agreed-upon plan would remain in effect. We would rely on Polyakov to decide if and when to break his silence. Our role would be to wait, reassured that knowledge of his secret past remained his and ours alone.

It had been four years since Polyakov's return to Moscow, when an unexpected event occurred in the now dormant case. A copy of *Okhota* arrived at headquarters. It contained another Polyakov-authored article, but this one raised eyebrows. It was not about hunting for big game or similar topics about which he had previously written. It was a recipe for coot, and contained detailed instructions and ingredients for preparation. Some viewed the article as an anomaly and, therefore, possibly a signal from Polyakov that he not only was alive but also was somehow trying to re-establish our communications link. Others were more pessimistic, but agreed that the theory should be pursued. His *Okhota* articles and the thousands of pages of cables and transcripts were scoured for answers. A hint was found in the operational files. During a brief conversation in the mid-1970s, Paul D and Polyakov discussed possibly using *Okhota* to establish communications should other options fail.

After much review and testing of the coot recipe ingredients, it was determined that they could be used for secret writing. Extrapolating from these discoveries, we could send a letter to the editor of *Okhota*, with questions for Polyakov on his article. The benign correspondence would contain secret writing that Polyakov could develop using the ingredients he had provided in the recipe. But should we proceed, given that our hypothesis was based on few facts and a great deal of conjecture? Burton Gerber, then chief of SE Division, made the final decision. The risks to this noble man were too great. We would take no action that might put his life in further jeopardy. He had reached mandatory retirement age and we would let him live in peace. The final chapter had been written in the Polyakov case, or so we thought.

One year later Ames volunteered to the KGB and identified General Polyakov, among many others, as an American spy. The roll-up of our assets began in June 1985. By 1986 we were forced to concede that there was a possibility that Polyakov was among the missing. In mid-1986 one of his sons, a Soviet Ministry of Foreign Affairs officer stationed in New Delhi, left for Moscow on what we assumed but could not confirm was home leave. He did not return to India. About the same time Polyakov's articles suddenly stopped appearing in *Okhota*. Lastly, there was an unsourced report about the arrest of a GRU general who had served in Greece. While Polyakov had never served in Greece, it was discussed as a possible assignment for him in the 1960s, and that he was a general could not be ignored.

In late 1988 we unofficially learned that Polyakov had been arrested. Several years later the Soviets officially announced that on 15 March 1988 (coincidentally, the Ides of March) General Dmitriy Fedorovich Polyakov was executed for espionage.

To many who never met Polyakov but supported the operation, and to his case officers who remained, the loss of this man was inexpressible. Polyakov, his contributions, and the sheer number of his years of service had become legend. He was immune from the inherent dangers of the dark side of espionage. It was difficult to accept that he was gone; it was more difficult to accept that he had died such a grisly death. An even greater burden was the possibility that our actions or inactions had resulted in his unmasking. We could not repay him for his sacrifice or his family for their loss, but we did owe each an answer.

CHAPTER 7

EARLY MAJOR CASES

A LEKSEY ISIDOROVICH KULAK, a KGB scientific and technical officer, may have been the only KGB or GRU source who outwitted the KGB, Robert Hanssen, Rick Ames, and author Jay Epstein. He did so by reportedly dying of natural causes before the KGB reacted to knowledge of his fifteen years of spying for the United States. That he was a Hero of the Soviet Union recipient, the Russian equivalent of a Medal of Honor, and was a legendary figure within the corridors of the First Chief Directorate were believed to have also played a role in delaying the arrest.

In March 1962 Kulak, later encrypted FEDORA by the FBI for internal use, and JADE for correspondence to and from the CIA, walked into the FBI field office in New York City and volunteered his services to American intelligence in exchange for cash. An odd duck in the world of espionage, he was more scientist than KGB case officer, and later asked the FBI for assistance in the form of double agents. (On occasion the FBI and CIA provided double or "controlled" agents to their recruited KGB and GRU sources to enhance the source's operational record with his parent service. The double agent ostensibly agreed to cooperate with and provide information to the source and his organization, but in actuality was under the direction and control of the CIA or FBI. Such operations were always handled with the source's input, and the double agent was never aware of the source's clandestine relationship with American intelligence.)

For thirteen years Kulak, whose CIA code name was CKKAYO, served in the United States on two separate tours. Between these tours he was assigned to Moscow, but we had no contact with him there. During the entire period of his U.S. assignments, the CIA's knowledge of his cooperation with the FBI was limited to general-interest counter-intelligence reporting and some positive intelligence. With the presumed exception of Angleton, the CIA was unaware of any operational details of the case such as meeting arrangements, debriefing language, and documentary production if any.

What caused this bureaucratically polite but distant relationship between the two organizations on the Kulak case? It could be summed up in two words: bona fides. As with Polyakov, Kulak was a target of Angleton's and his cadre of Monster Plot theorists, initially simply because he was a KGB officer who volunteered within months of Polyakov's approach. As they viewed it, this could not be a coincidence; this was the hidden hand of the KGB directing the operation. Conversely, Hoover and his special agents believed that Kulak (as Polyakov) was the genuine article, and resented Angleton's, ergo the CIA's, intrusion in an FBI operation about which they knew little. The rift only widened following the defection of KGB officer Nosenko in 1964 and subsequent reporting by Kulak that supported Nosenko's legitimacy, a position Angleton never accepted.

Following the removal of Angleton as Chief of the Counter-intelligence Staff in December 1974 and his subsequent retirement in 1975, the official CIA position on Kulak's bona fides began to take a 180-degree turn. Angleton was replaced by George Kalaris, who brought in career SE Division reports officer Leonard McCoy as his deputy. Earlier in his career McCoy, a renowned authority on Soviet military and political matters, had incurred the wrath of the Angletonians for his support of the bona fides of Nosenko, Polyakov, and others. He also believed that Kulak's bona fides were supported by the information the FBI had supplied to the CIA, even though it was limited in volume and scope.

At the time the CIA began to rethink its official position on Kulak, so too did the FBI. In a bizarre twist senior FBI Special Agent and counterintelligence expert James Nolan conducted a review of the Kulak case and concluded that it had been a KGB-controlled operation from inception. The FBI now believed that Hoover's premier source was a phoney.

At CIA headquarters news of the Bureau's about-face was greeted with disbelief and bewilderment. McCoy decided to challenge their findings and requested CIA access to the FBI files on the Kulak operation. In an unprecedented move, the FBI agreed. McCoy selected Cynthia Hausmann, a senior division case officer and counterintelligence specialist, and Sandy as the members of the CIA team. Issued FBI non-escort visitor badges two and three, the women spent four months reviewing the Kulak material at FBI headquarters under the watchful eye of Larry McWilliams, a crusty outspoken special agent and supporter of Nolan's theories of the case.

Cynthia and Sandy were provided with summary statements of Kulak's reporting, which included agent leads, KGB organization, and modus operandi. Repeated attempts to see meeting transcripts with verbatim source comments were met with a polite but forceful no. According to McWilliams, they would serve no useful purpose. The Bureau had accurately reflected Kulak's remarks in the summaries. After several months McWilliams acceded to the request and gave them partial transcripts of discussions of selected sensitive counterintelligence issues. However, to their chagrin they learned that many meetings had not been taped and others had either not been transcribed or the tapes were no longer available. In sum, a complete record of Kulak's reporting in his own words did not exist even at the FBI.

Early congenial discussions among the three began to disintegrate into daily lectures from McWilliams that Kulak was bad because almost every operation he described was handled contrary to standard FBI procedure. "The FBI would not do it that way," was his comment and appeared to be a large part of the FBI's or at least McWilliams' basis for concluding that Kulak was a controlled source. Despite numerous attempts to convince him that the KGB was not the FBI and had different rules and regulations for engagement, McWilliams refused to concede the point. The KGB had fooled the FBI for years, but no longer. That McCoy sent two women to review his and Nolan's work only inflamed him more. As he often pointed out, the CIA could do what it wanted with respect to female professionals, but he was from the Hoover school and women did not belong in such ranks.

Upon the ladies' return to CIA headquarters, Cynthia drafted a report of their findings and conclusions regarding Kulak's bona fides. Specifically,

Kulak had been a legitimate penetration of the KGB from his walk-in in New York in 1962. Of equal importance, the FBI had failed to recognize Kulak's value and importance as a source of positive intelligence, viewing him primarily from a narrow counterintelligence perspective. In early 1976 senior Agency management accepted the paper as the official CIA position on the bona fides of Kulak. The CIA and the FBI were still on opposite sides of the case.

Spring of 1976 brought a major change in the operation. Kulak, now fifty-six, was departing New York and returning to Moscow. The FBI and CIA believed that he would not be assigned abroad again because he was approaching mandatory retirement. SE Division officers Ben Pepper and Gus Hathaway, the latter scheduled for assignment to Moscow as Chief of Station, decided to take a stab at convincing the FBI to turn Kulak over to the CIA for internal handling. The FBI denied their request, claiming that Kulak had refused contact with the Agency in Moscow. The SE officers persisted and finally convinced the FBI to let Hathaway meet with Kulak and attempt to persuade him to communicate inside the Soviet Union.

Hathaway was successful. Kulak departed the United States in August 1976, trained in internal communication, equipped with a series of dead drop and signal sites, and ready to provide intelligence to the U.S. government.

Having had no operational history with Kulak and only a handful of meetings with him before his return, it was impossible for the CIA to predict whether he would communicate as promised or simply decide to destroy his package. To everyone's astonishment, on his first scheduled recontact in July 1977 he signaled that he was ready to load one of his dead drops. The package was retrieved and its contents were startling, not so much in the material passed but in what his note promised. Among the items was a list of Soviet officials in the United States working against the American scientific and technical target. The list was neatly hand printed and its detail would have taken Kulak hours to amass and prepare. Further, he stated that in the next exchange in the fall he would include the following: the identities and targets of all Soviet officials and scientists worldwide involved in the collection of U.S. scientific and technical information and the five- and ten-year operational plans of the KGB Scientific and Technical Directorate. The eccentric old scientist was prepared to provide the United States with the KGB blueprint ten years in advance on the top priority intelligence collection requirement of the day—technology transfer. All we had to do was wait for his signal, retrieve his package, and reap the intelligence bonanza, or so we believed.

On 15 July 1977, about a week after the recovery of Kulak's package, the KGB ambushed Moscow Station officer Martha Peterson while she was trying to communicate with CIA source Aleksandr Dmitriyevich Ogorodnik, a Soviet Ministry of Foreign Affairs officer recruited in Bogota. Two weeks later without incident the station picked up a package from Polyakov filled with hundreds of pages of documents. August was calm, but the first of September brought a second compromise. Station officer Vincent Crockett was arrested servicing a dead drop for CIA source Anatoliy Nikolayevich Filatov, a GRU officer recruited and handled in-place in Algiers. Shortly thereafter CIA Director Admiral Stansfield Turner ordered a stand-down of all Moscow Station operational activity. There would be no additional embarrassments to the administration. Moscow was closed for business until further notice.

Turner's edict was met with an uproar from SE Division and others in the Directorate of Operations. He could not be serious. No one, including the director, could or would shut down the collection of high-level intelligence from the Soviet Union. But Turner stood firm, only adding to the pandemonium when he set the parameters for reconsideration of his decision. Unless or until the directorate could guarantee that there would be no further compromises, the ban would remain in effect. Did we really have a director who did not understand basic tenets of espionage activity? It always involved calculated risk and always violated the laws of the target country. The director's demands could not be met.

Kulak became the central figure in the firestorm between the director and SE Division. In another month or so, we would know the KGB's shortcomings, their strengths, their specific targets, and the identities of all who were targeted against us in the scientific and technical field. At a minimum it would save untold millions in expenditures that would otherwise be necessary to uncover and counter Soviet efforts. These arguments did not impress or dissuade Turner. We had no recourse and only one option—wait to hear from Kulak and then do nothing.

Kulak signaled his intention to fill his dead drop right on schedule. Bound by Turner's directive, Moscow Station did not respond with a sign that it was prepared to retrieve the material. Again on schedule Kulak marked his signal site for a second time. Once more the station took no action. The CIA phase of the Kulak operation that had begun with such promise appeared to have ended in silence. The director had been obeyed, and the files were closed.

In 1983, while writing *The Agency: The Rise and Decline of the CIA,* author John Ranelagh interviewed Turner, who is quoted as stating: "My feeling with the DDO was to tell them I wanted to know when they were planning to take a risk above a certain threshold. And when they did, I'd ask what was the percentage risk of them or their agent getting caught. I wouldn't say 'use a different technique.' I didn't know techniques. But I would say I was willing or unwilling to take the risk."[1] On 11 December 1985, Turner wrote to Ranelagh as follows: "You suggest I was cautious about taking risks in the clandestine collection process. In four years there was only one risk the espionage branch asked me to take that I did not approve—sometimes we debated and refined the operation—but the spooks got all the support they asked for. The problem was they didn't have enough risky proposals."[2]

In his own book, *Secrecy and Democracy: The CIA in Transition,* published one year later, Turner stated, "the question, though, was which of the more sensitive operations I should personally control. Espionage operations came in such different forms, often of a kind that I found it almost impossible to write specific rules. I was able, however, to define certain categories of actions to be cleared with me. These included payments to agents when they exceed certain dollar amounts; recruitments of foreign agents at Cabinet level or above; dispensing any lethal material, such as explosives or poison requested by an agent who might feel he would be tortured if caught; any operation where the risks were high and exposure could seriously embarrass the United States."[3]

It was apparent to those involved in the Kulak operation that "exposure" was the operative word to Turner when he shut down Moscow Station activities. He had no problem with the earlier and successful Kulak and Polyakov dead drop retrievals in July, but after the Peterson and Crockett arrests the collection of intelligence in Moscow had become too risky.

In March 1978 Turner did an about-face and temporarily lifted his ban on Moscow Station to conduct the most daring and dangerous of operational acts—an attempt to establish personal contact with an asset and exfiltrate him from the Soviet Union. Kulak was that agent.

Distrust and dislike of Turner's decisions had reached such a level that many in SE Division were surprised at his sudden reversal of policy. However, in what may be a sanitized reference to Kulak, the rationale for his blessing of the impending operation can be found in his book: "The most daring exploit I witnessed in my four years as DCI was a successful effort by the Agency to protect the life of an agent who thought he was about to be arrested. In part this is a moral obligation; in part, it is a pragmatic matter, because it assures future agents that they will be taken care of if at all possible."[4]

In early 1978 Edward Jay Epstein published *Legend: The Secret World of Lee Harvey Oswald*. In the book Epstein described FBI source FEDORA in sufficient detail that KGB counterintelligence would be able to put him on a short list of suspected American spies. Among the facts Epstein presented were the following: FEDORA was a KGB First Chief Directorate officer; he specialized in scientific and technical intelligence collection against the United States; he was assigned to a cover position at the United Nations in New York; he volunteered to the FBI in March 1962; for more than six years he provided the FBI with information about Soviet espionage activities; in 1971 he told the FBI that Daniel Ellsberg's Pentagon Papers had been provided to Soviet intelligence; and at the time of Colby's removal of Angleton and McCoy's appointment to the CI staff (1974–75) FEDORA was still providing the FBI with information.[5]

News of Epstein's book stunned SE Division. It was incomprehensible that the existence of, let alone details about, a valued penetration of the KGB would appear in the public domain. While the investigation of such a leak was an FBI responsibility, an agent's life was potentially in grave danger and the CIA had to act immediately.

The operational plan called for Hathaway to "get black," that is, evade KGB surveillance and call Kulak at his home, hoping that he was there and that he would answer the phone. Hathaway would then briefly describe the situation and offer Kulak safe exit from the Soviet Union and asylum in the United States. Assuming Kulak's acceptance of the proposal, the actual exfiltration would begin. Everyone involved knew that under the circumstances the odds for success were not in our and our agent's favor. Such operations required months of detailed preparation and even then luck played an important role in any success. Moreover, Moscow Station had never attempted an exfiltration. Kulak would be the first.

The night before the operation's onset, a massive snowstorm hit the Washington, DC, area and a late evening at the office turned into an all-night stay. Weather in Moscow was no less harsh. With frigid temperatures and snow, Hathaway spent hours on the dark streets trying to lose KGB surveillance. He was forced to abort. The next evening he made a second attempt and this time he was successful. Kulak was home and immediately recognized Hathaway's voice. He was given the news and quietly responded without hesitation or fright. He thanked Hathaway for the notification and the offer, but said that he would be fine. The call ended.

Despite Kulak's conviction that he would be safe, we continued to be fearful that it was just a matter of time before he was arrested due to Epstein's revelations. However, that did not take place; for years we heard nothing, although we had a variety of sources. It was not until the early 1990s, long before we were aware of Hanssen's treason and before the case against Ames had been proven, that we received word about Kulak. He had died of natural causes about a decade earlier and more recently his portrait, which was prominently displayed because of his status as a Hero of the Soviet Union, had been removed from the hallways of the KGB. Kulak had been correct in his pronouncement to Hathaway. He knew that it would take more than his exposure in a book written by a Western author for the KGB to take action against a Hero of the Soviet Union. What he would have been unable to fathom, we suspect, was that the KGB would continue to conceal knowledge of his treason despite reporting from Hanssen and Ames. In the end the only price Kulak paid was the loss of his place on the KGB's wall of heroes.

●—●—●

Whether inside or outside of the world of espionage, seemingly insignificant events may later have profound impact. The following is such a story.

During Polyakov's home leave in 1968 Sandy was asked to inventory the contents of a large bank of five-drawer safes in her branch. Dust covered the files, which contained only non-record copies of official documents and therefore should have been destroyed years earlier. However, one folder caught her attention. Wedged among the inconsequential material in the bottom drawer of one safe was an official DO operational file (a 201) on a Soviet official named Nikolay Chernov. It contained only a few documents, including a visa request for temporary travel to New York in the 1960s and a reference to sensitive-source information identifying Chernov as a GRU officer. Who was this man and why was his seemingly forgotten 201 in a branch that did not retain such records and obviously had not looked at the file for years? Perplexed, but a new employee recently schooled in the need-to-know principle, Sandy simply took note of the Soviet's name, finished her task, and handed the pages of her inventory to the deputy branch chief.

One morning four years later, in 1972, an employee of Jeanne's in the division's Biographics Branch appeared in Sandy's office holding the file of a Nikolay Chernov and asking for a copy of the sensitive-source reporting referenced in the file. Chernov had requested a visa for a short trip to the West, including a stop in New York City.

Sandy immediately recognized the name as that of the subject of the mysterious 201 she had inventoried years before. This time she had the courage to tell her boss about the strange story of Chernov and his official file, which someone must have returned to the directorate's main files after her inventory. Later that day her chief related news shocking not only to her but also to him and a number of others in their chain of command. Chernov, code-named NICKNACK by the Bureau and later PDCLIP by the CIA, was a GRU technical officer who had volunteered to the FBI in the early 1960s and whose cooperation had been known only to a few former senior SE Division officers, obviously someone in the old branch that followed GRU cases, and, of course, Angleton.

The division immediately phoned the FBI to ensure they were aware of Chernov's planned travel, scheduled for the following week. They were not. A copy of the identical visa request had not yet made its way through their bureaucracy. Thankfully, the CIA had given the FBI sufficient time to plan and attempt to recontact Chernov, with whom they had not been in touch for about ten years. We were proud we could assist and they were appreciative of the help.

Several years passed before SE Division learned that the FBI had a successful exchange with Chernov and just how important that exchange had been. During a brief encounter with the FBI in the New York area Chernov turned over documentary material containing thousands of leads, known to the CIA and FBI as the MORINE leads, to heretofore unknown GRU agents abroad. The FBI, in turn, quickly and properly forwarded the material to the CIA through established channels at that time—directly to Angleton and his counterintelligence staff.

Unconscionably, Angleton ensured that for three years Chernov's gold mine of information remained buried and uninvestigated in the staff's files, because he was believed to be a Soviet-controlled source and part of the Monster Plot. The voluminous reporting was discovered by an individual working for George Kalaris, Angleton's replacement, after Angleton's 1975 departure.

The volume of the material was so great that Kalaris sought the assistance of SE Division's Counterintelligence Group in the research and dissemination of the reporting to intelligence services worldwide, a project still being carried out in the early 1980s. The information included but was not limited to the Serge Fabiew GRU spy ring that had been operating in France since 1963, and the former head of the Swiss National Air Defense forces, Brigadier Jean-Louis Jeanmaire, who became a GRU agent in 1961.[6]

In the early 1990s, some twenty years after his last contact with the FBI, Chernov was arrested in Moscow. In the more permissive post–Cold War atmosphere, he was sentenced to eight years but amnestied after less than a year. He was known to Ames and, presumably, Hanssen. One or both of them no doubt fingered him to the KGB. However, because this was a long dormant case, and Chernov had left the GRU many years earlier, the authorities delayed arresting him until they no longer faced a source-sensitivity problem.

●—●—●

In 1974 during his first tour abroad Leonid Georgiyevich Poleshchuk,[7] a young KGB political intelligence officer assigned to Kathmandu, Nepal, became a CIA asset. He was encrypted CKRUN at the time, with a later change to GTWEIGH. To some degree the circumstances of his recruitment mirrored his impulsive personality. A CIA case officer with whom he was in contact had developed him almost to the point of recruitment, but had to leave Nepal before he could make the formal offer.

Subsequently, Poleshchuk volunteered his services to his CIA friend's replacement. In a strange twist of fate it was Poleshchuk's boss, KGB Resident Seliverstov, who deserves the credit for pushing the junior officer over the edge and into the camp of the Main Enemy. He insisted that Poleshchuk pay for a bottle of whisky the latter intended to use with one of his developmental sources. This was the last straw for the rash Poleshchuk, who saw the resident as a tyrant—a habitual abuser of the system who left his subordinates to fend for themselves. Poleshchuk abruptly left the residency and contacted his acquaintance at the U.S. embassy. He later commented that but for a bottle of booze he might not have sought the American's counsel and assistance.

We later learned that Poleshchuk's motivation apparently went far beyond anger at a domineering boss, a view reportedly also held by a number of Seliverstov's subordinates over the years. In November 1973 Poleshchuk's father passed away after a long, painful struggle. Poleshchuk wanted to return home to attend the funeral. The KGB denied his request. The following month his only child, eleven-year-old Andrei, became ill, requiring hospitalization until early 1974. Poleshchuk again asked permission to leave Nepal. Once more the answer was no. It could easily be argued that the KGB itself deserves a great deal of the credit for Poleshchuk's decision to seek out the Americans, an action that he took within a year of his father's death and his son's illness.

Sandy was supporting the nascent Poleshchuk operation at headquarters when in early December 1974 Ben Pepper, chief of the Operations Branch in the division's Counterintelligence Group, popped into her office and asked if she would like to spend Christmas in Nepal. Local CIA Chief John B, who was Poleshchuk's new case officer, had requested headquarters' assistance. He wanted someone who knew the KGB, could set up case files, refine the guidance on requirements, author cables, and provide other support as required. Thrilled at the prospect of her first overseas assignment and with the blessing of her family, one week later she was on her way to Nepal.

Three days later Sandy arrived in Nepal anxious to meet John B, a man she had never seen and with whom she had no contact instructions. But how hard could it be to identify an American official from those greeting the daily Air Nepal flight from New Delhi? This was the end of the world, after all. Unfortunately, it was more difficult than expected and almost resulted in an operational disaster before she had been on the ground five minutes. Upon deplaning Sandy immediately saw a well-dressed Caucasian man in the mostly Nepalese crowd, who obviously had to be John B. She uttered a faint hello, but before she could identify herself by name the stranger began shouting greetings in Russian to a group behind her. Briefly wondering how she could mistake a Russian for an American diplomat, she quickly extricated herself from the Soviet contingent and bolted for the terminal building. There the elusive CIA chief suddenly appeared, introduced himself, and explained that they had to leave the airport immediately. He mumbled that he must avoid an acquaintance he had just seen. The mystery man turned out to be KGB Resident Seliverstov who was instrumental in our recruitment of Poleshchuk and who was none other than the Soviet gentleman Sandy had earlier approached. As luck would have it, they did not escape the KGB chief; he accosted John near his parked car and bluntly asked the identity of his visitor. Thinking on the fly, John introduced Sandy as a guest of the U.S. ambassador's wife. This appeared to satisfy Seliverstov and they all went their separate ways. What a way to start Christmas in Nepal.

For the Kathmandu officers involved with Poleshchuk and his various antics, the next month was a whirlwind of activity. This included meeting preparations, debriefings, initial planning for internal communications, and refinement of an exfiltration plan should Poleshchuk decide to defect rather than return to Moscow. The latter possibility was a daily concern. Poleshchuk was prone to act before he considered the consequences. It was well within the realm of possibility that he would get drunk, drive his KGB operational vehicle to John B's house, and say "let's go, I've just punched my resident in the nose." The office had spent considerable time and effort planning for such an event, taking into account the fishbowl-operating environment of Kathmandu and the limited available options even in a nonemergency situation. That plan was soon to be tested as part of a surprise birthday party John B's officers had planned for him, fitting his reputation as a legendary prankster.

Late one afternoon the pregnant wife of the deputy chief notified John that she had an inebriated Poleshchuk in her living room demanding to be taken to the United States. The chief flew into action, initiating each step of the exfiltration when he suddenly realized that there were flaws in the original plan and he would be forced to improvise. An hour later he appeared at his deputy's home to collect what he assumed was an even more distraught and anxious Poleshchuk. To John's officers' delight and his own anger, he was greeted with cheers of Happy Birthday. After a tirade of expletives, he soon calmed down when it was pointed out that, while he had been duped, the weaknesses of a flawed operational plan had been exposed and could be corrected.

Fortunately for all involved in the case, the revised exfiltration plan was never implemented for "the wild one," as Poleshchuk was affectionately dubbed. Rather, he left Kathmandu in 1975 with diamonds as payment for his services, an internal communications plan, and a promise to resume contact in the Soviet Union. For ten years there was no word from Poleshchuk until early 1985, when Sandy's and his paths again crossed.

One morning Sandy, then chief of SE External Operations for Africa, received a cable from Lagos describing a walk-in who said, "I come from the land of the tall mountains." The walk-in requested that this message be sent to Washington and promised they would know who he was. Sandy immediately recognized that it was Poleshchuk, the young KGB political intelligence officer whose case she had supported in Kathmandu in 1974. What were the odds that eleven years later they would be on the opposite ends of the same cable? Even more incredibly, Jeanne in Libreville received a copy of the cable and, like Sandy, recognized the case. As it happened, the CIA chief from Lagos was vacationing in Libreville to enjoy the beach and some French cuisine. His deputy thought he should be advised of the walk-in.

Headquarters immediately informed Lagos that they did indeed have a new source, provided them with the history of the case, and advised them to hold on for the ride of their life. This asset would try everyone's patience and the operation would require careful, detailed planning to ensure his safety.

After the first sit-down meeting with Poleshchuk it was clear that he was a changed man. Thankfully for all, headquarters' initial warnings were wrong and history had not repeated itself. Erased from Poleshchuk's personality were his earlier brashness, impulsiveness, immaturity, and self-centeredness. In its place his new handlers found a soft-spoken, reflective, cautious individual whose drinking had moderated and who would never consider a precipitous operational act that might compromise himself or his family. The "wild one" had metamorphosed into an ideal agent.

Additionally, he was no longer a political intelligence case officer but had switched to the counterintelligence line of the KGB, a specialty that would allow him fairly wide access to information on KGB penetrations of and operations against members of foreign intelligence services, particularly upon his reassignment to Moscow from Nigeria.

In late May 1985 a discussion took place at headquarters that would have a profound effect on the future of the Poleshchuk case. It involved his request for the $20,000 he was owed, his desire to take the money with him on his upcoming Moscow vacation, and his concern about smuggling the money past the KGB border control. Sandy and several others argued that the situation was a perfect opportunity to convince Poleshchuk of our ability to communicate securely inside the Soviet Union during his eventual permanent reassignment there, rather than sit back and wait another five or ten years before he was reassigned in the West.

The argument was straightforward. Just pass him the money via a dead drop that contained no spy paraphernalia and no secret messages. In a worst-case scenario, if he were caught with the money, the KGB would suspect criminal activity, but they would have no proof of espionage. There would be nothing to connect Poleshchuk to American intelligence assuming, of course, that the designated Moscow Station officer did not place the drop until he or she was surveillance free.

Rick Ames, as chief of the Soviet Branch of the Division's CI Group, had an advisory role in operational decisions involving division sources and developmental cases outside the Soviet Union. For the first time in Sandy's experience in the Africa Branch, Rick not only exercised his role on one of her cases, but did so forcefully. He was adamant in his disagreement on the passage of funds in Moscow and repeatedly argued that the potential risk of compromise to Poleshchuk was too great. Division chief Gerber sided with Sandy, and Poleshchuk agreed to retrieve his money via a Moscow dead drop.

In July 1985 Poleshchuk and his family departed Lagos for their vacation with an anticipated return to Nigeria in September. Poleshchuk failed to appear for his first scheduled recontact in late September. He was also a no-show for number two. Worry set in and on 2 October Milt Bearden, then deputy chief of SE Division, called Sandy to his office and showed her an excerpt of a cable from an unidentified field station. The reporting was obviously from a sensitive source and it was a DO officer's worst nightmare. Poleshchuk had been arrested. It would be Sandy's job to inform his field case officers.

How do you convey the sense of loss and the fear that we individually or collectively may have made the mistake or mistakes that cost this man his life? After much thought, anguish, and inability to say anything else, the message was simple and pointed. "There is no easy way to say this. GTWEIGH has been arrested." Everyone involved in the case from Lagos to Moscow to Langley remembered the day they learned of the tragedy. As we assumed at the time and learned later, the unmentionable consequences became a trial, a conviction on 12 June 1986, and a bullet to the head on 30 July 1986 for the thoughtful, reasoned man who by the time of our contact in Lagos had truly come to understand the risks on his path of treason.

What had gone wrong? The analysis began the next day. After a review of all aspects of the operation we concluded that the Moscow Station officer had been under KGB surveillance when he put the money down. Thus, the KGB was able to establish the link between Poleshchuk and the CIA. Ames had been right; the risk was too great. Nine years would pass before Sandy, the Moscow Station officer, Poleshchuk's Lagos case officers, Gerber, and others could publicly unload their burden of guilt for their agent's compromise. Poleshchuk's death was the direct result of Ames' treason. Early in his treasonous activities he informed the KGB about Poleshchuk's relationship with the CIA. Long before the Moscow Station officer loaded the dead drop, the KGB knew for whom it was intended, where it was located, and approximately when it would be retrieved.

General Rem Sergeyevich Krasilnikov, who directed KGB operations against CIA personnel and agents in Moscow from 1979 to 1992 while serving as chief of the American Department of the Second (Counterintelligence) Chief Directorate of the KGB, discusses the compromise of Poleshchuk in a recent book. Krasilnikov assigns initial responsibility for the loss of Poleshchuk to the CIA Moscow Station, which failed to note KGB surveillance and led them right to the spot where he placed a secret container for an unknown individual. On 2 August 1985 a heavy-set man of middle age, who turned out to be Poleshchuk, cleared the dead drop. In a subsequent investigation and trial, the details of Poleshchuk's treason were revealed. Not surprisingly,

Krasilnikov makes no mention of Ames' role in Poleshchuk's capture and, to the contrary, calls Ames a "scapegoat" for the failures of Moscow Station.[8]

However, Viktor Ivanovich Cherkashin, the senior KGB counterintelligence officer in Washington in 1985 and Ames' first case officer, contradicts Krasilnikov's account of the Poleshchuk loss. According to Cherkashin, Ames betrayed Poleshchuk. The KGB's story of the latter's unmasking was nothing more than an ornate fabrication by the Second Chief Directorate.[9] Ames, of course, freely admits that he betrayed Poleshchuk to the KGB.

Lieutenant Colonel Vladimir Mikhaylovich Piguzov, a KGB political intelligence officer code-named GTJOGGER, was recruited by the CIA in Indonesia in 1978 through a bizarre chain of events. A CIA case officer had developed a close friendship with Piguzov that subsequently led to a recruitment approach. Piguzov agreed to cooperate with his CIA friend, and headquarters and the field geared up to handle the new source. Then everything fell apart. Amid photographers and the local press, the Soviet ambassador to Indonesia lodged an official protest with the Indonesian government, accusing the United States of attempting to subvert Soviet diplomat Vladimir Piguzov. There was shock and disbelief in our office in Jakarta and at CIA headquarters. How could we have been so wrong about the nature of our officer's relationship with Piguzov and his commitment to cooperate?

Fortunately, all was not lost. Several days later Piguzov contacted our officer, informed him that he told his KGB security officer about our approach, and was now ready to work for the CIA. In explanation Piguzov reasoned that KGB counterintelligence would never suspect him of being an American spy because he had reported our advances, claiming that he had turned them down. He was now above reproach.

For the remainder of his tour in Jakarta Piguzov provided information on KGB officers and agent operations in Indonesia, to include those being run by the KGB residency in Jakarta and the sub-residency in Surabaya as well as in other Southeast Asian countries. One of the most important agent leads provided by Piguzov was that to David Henry Barnett. Barnett, a former CIA officer, had resigned in 1970 after completion of a tour in

Indonesia. He remained in the area and, in late 1976, following the failure of a business venture and faced with large debt, he approached the KGB and offered to sell them classified information. During the period of his cooperation with the Soviets he provided details on a CIA collection program targeted against Soviet military weapons, and identified CIA case officers and assets. The KGB wanted him to re-apply to the CIA but, faced with the prospect of being polygraphed, he demurred. He had, however, put out feelers to other U.S. government components.

Barnett was indicted on espionage charges on 24 October 1980. He pled guilty and was sentenced to eighteen years in federal prison. He was paroled in 1990 after serving approximately ten years.[10]

After completion of his tour in Jakarta, Piguzov returned to Moscow, where he was assigned to the Andropov Institute, the KGB training academy. He eventually assumed the senior position of secretary of the Communist Party at the Institute, a position he held at the time of his February 1987 arrest. Having been given up by Ames in the summer of 1985, Piguzov was subsequently tried and executed.

Boris Nikolayevich Yuzhin, encrypted KAHLUA by the FBI and GTTWINE by the CIA, is one of the luckiest men alive. A KGB officer in San Francisco under TASS journalist cover, he was recruited by the FBI in 1979 and run by them for the next three years. The CIA played a subordinate but important role in this operation, because one of our officers, Colin T, participated in some of the meetings to obtain information for dissemination to the U.S. intelligence community. We also provided technical support in the form of a miniature spy camera that Yuzhin used to photograph documents. Alas, he was subsequently obliged to confess to his FBI handler that he had lost this camera somewhere in the Soviet consulate.

In 1982, Yuzhin returned to Moscow for a new assignment. His FBI handlers did not want the CIA to run him in the Soviet Union, and he had not been issued any means of internal communication. We heard nothing about him until the defection of KGB CI officer Vitaliy Sergeyevich Yurchenko at the beginning of August 1985. Yurchenko reported that the KGB had found the spy camera in a recreation room in the Soviet consulate and had launched an extensive CI investigation. This inquiry was later bolstered by some vague reporting from Edward Lee Howard, the former CIA officer who volunteered to the KGB in 1984. Eventually the field of suspects had been narrowed to a very few. One of those was Yuzhin.

Yuzhin was arrested in 1986, tried and convicted, and sentenced to prison. He was released in 1991 as part of Boris Yeltsin's general amnesty. In retrospect, it is amazing that he survived. He was first compromised by his own carelessness, then by the treasonous activities of the CIA's Howard and Ames, and the FBI's Pitts and Hanssen.

Sergey Ivanovich Bokhan, a GRU colonel run by the CIA during two tours in Athens, Greece, was one of the few agents who survived the wholesale arrests, imprisonments, trials, and executions that began in the summer of 1985. That he was not among the missing or the known compromised can be attributed to his fear in late May 1985 that he was being recalled to Moscow on a ruse. Burton Gerber, chief of SE Division, and Dave Forden, our chief in Athens, agreed that something was amiss shortly after Bokhan signaled for an emergency meeting. He informed us that he had received a message from his brother in Moscow asking him to return to deal with some problems connected with his son, who was a cadet at a Soviet military academy. The brother knew of no issues and the CIA abetted Bokhan's departure from Greece followed by his arrival in the United States, where he lives today.

To this day, however, as with Gordievsky, a mystery surrounds Bokhan's possible compromise. (The Gordievsky riddle is described in Chapter 17.) Ames has insisted that he did not give up major CIA and FBI assets until 13 June 1985, which was about three weeks after Bokhan's precipitate departure from Greece. Either Ames identified Bokhan to the KGB earlier than he admitted, or Bokhan and we incorrectly interpreted the message from Moscow. A third possibility exists, as it does with Gordievsky. Bokhan was betrayed by someone or something else and the KGB's plan to bring him home failed. The truth remains unknown, at least to Sandy and Jeanne because we have no current access to information on the subject.

The story of Bokhan's cooperation with the CIA began in Athens in the spring of 1976 during his first tour abroad. The circumstances of his recruitment could well have been titled "Foreign Language Mishaps Abroad" or "Sign Language Sometimes Works." A CIA station officer had struck up an acquaintance with Bokhan, based on their mutual interest in tennis. They played periodically, but conversation was limited because the case officer spoke no Russian and only a little Greek. Bokhan spoke Greek but little English. After one such get-together, the CIA officer returned to the CIA station and reported: "I know I pitched him and I think he said yes and I think he pitched me and I know I said no." A Russian-speaking officer attended the next meeting and so began the long relationship between Bokhan and the CIA. He had indeed said yes to the recruitment pitch. He was encrypted CKWORTH, later changed to GTBLIZZARD.

SE Division officer Dick C was sent to Athens in the summer of 1976 to handle Bokhan for the duration of the latter's assignment. Meetings were overtly recorded and held approximately every other week in three or four different safe houses, according to a rotating schedule. Bokhan provided information on GRU operations and personnel in Greece and elsewhere in the region, photographed GRU correspondence to and from Moscow using a CIA custom-made camera that looked like a candy cane key fob, and furnished copies of the unclassified version of the Soviet publication *Military Thought*, not generally available in the West.

One of Bokhan's most famous agent leads was to an individual who provided the GRU with the top secret instruction manual for the U.S. spy satellite known as the KH-11. According to Bokhan, one afternoon in 1977 he walked into the GRU residency's work space to find Mikhail Zavaliy, a fellow residency officer under naval attaché cover, working intently on a cable to Moscow. When Zavaliy was summoned to the resident's office, Bokhan stole a peek at the message Zavaliy had begun to write. Zavaliy had just received a copy of the manual for the KH-ll. Bokhan could provide no further details other than that the word "Rugger" appeared in Zavaliy's draft. Bokhan also did not know who or what Rugger was, but speculated that perhaps it was an individual's last name. Bokhan signaled for an unscheduled meeting and passed the information to Dick C.

Bokhan's lead was passed to the FBI, which eventually arrested William Kampiles, a former CIA entry-level employee assigned to the Directorate of Intelligence Watch Office, in August 1978 and charged him with six counts of espionage. As it turned out, Rugger was simply the logo that appeared on the shirt Kampiles wore during his meeting with Zavaliy in Athens. Kampiles was convicted and sentenced to forty years in prison. In the late 1990s he was scheduled to be released after serving nearly nineteen years of his original sentence.

While Bokhan always appeared for meetings on time and prepared for work, his love for and purchases of consumer goods with his CIA gains became legendary at headquarters and remained a constant tug-of-war between case officer and agent. Dick C often reminded Bokhan of the need to curb his spending so his unexplained apparent affluence would not attract the attention of KGB security, but Bokhan was equally steadfast in his numerous requests for more money. On one occasion he noted that, according to recent news accounts, trash workers in New York City were on strike with a demand for higher wages. As Bokhan correctly reminded Dick and those at CIA headquarters, the New York trash collectors already made more than he and "I'm not giving you garbage."

Despite his protestations, Dick C limited Bokhan to a thousand dollars a month in cash, with another thousand deposited to an escrow account maintained at CIA Headquarters. However, true to form Bokhan continued to spend all that he was given on everything from expensive shoes to a fur coat for his wife, an exercise cycle, and gifts for his superiors at GRU headquarters.

Bokhan and his family left Athens by train in late summer 1978 en route to permanent reassignment in Moscow. He arrived at the railroad station laden with numerous suitcases containing the spoils of his CIA labor. There he and his family received a rousing send-off from members of the local Soviet embassy. Dick C, heavily disguised as a filthy, impoverished European hippie, silently watched the entire scene while sitting on the ground at the end of the station platform to ensure that Bokhan was free of KGB escort. He was.

Before his departure, Bokhan was trained in internal communications and issued materials that included a pre-arranged signal by which he could indicate that he was alive and well. He activated this signal about a year after his return to the Soviet Union but no further word was received from him until 1982, when he returned to Athens for his second tour, now a full colonel and deputy GRU resident. He followed his Athens recontact instructions perfectly, and Dick C, who was occupied with new challenges, was sent to Greece to make the initial contact and introduce Bokhan to a new CIA case officer. The operation proceeded smoothly and productively until May 1985, when the fateful cable arrived from Moscow that precipitated his escape, thus changing his life, that of the son whom he left in Moscow, and that of the daughter and wife whom he left in Athens.

•—•—•

The case of Adolf Grigoryevich Tolkachev demonstrates how it was possible for the CIA Station in Moscow to conduct regular personal meetings with a Soviet military electronics expert in the heart of Moscow and, in so doing, produce reams of high-quality intelligence. It also shows how easily such an important operation can be brought to an untimely end, with drastic consequences to the Soviet scientist in question, by the acts of a CIA traitor.[11]

Tolkachev (first encrypted CKSPHERE, later GTVANQUISH) made his initial approach in January 1977, by passing a note to then–Chief of Station Bob Fulton, who was filling his tank at a Moscow gas station. The note, while indicating the bearer's wish for a confidential discussion with an American official, did not give any precise details about what the individual could or would do for us. Therefore it was decided not to reply to his overture.[12]

Tolkachev would make five more approaches, of increasing specificity, before CIA headquarters approved plans to respond to him. The CIA was well aware that the KGB Second Chief Directorate, which ran operations against our station in Moscow, had a well-developed program to place "dangles" or false volunteers in our path. This was done for several purposes: to tie up the slender resources of our small Station, to uncover our personnel and methods of operation, to get active officers declared persona non grata, and to increase our understandable reluctance to deal with such volunteers. The KGB knew full well that some of the most dangerous cases, among them GRU colonel Oleg Penkovsky and KGB officer Aleksandr Cherepanov, had begun in this way. Tolkachev himself realized the problem, telling us in a February 1978 note that he seemed to be caught in a vicious circle. For his own safety, he could not tell us too much about himself and his access. Yet without this information we appeared to look at him as a "provocation."

More than one year after Tolkachev's original attempt to make contact, he received his first response from us—a telephone call from station officer John Guilsher, a fluent Russian speaker. By this time Tolkachev had produced detailed intelligence related to Soviet military aircraft and fully identified himself. Gardner ("Gus") Hathaway, who had replaced Fulton as Chief of Station, had pushed for this move, and had finally convinced headquarters. This was only a halfway measure, however, because headquarters would not approve a personal meeting, preferring instead a system of secret writing letters and dead drops. Not until January 1979 did Guilsher finally get the green light for a personal meeting. This took place on New Year's Day, when the two met by pre-arrangement and walked around on the freezing Moscow streets. As described in the section above on Kulak, this was the period when DCI Turner disapproved of other attempts to conduct personal meetings in Moscow.

More than twenty personal meetings took place in the next five years, either on the street or in Tolkachev's car. There were several rocky periods, to include a major security investigation at Tolkachev's place of employment, and the periodic inability of station officers to evade KGB surveillance. (Guilsher left Moscow in 1980.) During these five years, Tolkachev produced hundreds of rolls of film, some taken with a regular 35-mm camera, and some with CIA-manufactured equipment. Like Polyakov before him, he sometimes complained about problems with CIA-issued gear. He also passed hundreds of pages of detailed written notes. The reaction of U.S. military analysts was highly enthusiastic. Tolkachev provided details on Soviet military weaponry long before it was deployed, and thus long before information on the systems could be picked up by technical collection. It sometimes changed the direction of our own research and development and, by so doing, saved the U.S. government billions of dollars. Indeed, his production was so voluminous and so significant that it was still being exploited by a task force as late as 1990.

What was Tolkachev's motivation for this intense, almost compulsive, desire to provide us with intelligence damaging to his own country? During the life of the operation he wrote us a number of personal notes. In them he explained that he was not a Communist, and that, if he had not had a security clearance, he would have been active as a dissident. In this connection, he mentioned that his wife's family had suffered during the Stalinist purges. Another family factor was providing for his only son, to include items of

Western manufacture not available in the USSR. In general, one gets the impression of a close-knit family. Yet money was an important factor. He requested immense sums from us, and was unhappy when we did not accede to his demands. To our explanations that we were concerned with his security, and did not want him to appear to be unduly affluent, he responded that he did not want the money to spend, but to reassure himself that we considered him of high value. (This theme also appears in the Smetanin operation.)

Our last personal meeting with Tolkachev took place in January 1985. We hoped to meet him in March 1985, but were unsuccessful in our attempts to arrange a contact. On 13 June station officer Paul Stombaugh was detained by the KGB and taken off to KGB headquarters at the Lubyanka, where he was held for some hours before being released. Stombaugh had been on his way to a scheduled meeting with Tolkachev. The inevitable conclusion was that Tolkachev had been arrested. This turned out to be the case. On 20 September 1985 the Soviet media reported on the event, describing Tolkachev as a staff member at one of Moscow's research institutes who had been arrested in June trying to pass secret materials to the United States. The next year they issued a report that he had been executed for high treason.

It is a virtual certainty that Tolkachev was compromised by Edward Lee Howard, either in late 1984 or early 1985. Howard had been made aware of the operation in preparation for his planned assignment to Moscow in 1983. Ames knew almost nothing abut the case, certainly not enough to pinpoint Tolkachev before the latter's arrest. Neither Sandy nor Jeanne knew anything about it either because it was the most carefully compartmentalized of all SE operations. Ironically, after the June arrest of Stombaugh, Ames was handed the Tolkachev files and asked to prepare an analysis of what had gone wrong. He never finished his task because he was diverted to the debriefing of Yurchenko, the KGB CI officer who defected at the beginning of August, and subsequently began Italian-language training. However, in the unlikely event that the KGB had any unanswered questions after Howard's reporting, a search of Tolkachev's office and residences, and revelations during his post-arrest interrogation, Ames would have been in a position to fill the gaps.

●—●—●

For those who participated in the Viktor Ivanovich Sheymov operation, regardless of their role, it was the operational experience of a lifetime—a roller coaster ride of exhilaration and intense anxiety. The story began on Halloween night 1979 in Warsaw, Poland, when Sheymov walked into the American Embassy and offered his services in exchange for the exfiltration of his wife, their young daughter, and himself from the Soviet Union and resettlement in the United States.[13]

Warsaw's cable to Washington was a correct statement of the facts, but they did not have the background to comprehend fully the significance and the impact this man would have in the world of intelligence. Sheymov was an officer of the KGB's Eighth Chief Directorate, representing and working in the heart of the organization—its cipher communications. The employees of this directorate, and their activities, were so protected and secretive whether at home or abroad that the U.S. government had only a general knowledge of their professional lives and duties.

Simply stated, initially Sheymov could have told us anything about the inner workings of the Eighth Chief Directorate because we had no collateral information against which to check his statements. However, given his comments about his position and access, and the personal documents and information he provided, his bona fides were immediately established. Sheymov was one of the KGB's most valuable assets and we knew that he represented the ultimate prize for us. We acknowledged his worth by giving him the CIA cryptonym CKUTOPIA (later changed to CKQUARTZ) and the interagency designation TIEBREAKER.

The thrill of that first day did not diminish, but our focus immediately became the seemingly impossible pledge we had made to him, which we were determined to honor. The hurdles were many and monumental. First, few could be made aware of the very existence of Sheymov, but many had to be included to effect his request. Worse, he had demanded exfiltration not for one person but for three, including a five-year-old child. (As detailed earlier, we had planned Kulak's removal from the USSR but had not had to carry it out.) To add another element of danger, primarily for Sheymov, we had to conduct face-to-face meetings with him in Moscow to work out the details of the exfiltration. He had rejected a series of dead drops to exchange information because of time constraints and the magnitude of the operation. Finally add the frigid Moscow winter to a number of the personal meetings, Sheymov's work schedule for the

KGB, to include travel to Yemen and possibly other trips, and a five-to-six-month window to complete the operation.

A day or two after his walk-in in Warsaw Sheymov returned to Moscow and shortly thereafter left for Yemen on KGB business. At CIA headquarters cable traffic flew back and forth to Moscow Station and meeting after meeting was convened to find answers to the most basic operational questions. What border should we use for the crossing? How should the family get to a pick-up point with our officer or officers? What type of conveyance should we use to attempt the border crossing? How should we secrete the family members in the vehicle? Slowly the framework of a plan emerged. Next we had to address the personal details related to the Sheymov family. These numbered in the hundreds, were equally critical, and were often debated ad nauseam. Many of them required that Sheymov and his family maintain a normal pattern of activity.

One caused great consternation. The problem was simple. How do you keep a five-year-old quiet in cramped quarters on a trip that could last a number of hours? In a bureaucracy, the solution was not straightforward. A disagreement erupted between SE Division and a support component that could not be resolved. Thankfully, without communication with us Sheymov understood the problem and he alone came to the rescue. As he relates in his book, he had a conversation with his wife Olga: "Elena could be a major problem during the operation. I'm afraid we have no alternative but to sedate her with some kind of sleeping pill during the actual border crossing. . . . By definition, a five-year-old child is completely unpredictable and we can't hope for the best. There's too much at stake."[14]

We have chosen not to relate the details of the spring 1980 exfiltration nor Sheymov's ultimate contribution to the U.S. government. Suffice it to say that the former was flawless and the latter extraordinary. What was and remains important is that three human beings risked all. Everyone involved in the operation from the CIA to the Sheymov family deserves credit for the success of such a perilous operation, including the gods of good luck and good fortune.

CHAPTER 8

LATER MAJOR CASES

THE CIA HAD NO MONOPOLY on running good cases against the KGB during the Cold War. As has been mentioned separately, the British SIS handled Oleg Gordievsky in place for many years. There are other examples not mentioned in this book run by other services. The following story outlines how the French were able to maintain frequent contact with a KGB scientific and technical specialist in Moscow for a couple of years, thereby acquiring a large amount of very valuable documents, until the asset caused his own downfall.

In November 1980 a French businessman telephoned Raymond Nart, a senior officer of the French internal service, the Direction de la Surveillance du Territoire, or DST. Nart and the businessman were friends and the businessman wanted Nart to come by his office. When the two met, the businessman showed Nart a postcard, mailed from Eastern Europe. The writer, a KGB officer named Vladimir Ippolitovich Vetrov, had been stationed in Paris from 1965 to 1970 and, while there, had been acquainted with the businessman. Now, after a hiatus of several years, Vetrov was trying to renew the contact and stated in his card that he hoped to see the businessman as quickly as possible.[1]

Both Nart and the businessman recognized the possibility that Vetrov, who had become enamored with France during his assignment there, wanted to work with the French. However, while they were working out a secure recontact plan, Vetrov made another move. In February

1981, he attended a commercial exhibit in Moscow and, like Penkovskiy and Tolkachev before him, passed a note to a Westerner. The recipient on this occasion was a Frenchman. The note requested a meeting and included Vetrov's telephone number. Luckily, the Frenchman duly passed the note to the DST when he returned to Paris.

In response to the note, Nart and his colleagues dispatched a French engineer known to them by reputation. He was asked to go to Moscow and to telephone Vetrov, which he did. The two met in early March and Vetrov provided both information and documents. He continued to do so during subsequent meetings. In April, however, realizing the danger to the engineer because he of course did not have diplomatic immunity, the DST arranged for the military attaché at the French embassy in Moscow, an individual favorably known to Nart, to take over the case. Highly fruitful meetings between Vetrov, who by now had been encrypted FAREWELL by the DST, continued until late 1981. The attaché then left for Paris on Christmas leave. He had an appointment with Vetrov after his return but Vetrov did not appear.

When Vetrov started producing reams of Russian-language documents, the DST was faced with a problem. They did not have a cadre expert in both the language and the technical substance. Furthermore, they wanted to provide Vetrov with a miniature camera to minimize the risk of his document photography and did not have state-of-the-art equipment. Therefore, they decided to approach the CIA, which provided the requested technical and non-technical translations and analytical support but did not participate directly in the operation. Jeanne remembers a cart piled high with photocopies being rolled past her door in SE CI in the summer of 1981, and soon she became involved with editing some of the translated material.

In all, during the life of the operation Vetrov produced more than three thousand secret and top secret documents emanating not only from the Directorate T (Science and Technology) of the KGB, but also from the Military-Industrial Commission (VPK) of the USSR Council of Ministers. As explained in the section on Polyakov, the VPK coordinated and controlled all research, design, development, testing, and production of Soviet military equipment and systems. An integral part of the VPK's responsibility was the issuance of collection requirements on military matters for all Soviet government agencies from the KGB and GRU to the

Ministry of Foreign Affairs and the Ministry of Foreign Trade. VPK documents were highly valuable to CIA and Department of Defense analysts because they showed the gaps in the Soviet Union's military and industrial might. Polyakov produced some for us, as did Kulak. We also got some watered-down requirements from an East European source. The KGB operational documents, on the other hand, showed what clandestine activities the KGB—and the GRU and the East European services—were undertaking to close those gaps. In other words, they contained a vast number of espionage leads. Those leads were still being investigated several years after the case came to its untimely close.

Considering the circumstances of the meetings with Vetrov, it is understandable that we do not have a clear view of his motivations. He was undoubtedly a Francophile, but he did not want to defect and spend the rest of his life amusing himself in Parisian cafés and restaurants. Revenge was a definite factor, but he was an undisciplined individual who could have butted up against the KGB bureaucracy in any number of ways. According to Yurchenko, who participated in his interrogation, Vetrov wrote a long document vilifying the Soviet system as a whole and the KGB in particular, saying that the system was totally rotten.

The unfortunate denouement of the FAREWELL operation cannot be attributed to a Western traitor or to clever KGB scrutiny. Alas, Vetrov caused his own downfall. The story is a sensational one. Because it was the subject of much corridor gossip in the KGB, several versions have come down to us. Therefore, the following details may not be entirely correct, but the gist of the story is pretty clear. Vetrov was having an affair with a KGB secretary named Lyudmila. One cold night they were in his parked car, indulging in some dalliance. Someone knocked on the window. It turned out to be a militiaman (or Lyudmila's husband or some other lover of hers). Vetrov, who was drunk and who had a gun, shot and killed the man. He also tried to kill Lyudmila, but failed. She was able to testify against him. He was convicted of murder and sentenced to prison. While there he said something to a fellow inmate or a guard about his espionage activity on behalf of the French. According to one story, the fellow inmate was about to be released and Vetrov wanted him to contact the French embassy in Moscow. In any event, Vetrov was tried again, this time for espionage. He was sentenced to death and duly executed early in 1983.

● — ● — ●

In 1982 GRU colonel Vladimir Mikhaylovich Vasilyev, under cover as a Soviet military attaché, volunteered to a U.S. military representative in Budapest, Hungary, then part of the Soviet Bloc. The military turned him over to the CIA to handle, a particularly delicate job in a Communist country where all Western representatives, and particularly intelligence officers, were under considerable surveillance. The CIA encrypted him GTACCORD. The turnover did not please Vasilyev who, as a military man, preferred to deal with his uniformed counterparts, because he knew them personally and had contact with them as part of his normal duties. That the CIA officer who became his new handler was a woman and a civilian probably did not help matters. Nonetheless, the CIA—with substantial U.S. military assistance—managed to keep in limited but productive contact with Vasilyev until he returned to Moscow on a routine change of station in the summer of 1984.

Vasilyev provided a variety of intelligence to the CIA. However, because communications with him were difficult and infrequent, we did not always understand the nature of his access nor do we have a clear view of his motivation. Among the most significant items he passed were copies of top secret documents emanating from the U.S. Army in Germany. Since 1978 the CIA had been aware, from East European sources, that there was massive leakage from U.S. forces in Germany to the Hungarians, but our sources' reporting was oral. The anecdotal and somewhat vague information had duly been passed to our military counterintelligence and to the FBI. An investigation had been opened but had not borne fruit. Now we had the actual documents, and they were chilling; they outlined in detail what the Western response would be to a Soviet invasion. Vasilyev had no idea who the source of the top secret documents was, but he knew that Hungarian military intelligence immediately passed the documents to the GRU in Budapest, that the GRU had them flown to its headquarters in Moscow on a priority basis, and that the GRU was footing the bill for the operation.

In brief, the information provided by Vasilyev dealt the final blow to the espionage activities of former U.S. Army sergeant Clyde Conrad and his partners in crime. Conrad was arrested in Germany, where he had retired, in August 1988 thanks to cooperation between U.S. military counterintelligence and the German criminal police. He was tried in a German court in early 1990 and sentenced to life in prison. This case, probably because it was run by East Europeans and not by the Soviet Union, has never received the attention it deserves. As former CIA Associate Deputy Director for Operations (ADDO)/CI Paul Redmond is fond of remarking, if there had been a hot war we would have lost because Conrad had compromised all the plans for the defense of Western Europe.[2]

Vasilyev was compromised in two stages. His first betrayer was Edward Lee Howard. According to Yurchenko, during Howard's first meeting with the KGB, which took place in Vienna probably in late 1984, he reported on an unnamed "angry colonel" who was being run by the CIA in Budapest. Howard was accurate in that Vasilyev had complained angrily about the way we were handling him. Whether Howard was under the misapprehension that Vasilyev was from the KGB, or whether the KGB made an unwarranted assumption, is unknown. In any event, this report unleashed an investigation of all the KGB colonels in Budapest, of which there were several. As far as we know, no special attention was paid to GRU colonels. And, as it happened, Vasilyev had already left for a new post in Moscow by the time the investigation got under way.

The reporting from Ames was much more definitive. Ames would have had his facts straight because much of this case was handled by SE CI, where he worked, and he would have had access to the cable traffic. One of his subordinates had been responsible for the translation of the written messages we exchanged with Vasilyev. The most probable date for Ames' initial betrayal of Vasilyev is 13 June 1985. However, according to everything we have heard, Vasilyev was not arrested until early June 1986. Like others, he was subsequently tried and executed.

Much has been made of the one-year gap between Ames' reporting on Vasilyev and his arrest. When he left for Moscow, Vasilyev had a detailed plan for internal communications, which he began to implement. In August 1985, when we had the benefit of Yurchenko's reporting and when we began to realize that we were having other difficulties in our Soviet operations, a debate opened as to whether we should continue to receive materials from Vasilyev. However, after receiving our green light, on 11 December he dropped a package to us. This was our last contact with him.

There are some, for instance the interagency Ames Damage Assessment Team convened after Ames' 1994 arrest, who have concluded that the documents in this package were manufactured by the KGB to mislead us as to Vasilyev's well-being and continued access. To be sure, as described elsewhere in this book, the KGB undoubtedly did undertake such deception operations. However, this package contained valuable intelligence covering a broad range of topics and emanating from a variety of Soviet official institutions. It was not CI-related and did not contain any material that would mislead us in our investigations.

Some will say that it would have been impossible for Vasilyev, who had been compromised several months earlier, to put down a genuine drop without being observed and arrested by the KGB. Yet even the KGB had its limitations. Because of reporting from Howard, Ames, and Hanssen, they were forced to open perhaps as many as twenty espionage investigations against U.S. penetrations of their country's secrets. Resources must have been strained to the limit. Furthermore, they would have had to establish some sort of priority list. In retrospect, we can see that the highest priority was given to our KGB and GRU assets abroad, who were out of their control. It was necessary to lure them back to the Soviet Union, so they could be arrested, and this had to be done using various believable pretexts. If the KGB had started mass arrests in Moscow, our assets abroad would presumably have learned of these actions and asked us to arrange their orderly defections. Only when the KGB's first priority task was accomplished, which happened in mid-November with the orchestrated departure of Varenik from Germany, could it start giving undivided attention to the second priority—persons inside the Soviet Union who had some means of communicating with us. Vasilyev belonged in this group.

By way of comparison, when the FBI opened its full-scale investigation of Rick Ames in the spring of 1993, this was the major undertaking of the Washington Metropolitan Field Office and much of the local FBI's resources were allocated to it. Yet the FBI did not surveil Ames twenty-four hours a day, seven days a week. First of all, surveilling a trained intelligence officer is no easy job. If the suspect, because of his training and experience, detects that he is under surveillance, he might flee the country. At best, he might just cease any operational activity. Obviously, the FBI did not want this to happen, so they hung back at times, depending on telephone coverage to keep abreast of Ames' comings and goings. They made one mistake, however. On 7 September the surveillance team deployed to Ames' residence early in the morning as usual. However, when they got there shortly after 6:30, they saw that Ames' car was sitting in the driveway instead of the garage. They deduced that he had gone out, and they were right. It was later ascertained that he had signaled to his KGB handlers by making a chalk mark on a mailbox. Later that day they lost him again for an hour when their radio system broke down. We do not find it surprising that the Moscow KGB, with all the investigations being handled, might have had the same sort of problems and limitations that the Washington FBI did.

•——•——•

Gennadiy Aleksandrovich Smetanin, a GRU officer under military attaché cover in Lisbon, Portugal, volunteered to the CIA in late 1983. He was handled by our Lisbon office, which had personal meetings with him under the guise of tennis dates. There are two unusual aspects to this case. First of all, it is a rare example of a spouse also cooperating with the CIA. Mrs. Smetanin, who worked in the consular section of the Soviet embassy, did not have access to real state secrets but she shared with us the information that came across her desk. She also participated in at least one meeting with her husband's CIA handlers.

The second unusual aspect of the case involves the polygraph. It was not customary to polygraph our Soviet assets. However, early in our relationship with Smetanin he demanded the sum of $330,000 saying that he had embezzled it from GRU funds in Lisbon. (As an aside, neither Sandy nor Jeanne was around when that happened. Both were very familiar with GRU regulations and practices, and knew that it was totally unlikely that the GRU would have anywhere near that amount of cash locally. Only a few years earlier, Polyakov's large residency had a limit of $10,000.) Anyway, this was during the Casey era. He was consulted and decided that Smetanin could have the money if he passed a polygraph. A polygrapher was duly summoned to Lisbon, Smetanin submitted to the examination, the polygrapher was satisfied with the results, and Smetanin got his money.[3] Sad to say, Smetanin's request for a large sum was just his way of testing us. He never spent the bulk of the money.

In the summer of 1985 Smetanin and his wife were due for a normal home leave. He was supposed to meet his handler in Lisbon on 4 October, after his return, but never showed up. According to stories we heard later, he was arrested as he was about to take the train back to Portugal. As was the norm, he was tried and executed. His wife was sentenced to five years in prison. His downfall is directly attributable to Ames, who knew the case well and compromised it in the "big dump."

Ames did not confine his identification of American assets simply to those recruited and handled by the CIA. Two important FBI sources in Washington, DC, were also among those he chose to sacrifice. According to his own statements, in June 1985 he informed the KGB that Valeriy Fedorovich Martynov, a KGB scientific and technical officer, and Sergey Mikhaylovich Motorin, a KGB political intelligence officer who was an "active measures" specialist, were spying for the Americans. (Active measures is the Russian term for what is called covert action in the West, and entails, among other things, disseminating rumors and lies designed to discredit or disrupt governments and individuals hostile to the USSR.) Approximately four months later, in October 1985, Ames' reporting on Martynov and Motorin was confirmed by a write-in to the Soviet embassy in Washington, DC—FBI Special Agent Robert Hanssen.

Martynov arrived in the United States in the fall of 1980, assigned to the cover position of an embassy third secretary. A year or two after his arrival he caught the attention of a CIA case officer working in the Agency's Washington field office. The case officer had met Martynov at a series of scientific presentations and immediately concluded that he was far from the typical standoffish, stern-faced Russian diplomat serving on the territory of the Main Enemy. Quite the contrary—he was affable, self-confident, and socially comfortable among strangers. The case officer felt he deserved further attention from U.S. intelligence.

The CIA case officer's assessment was provided to officials in the newly created FBI/CIA joint operations unit known as COURTSHIP, one of whom was Diana Worthen, a major player in the future Ames investigation. Martynov became one of the unit's primary targets and after approximately a year of pursuit he was recruited as a penetration of the KGB.

Code-named GTGENTILE by CIA and PIMENTA by the FBI, Martynov was handled jointly by the two services. (As an aside, the FBI chose the code name PIMENTA in honor of Ben Pepper, a CIA officer who had been a driving force in setting up the joint unit.) His FBI case officer was Jim Holt, who six years later would join the CIA/FBI task force to search for the answer to the compromise of his agent as well as others. Martynov's CIA case officer was Rod Carlson, a senior officer with a great deal of experience working against the Soviet target. As we explain later in this book, Carlson later became Ames' chief when Ames was assigned as Soviet branch chief in SE Division's CI Group, a position that allowed Ames access to and intimate knowledge of the sources he would later betray, obviously including Carlson's.

Holt and Carlson met with Martynov twice a month for the next three years, during which time he provided information on the residency's scientific and technical officers, including their activities and targets, and identified other members of the local KGB contingent. In his book *Spy Handler*, Viktor Ivanovich Cherkashin, KGB CI chief in Washington at the time and the individual to whom both Ames and Hanssen volunteered, stated that Martynov turned out to be the mole he began looking for in 1984. Early in that year Cherkashin began to conclude that someone in the residency was telling the FBI who was KGB and who was not. He based his conclusion on his analysis of FBI radio intercepts, which showed that the FBI had changed its surveillance patterns and was following only KGB officers, allowing non-intelligence officials to go about their business without coverage. To Cherkashin's irritation, KGB higher-ups found his analysis unconvincing.[4]

Despite Martynov's compromise by Ames before mid-1985 and by Hanssen in October of that year, the KGB was forced to keep him at his post in Washington for a period and let him carry out his normal duties. Again, according to Cherkashin's memoirs,[5] this was not from a lack of trying. They faced a dilemma. The KGB desperately wanted to return Martynov to Moscow, but they had to do so without raising his suspicions, which would surely result in his and his family's defection. Home leave was not an option. He had just returned from Moscow in the spring. Using ploys such as fictitious family problems in Moscow or an awards ceremony would not work. As an intelligence officer, Martynov would recognize them for what they were—ruses indicating that he was in serious trouble. On 2 November 1985 Cherkashin was presented with the solution to the KGB's dilemma. Vitaliy Sergeyevich Yurchenko, the senior KGB counterintelligence officer who had defected in August 1985, appeared at the gate of the Soviet embassy residential compound wanting to return permanently to the Soviet Union. Yurchenko would be accompanied to Moscow by an honor guard of four, and Martynov would be one of the privileged.

On 6 November Martynov boarded the Aeroflot flight for Moscow. Immediately upon arrival he was arrested and taken directly to Lefortovo prison. His wife and children returned to Moscow several weeks later, after being told that he had injured his leg. A similar tale was put out by the KGB to cover what had really happened, and a version came to the CIA's attention. Specifically, the story was that Martynov was unable to travel and would remain in Moscow due to the flare-up of an old soccer injury that required surgery.

Martynov was tried and sentenced to death in the spring of 1987. He was executed later that year. By virtue of his position, Cherkashin was the central figure in the wrap-up of Martynov. He later wrote that he knew that Martynov, a gentle man whom he liked, was boarding a flight to his death. For Cherkashin personally, "It was one of the events in my career I most questioned."[6]

The recruitment of Sergey Mikhaylovich Motorin combined all aspects of a classic FBI counterintelligence operation—persistence, opportunism, and exploitation. He was not a volunteer and we submit he had probably never dreamt of committing treason.

Motorin's arrival in Washington on his first overseas tour coincided with that of Martynov, but they took different paths to cooperation with the Americans. Motorin's was caused by personal weaknesses that came to the attention of the FBI and that they used as leverage to convince him that he had no choice but to accede to their requests. As he came to understand, his only alternative was return to the Soviet Union where he would face disgrace, certain dismissal from the KGB, and possible criminal charges. In late 1982, after a lengthy period of FBI cajoling and prodding, he agreed to cooperate.

The FBI had to strike a delicate balance in the recruitment process of Motorin. In some circles exploitation of an individual's shortcomings is viewed as blackmail. The moral debate aside, such tactics often result in an uncooperative and unreliable asset, because participation has been coerced, not offered. In this particular case the FBI was fortunate. Motorin, although a junior officer with limited access, provided all within his purview. As an organization, the FBI deserves complete credit for the success of this operation.

What were Motorin's vulnerabilities? A tall, handsome man, Motorin loved to party and was not always discreet in his relationships with members of the opposite sex. However, this behavior alone did not result in his eventual recruitment. The FBI observed him trading his KGB operational allowance of vodka and other items for stereo equipment. At this point in the operation they inserted Special Agent Mike Morton, who identified himself as a government employee. Motorin flippantly dismissed the picture Morton painted of his situation, and so began Morton's relentless pursuit of the KGB major. All around Washington, and at every possible opportunity, Morton appeared unexpectedly in Motorin's path, showing him photographs and reminding him that the FBI knew about the women and the vodka.

The FBI selected Special Agent James Stassinos as Motorin's case officer. Stassinos assigned him the code name DIONYSUS, the Greek god of wine, fertility, and orgies, which was later changed to MEGAS. At CIA he was known as GTGAUZE. The CIA did not have any operational involvement in this case, which was handled solely by the FBI. However, we were responsible for disseminating his production to the intelligence community.

Meetings between Stassinos and Motorin continued until the latter's return to Moscow in January 1985. He did not have any internal communications, but the FBI did have discussions with the CIA as to whether he should have that capability. Fatefully, Ames participated in these talks and, therefore, knew the case quite well. As noted previously, in October 1985 Hanssen followed Ames' lead and identified Motorin as an FBI penetration of the KGB. With no hope of extraction, his fate was sealed.

Motorin was arrested in mid-January 1986, but later made phone calls to a former girlfriend in Washington at the behest of the KGB. These calls were simply another attempt by the KGB to deceive the CIA and

FBI regarding their lost agents. In Motorin's case, he was alive but certainly not well. Under arrest and facing trial, he was later executed as punishment for treason against the State.

Cherkashin addressed the KGB's killing of Motorin specifically, and the others generally, stating that he believed that "execution was wrong and entirely unnecessary." Motorin appears to bother him particularly, because this young officer knew almost nothing of significance and therefore did little damage to the Soviet Union. In Cherkashin's own words, "I remain completely convinced that the spies Ames betrayed should have been fired and deprived of their pensions, but no more. What further harm could they have done?"[7]

When we began our investigation of the 1985 compromises, one of the most baffling cases that we had to look at was the operation involving Gennadiy Grigoryevich Varenik. The case only lasted a few months. It was run tightly and professionally by CIA officer Charles (Chuck) Leven, and documented in detail. How could it have gone wrong?

Varenik was stationed at the Soviet embassy in Bonn, serving as a KGB Illegals Support officer. During his tour, he had become acquainted with a CIA case officer also stationed in Bonn. They had a cordial friendship, but this did not develop into a clandestine relationship. Eventually the CIA officer was reassigned to another European post. In March 1985, Varenik made a telephone call to this officer at his new post and said he wanted to arrange a personal meeting. This overture soon resulted in Varenik's recruitment in Bonn and extensive debriefings on the KGB's Illegals program and related matters. He was encrypted GTFITNESS.

One of the first items Varenik was eager to impart to us was the story of the KGB's "mini-bombs" operation, in which he was a participant. The operation, which was still in the planning stages, involved planting small bombs in venues such as restaurants and bars frequented by U.S. servicemen. As he understood it, this would result in the deaths of innocent men, women, and children, which he found totally unacceptable. The KGB's plan was to blame the bombs on German terrorists, thereby leaving the impression that the U.S. military was unwanted, and that the German government could not protect them. The hoped-for result was to sour U.S.–German relations.

When this reporting arrived at CIA headquarters, Director Casey immediately brought it to the attention of President Reagan, who saw it as further proof that the Evil Empire really did exist. While Varenik and Leven both believed that the KGB's operation would result in a loss of life, in retrospect one wonders a bit. Jeanne, who read the reporting with care, feels that it is susceptible to a more benign interpretation. These were indeed mini-bombs, which might only be capable of scaring people or at most inflicting superficial injuries. It seems strange that the KGB would run such a high-risk low-gain operation in a NATO country. The political fallout, were it to be discovered that the KGB was deliberately killing U.S. and German citizens, would be immense. In any event, it was a hare-brained scheme that the KGB planners should never have seriously entertained.

In early November Varenik was asked to attend a conference in East Berlin. He was also told that the mini-bomb project had been shelved for the present. (Of course, by this time the KGB had the benefit of Ames' reporting and knew about the fury with which the story had been received at the highest levels of the U.S. government. No doubt they assumed that Varenik would immediately pass to his CIA contact anything he learned about the mini-bomb project. They thus had a perfect vehicle for calming the situation.)

A few days later, after a short meeting with Leven to pass his information, Varenik left for East Berlin. He was immediately bundled on board a plane for Moscow. Needless to say, he never returned to Bonn. His wife and small children eventually followed him to Moscow. Like the others, he was tried and executed.

The majority of sources run by the CIA and FBI were met overseas, at least some of the time, and we were able to glean a fairly accurate idea of their motivation, access, and ability to withstand the rigors of espionage activity. Adolf Grigoryevich Tolkachev is an exception because he was not allowed to leave the Soviet Union. However, there were numerous personal meetings with him, supplemented by lengthy written communications, over a long span of time. This was not the situation with Sergey Vorontsov. We had only two meetings with him. We did not even know his name, or his assignment within the KGB.

Vorontsov, encrypted GTCOWL, volunteered to the CIA Station in Moscow using a State Department official as an intermediary. The first meeting with him was held in early 1984. There was a second meeting with him shortly thereafter. The station officer who handled this meeting was Mike Sellers. There was then a long gap in contact.

When Vorontsov first established contact with the CIA, he refused to identify himself, preferring to be known simply as "Stas." He intimated that he was from the Second Chief Directorate of the KGB, a high-priority target for CIA because this directorate was responsible for internal counterintelligence, to include operations against our CIA Station in Moscow. Some believed that he was exaggerating his access, and that in reality he was assigned to the Moscow City Directorate, a target that did not rank as high in the CIA's priorities.

Paul Stombaugh, who had been expelled from the Soviet Union in June 1985 in connection with the Tolkachev case, was working in the SE Division internal operations group at the time. He wrote a memorandum supporting the theory that Vorontsov was from the Moscow City Directorate, which turned out to be the truth. This put him into conflict with Ames, who considered himself one of the Agency's greatest experts on the KGB. Also, it was Ames' job to decide such questions and he felt that Stombaugh was invading his turf. Ames disputed Stombaugh's theory, and an argument ensued. The only importance of this minor dust-up was that it sealed Vorontsov's fate because Ames studied the case carefully in support of his mistaken insistence that Vorontsov worked in the Second Chief Directorate.

During the short life of this operation, Vorontsov produced one item that resonated throughout the U.S. government. He gave Sellers a packet of what is commonly known in intelligence circles as "spy dust" and whose scientific initials are NPPD. This is an invisible chemical agent used by the KGB to track the whereabouts of CIA Moscow Station personnel. We had known about the substance since at least the 1960s, but now we had a sample that could be submitted for analysis. Early tests suggested that NPPD was mutagenic, or possibly even carcinogenic. The media picked up the story and had a field day. The State Department protested that its personnel were being poisoned. However, the story eventually died down as there was no evidence that anyone had been harmed, and the Soviets loudly decried the possibility.

For various reasons, we did not meet with Vorontsov after the spring of 1984. The next meeting was scheduled for 10 March 1986 in a Moscow alleyway. When Sellers appeared, he was arrested by a squad of KGB officers, and taken to the KGB central offices at the Lubyanka. A few hours later he was released, when the U.S. embassy was able to establish his diplomatic immunity to Soviet satisfaction. Sellers was declared persona non grata and expelled from the Soviet Union.

As an aside, when Sellers was arrested he had with him a list of questions to ask Vorontsov. Prominent among them was: "What happened to Raoul Wallenberg?" This was an unanswered forty-year-old question, which had long obsessed Swedish officialdom and some senior members of the U.S. government, including Director Casey. Wallenberg was a Swedish diplomat assigned to Budapest toward the end of World War II who was responsible for saving a large number of Jews. When the Red Army rolled into the capital, Wallenberg disappeared. Over the years there were persistent rumors that he was still alive in a Soviet prison, unlikely as that may have been. Anyway, Casey, perhaps more attuned to political realities than to current priorities, insisted that the matter be broached. That such a question might be asked of a defector who is being debriefed at length in a Washington safehouse is understandable. That precious time in a Moscow alleyway under highly dangerous circumstances was to be taken up by this venerable enigma is much less so. (As it happens, Wallenberg had died in 1947 in prison. The Soviet government finally admitted to this in 1989, although not everyone accepts their story.)

Vorontsov was executed. It was only through the protest note issued by the Soviet government that we were finally able to identify the mysterious Stas. The note provided Vorontsov's true surname.

CHAPTER 9

THINGS BEGIN TO GO WRONG

THE SPRING OF 1985 saw the beginning of the end of the Cold War. In March Konstantin Chernenko died, and Mikhail Gorbachev became General Secretary of the Communist Party of the Soviet Union. The era of glasnost and perestroika was about to begin. This year has also been dubbed the "Year of the Spy" because of events that were publicly aired at the time, such as the arrest of U.S. Navy communications technician John Walker and his ring, the defection/redefection of Vitaliy Sergeyevich Yurchenko, and the flight of Edward Lee Howard. Little did anyone know, however, that fifteen years would pass before we learned just how much of a Year of the Spy it had really been.

While things were changing in Moscow, it was still too early for the CIA, and SE Division specifically, to alter its priorities. Work against Soviet and East European targets was being carried out as usual. At this point, we were feeling very proud of ourselves. Over the years we had built up our stable of reporting sources and had uncovered many of the USSR's major secrets. We had been so successful against the KGB and the GRU that it was no exaggeration to say that we knew more about these organizations than any individual officer in them. We had no idea that we were headed for disaster.

The first intimation that something might be wrong occurred in late May. (Throughout the following narrative, we have tried to make a distinction between when an event occurred, and when we learned about it.

This is an important differentiation because the KGB was trying to conceal what was going on from us, and sometimes succeeded. Therefore, a person could be arrested in 1985 and we might not hear about it until more than a year had passed.) Sergey Ivanovich Bokhan, the GRU officer who had been working for us in Athens, told us that he had been recalled to Moscow to take care of a problem involving his son. We suspected that he might be under suspicion and advised him to defect, which he did.

The next month our unease was appreciably heightened. On 13 June Moscow Station CIA officer Paul Stombaugh was arrested by the KGB on the street as he was attempting to meet with Adolf Tolkachev, who had volunteered to the CIA in Moscow in 1977 and had provided reams of highly important information. Although we did not know it at the time, he had been arrested on the 9th.

The next noteworthy event was the defection of Vitaliy Sergeyevich Yurchenko, a senior KGB CI officer, in Rome on 1 August. He was immediately brought to the United States and was considered an especially valuable defector, because he had previously served in the KGB residency in Washington, DC. Among the important reporting he provided was some information about a former CIA officer who had volunteered to the KGB after being dismissed from the Agency. He had been debriefed by the KGB at length in Vienna in the fall of 1984. Although Yurchenko did not know the man's name, it was almost immediately evident that he was describing Edward Lee Howard. Howard had worked in SE Division's branch responsible for operations inside the Soviet Union until May 1983, when he was unceremoniously dismissed because a polygraph examination indicated extensive drug use, alcohol abuse, and petty theft.[1]

According to Yurchenko, Howard had told the KGB everything he had learned while assigned to the internal Soviet operations component. This included an imprecise lead to an "angry colonel" in Budapest who was working for the CIA. Based on Howard's reporting, we realized that he was describing the case of GRU officer Vladimir Vasilyev.

Another KGB CI investigation related to us by Yurchenko involved a spy camera that the KGB had found in a recreation room in the Soviet consulate in San Francisco a few years previously. An extensive inquiry was undertaken, later bolstered by some vague reporting from Howard. Eventually the field of suspects had been narrowed to a very few. One of those was Boris Nikolayevich Yuzhin, a KGB officer under TASS cover.

This was disturbing news. Yuzhin had been recruited by the FBI in the 1970s. The CIA had supplied the spy camera, which indeed Yuzhin had lost in the Soviet consulate. Yuzhin had returned to Moscow in 1982. His FBI handlers did not want the CIA to run him in the Soviet Union, and he had not been issued any means of internal communication. Luckily for him as it turned out, there was no damning evidence that a KGB investigation could uncover.

While Howard's treason was a terrible blow, in one way it was a comfort. It explained the operational demise of Tolkachev, because Howard had been slated for a Moscow assignment. One of his duties there would have been to handle Tolkachev, and he had read Tolkachev's file. It also more or less explained the possibility that Bokhan was under suspicion when he defected. He had been working for the CIA for many years, since 1975. Therefore Howard could have learned about his case at some point. Further, it explained the anomalies discovered in GTTAW. GTTAW was a technical operation involving a tap into Soviet classified landlines. To service the tap, a Moscow Station officer had to "get black" and then go down a manhole to the tap's location to retrieve the tapes. Howard had been trained to undertake this duty and knew all the details.[2]

Another tidbit from Yurchenko concerned Oleg Antonovich Gordievsky, a senior KGB officer who had been the deputy resident in London. According to Yurchenko, Gordievsky had been recalled in May 1985 because of some suspicions. He had been interrogated but had not confessed and had not been arrested. This was an interesting piece of news. The British, who had recruited Gordievsky in Copenhagen in the mid-1970s, had shared some of his production with the CIA and FBI, but had not identified their source. We, however, had figured out that Gordievsky must have been the person who was supplying the information to the British and encrypted him GTTICKLE. That he had been recalled in May did not, however, unduly concern us because this was not our case and it was, again, an operation that had been running for many years. As some readers may know, the British exfiltrated Gordievsky shortly before Yurchenko's defection. They did not inform us of their noteworthy coup until some time after the event. Today he lives in Great Britain and has made a new life for himself as a successful author and lecturer.

Yurchenko also told us about a secret trip that Viktor Ivanovich Cherkashin, the KGB CI chief in Washington, had made in the spring of

1985. He had eluded FBI coverage and left the United States without their knowledge. Once he got to Moscow he had an interview with the top KGB leadership. Yurchenko did not know the reason for this trip, although he believed it must have been of considerable significance. We in the CIA speculated about this incident. One explanation that seemed plausible at the time was that he had been called to Moscow to discuss the future handling of Howard, who at the time was living in Santa Fe, New Mexico.

In October we learned of another major compromise. KGB CI officer Leonid Georgiyevich Poleshchuk had been arrested when he tried to pick up a dead drop we had put down for him in Moscow. Yet another unsettling event took place that same month. GRU officer Gennadiy Aleksandrovich Smetanin, who had volunteered to the CIA in Lisbon in late 1983, did not return from a scheduled home leave. We never had contact with him again and did not know what had become of him until sometime in the next year. What was especially perturbing about this case was that Howard could not have known about it. It started after he had left the Agency.

In the meantime, the Howard case came to a boil. On 19 September 1985, the FBI interviewed him based on Yurchenko's reporting. He refused to cooperate until he could consult a lawyer. Two days later, he tricked FBI surveillance and fled the country. He is believed to have crossed over into the Soviet Union shortly thereafter, thus making himself available for intensive and extensive KGB debriefings.

In the meantime, Yurchenko re-defected. He left for Moscow in a hail of publicity on 6 November, protesting that the CIA had drugged and kidnapped him. Especially pertinent to the present narrative is that one of the KGB officers assigned to escort him back to the USSR was Valeriy Fedorovich Martynov, who had been recruited by the FBI in early 1982, and was subsequently handled as a joint FBI/CIA asset. He did not return to Washington after his escort duties were finished. The word was out that an old knee injury had flared up and he might need surgery.

The last asset to disappear from our screen in 1985 was KGB Illegals Support specialist Gennadiy Grigoryevich Varenik. Varenik, stationed in Bonn, had volunteered to the CIA in March of that year. He missed a meeting that he was supposed to have had with us in mid-November and we never had contact with him again. Dismayingly, this was a case that had been tightly held and had lasted only a few months.

There was only one reassuring entry in this escalating catalog of disappearances. On 11 December Vladimir Mikhaylovich Vasilyev, the GRU "angry colonel" we had run in Budapest and who had later been reassigned to Moscow, successfully dead-dropped a package to us. The contents were such that no one involved in the operation believed that this could have been a KGB ploy.

Before the year closed, Director Casey was briefed on what we knew to that point about what seemed to be wrong in a broad array of our Soviet cases. He directed John Stein to conduct a study on the subject. Stein was a logical choice because he had served as deputy chief of SE Division, as deputy director for operations, and as inspector general. Furthermore, he was available, marking time until taking up his next assignment as chief in Seoul.

Soviet and East European Division chief Burton Gerber wrote a memorandum to Stein, outlining the problem and listing the cases that he should review. In early 1986, Stein prepared his report. Some recall he concluded that there was no overarching connection between the compromised cases known to us at this time. Each one contained the seeds of its own destruction. Stein himself remembers that he came to the tentative conclusion that a compromise of our communications was the most likely explanation. Unfortunately, despite repeated searches, no copy of this report has ever been found. Thus, what Stein actually said remains a mystery. However, Stein's reference to a compromise of our communications is not surprising because the Walker case was very much on everyone's mind at the time.

John Anthony Walker Jr., a communications specialist in the U.S. Navy, volunteered to the KGB in December 1967. For almost twenty years he provided cryptographic materials to the KGB, eventually involving his brother, his son, and his best friend, Jerry Whitworth. He was arrested in May 1985 by the FBI based on a tip from his wife. This was an extremely damaging case and, despite NSA's assurances to the contrary, many in the CIA were concerned that the KGB might have been able to compromise CIA's secure electronic communications.[3]

This is perhaps a good juncture to describe the makeup of the components that were to be involved in the search for the solution to what had gone wrong in 1985, and to sketch the key players. The Soviet and East European Division had been headed by Burton Gerber since June

1984, when he succeeded Dave Forden. Gerber, a tall, black-haired craggy Midwesterner, knew he was in a serious business and took it seriously. He had a razor-sharp memory, followed all the events on his watch with a close eye, and, although he tried conscientiously, found it difficult to delegate authority. An SE professional, he had served as chief in Sofia, Bulgaria, and Moscow. Wolves were his avocation, and pictures and artifacts of them decorated his office.

Ken Wesolik was Burton's first deputy. A seasoned SE hand, he was slated for the Chief of Station, Moscow, position but had to bow out for health reasons and moved on to become head of the Directorate's Information Management staff. He was replaced by Milt Bearden in July 1985. Milt, though well liked at the time, was an outsider from Africa Division with no tours in the USSR or Eastern Europe. He was perhaps more suited to Third World derring-do than to trying to outwit the wily and experienced KGB. In any event, he stayed in the job only ten months, departing for Islamabad to take over the CIA's Afghan program in May 1986.

Paul Redmond was chief of the CI Group in SE Division. A Boston Irishman, Harvard graduate, and catalytic rather than analytic, he was full of energy, always eager to forge ahead, although not foolhardy. He was also dogged and impatient at the same time. Like most of his peers, he had served in Eastern Europe—in his case, as chief in Zagreb. Later, Redmond moved up to become deputy chief of SE.

The role of SE Division was to run operations against the Soviet and East European target, as earlier described. The counterintelligence component of the division ran selected operations involving Soviet intelligence officers, performed CI analysis of the division's operations, and produced CI reporting. The Division did not have any responsibility for investigating penetrations of the Agency, a function that was carried out by the CI staff and the Office of Security.

In 1985 the chief of the CI staff was David Blee. A Near East specialist, he had served for a term as chief of SE Division, and as associate deputy director for Operations. In the spring of 1985, Blee retired and was replaced by Gardner "Gus" Hathaway, who remained a central player for several years in the search for what had gone wrong. A courtly Virginia gentleman and a World War II combat veteran, having marched up from the south of France as part of the pincer movement in support of the

1944 D-day invasion, Hathaway was another SE professional. Like Gerber after him, he had served as chief of station, Moscow and as chief of SE Division. Hathaway, Gerber, and Redmond are the three senior officers who were closest to the hunt for the mole, and who cared most about catching him. Redmond has received proper recognition for his contribution but, sadly, Hathaway and Gerber have been overlooked.

The Office of Security also did its part. While we in the CI staff primarily took an analytical approach, Security carried out investigations, commencing with people who had served in Moscow. Ray Reardon, who had a broader outlook than many of his colleagues in Security and who later became deputy chief of that component, was in charge of this effort. Among the officers who worked for Reardon was a young man named Dan Payne, who will play a major role in this story.

FIRST ATTEMPTS

N OW THAT MOST OF THOSE who were privy to the information about the lost cases were convinced that, whatever its nature, something was seriously wrong, the question was: What should we do about it? Defensively, the answer was to institute, in Redmond's phrase, draconian compartmentation. This was the inception of what became known as the "back room." It was necessitated by the appearance of a new Soviet source in January 1986 and Gerber's personal crusade that this one be kept alive. Because one of the theories was that we had a mole in our midst, knowledge of the new asset's existence was limited to a select few. Another prominent theory was that our communications had been compromised, so the decision was made to handle him without recourse to any of our electronic links. Dick C, an experienced SE officer who, like many others who appear in this story, had served in Moscow and spoke Russian, traveled indirectly from Washington to the new source's location, transiting several countries en route and using various methods of transportation. Dick never appeared at the local U.S. embassy and any required field support was handled by a single officer from the CIA station in that country, who met him briefly in some secure location. After meetings with the asset in a safe house, Dick returned to his hotel room, where he transferred his written notes to a laptop computer and then encrypted them. Following completion of each meeting schedule, Dick returned to Washington, where the reporting was decrypted.

Offensively, it was decided to undertake two probes. In the first, Milt Bearden went to Nairobi and proudly reported back through our communications channels that he had recruited a specific KGB officer. Actually, he had done nothing of the kind. The reporting was a test of the security of our communications, the thought being that if the KGB was reading them, the KGB officer would be sent home in short order. Nothing of that nature happened. He remained in Nairobi for another year or two.

A similar probe of our communications involved Moscow. Barry Royden, deputy chief of the CI staff, went to Moscow to brief COS Murat N that he would be getting a cable to the effect that we had recruited a named KGB officer in Bangkok. The cable duly arrived in Moscow Station after Royden's trip. Again the information was not true. The outcome was the same as the Nairobi probe. The KGB officer remained in place for a substantial period.

In mid-January 1986 a seeming breakthrough occurred. A self-declared KGB officer volunteered to CIA via a letter to one of our officers in Bonn. This volunteer, who never had a formal CIA cryptonym but who was referred to as Mister X, told us that we had a mole in our communications component, which was located outside the Washington area. He further conveyed the news that Gennadiy Grigoryevich Varenik had been caught because his father found his spy gear. Through the summer of 1986 Mister X sent us a total of six letters, four of which repeated the theme that we should be looking to our communications component for the source of our compromises. In response to his request we dead-dropped considerable sums of money to him in East Germany.

This case was handled like the other 1986 European volunteer case. When the first cable came in announcing this supposed breakthrough, Redmond got on a plane, flew to Europe, and then, in the interests of speed, took a long-distance—and highly expensive—taxi ride. He wanted to prevent any possible follow-up electronic communications. From then on the case was handled without cable traffic and was subject to further compartmentation.

Eventually it was concluded that Mister X did not exist, and that the letters had been a KGB attempt to deceive us. If so, the answer to our problems was not to be found in our separately located communications component, but we were no closer to determining where it might be.

While Mister X was peddling his bogus reporting, we continued to learn of the compromise of our operations. In late January 1986, a GTABSORB shipment was opened by customs officials in the USSR. GTABSORB was a clever CIA technical operation involving the shipment of containers shaped as flowerpots on the Trans-Siberian railroad. Concealed in the containers were sensors that allowed us to monitor nuclear activity.

On 10 March 1986, Moscow Station officer Mike Sellers was ambushed trying to meet Sergey Vorontsov. Vorontsov, an officer in the KGB's Moscow City Directorate, had volunteered to us in 1984.

Two months later, on 7 May, Moscow Station officer Erik Sites was ambushed trying to meet with GTEASTBOUND, an engineer from Novosibirsk. At the time, we considered that GTEASTBOUND was a bona fide case, and we included it in our analysis. Later, however, we came to the conclusion that it had been a dangle to our station and never valid at all.

Meanwhile, on 4 April, Sergey Mikhaylovich Motorin, the KGB covert action specialist who had been assigned to Washington, DC, until January 1985, called his girlfriend at the Soviet embassy. This indicated to us that he was not compromised. It was a rare piece of good news. In October, however, we learned that both Motorin and Valeriy Fedorovich Martynov, the KGB scientific and technical officer who was being run jointly with the FBI, had been arrested some months before. Motorin's calls to his girlfriend were presumably made under KGB duress to mislead us.

While some prior attempts had been made to determine what was wrong, it was not until late October 1986 that the first organized efforts were undertaken. Jeanne returned from her tour in Libreville to work for Gus Hathaway, then–chief of the CI staff. Hathaway was in charge of the investigation and he appointed Jeanne as chief of the small group that would be carrying out the analytical work. The unit was entitled the Special Task Force, CI/STF for short.

Gus chose Ben Pepper, a retired SE operations officer who had been chief of SE's counterintelligence component in the late 1970s; Dan N, another retired officer, who had vast experience in the CI staff; and Fran Smith, who transferred from her job as chief of the branch in SE Division that ran our operations inside the Soviet Union. Ben had a wealth of historical knowledge of SE operations and their counterintelligence ramifications but he was somewhat out of date and had to do some extensive reading to become current. The same was true for Dan, whose area of expertise was China. Fran was the best prepared, possessing up-to-date and in-depth familiarity with the operations that SE had been running in recent years.

When Jeanne arrived in the CI staff, she was shown to her office, just a few doors away from where Gus sat. The office contained an empty safe, a desk and chair, and a manual typewriter. The manual typewriter was explained by the fact that David Blee, the previous chief of the CI staff, had disliked and distrusted computers, and did not want them around. (Blee also had a problem dealing with women, and never gave them an even break. Among a number of others, Jeanne and Sandy were subjected to his discriminatory treatment. Both took it with amusement or a shrug of the shoulders because by the 1980s it was obvious he was out of step with the times.) Gus was a more open-minded person and, when asked, readily agreed to provide a stand-alone computer for the unit. Thanks to him, we were able to carry out the first computer-assisted counterintelligence investigation in CIA history.

The first order of business was a review of the files on the cases that had been, or at least might have been, compromised. This was a labor-intensive process, for two reasons. First, it was SE's policy to document its cases in minute detail. This meant that there could be ten, fifteen, or more thickly packed file folders for each case. Secondly, we did not know what we were looking for. We took copious notes, and prepared individual chronologies, including every fact that we thought might be useful in an investigation.

Jeanne's job was to enter all of this material into a computer database. She devised one that eventually had some forty-eight fields, including the obvious ones such as name of the asset, date the case began, date it ended (insofar as we could determine it), places where operational activity took place, names of case officers involved, units providing technical support, whether the case was known to other organizations in the intelligence community, whether it was known to any friendly liaison services, whether any compromising materials had passed through our pouch system, and so forth. Deliberately, we made this database as broad-ranging as possible. Thus we also included cases that, as far as we knew, were experiencing no problems.

While we tried to cover everything, we made at least one error of omission—we did not enter the type of currency used to pay each asset. Only later did it occur to us that rubles were not a convertible currency, and had to be obtained clandestinely. It was possible that the rubles could be tagged in some way and the chain of acquisition contaminated. Once we realized this, we had to go back through all the files to determine who had been paid in rubles and who had not. This was of no investigative use in the long run, but it is an example of how our time was consumed.

In the meantime, Ray Reardon's group in the Office of Security was starting some investigative work. First they compiled a list of every CIA employee who had resigned, retired, or died in the 1985–86 period. This was in support of the theory that the KGB would not have been so quick to roll up the compromised cases if they had a goose who was continuing to lay golden eggs for them. On the other hand, if they had received their information as a one-time shot, perhaps from someone who was no longer in a position of access, they would be less hesitant. The list was scoured in an effort to determine if any of the individuals on it were likely to have been in positions that would have given them access to the compromised cases. This venture did not lead to any useful outcome. It was just one of those things that had to be done.

Even at this early date, Moscow Station was believed to be germane to any investigation. We knew that the internal KGB had considered us the main enemy since 1945 and that they had dedicated a large percentage of their manpower and expertise to uncovering our operations, by either surveillance, technical operations, or attempts to subvert our personnel. As far as we could tell, they had had little success, which was quite worrying in itself. We wondered what was out there that we were not seeing.

With this in mind, the Office of Security started a program to interview CIA personnel who had been stationed in Moscow, or had undertaken official travel there, in 1985 and 1986. Dan Payne was the officer responsible for this program and he continued it for a year or two. Like many of the other endeavors undertaken in this period, his efforts did not lead to any breakthroughs. However, it was useful in that it increased our understanding of what was what, and who was who, in Moscow at the time.

At this same time we initiated a re-review of some CI leads received in the 1973–75 period, both by CI/STF and the Office of Security. The leads, which pointed to a possible penetration of CIA, had never been resolved, and it was thought that the information covering this earlier period might somehow be connected with the 1985–86 compromises. Although we could not know it at this juncture, this was another chimera that wasted our time.

Meanwhile, the FBI had become energized when it learned of the loss of its two most important cases—Martynov and Motorin. In the fall of 1986, they set up a unit entitled the ANLACE Task Force, headed by Tim Caruso. Caruso was a gray man who always wore a gray suit. It was obvious that he was no friend of the CIA but had been told to cooperate with us, probably by Don Stuckey, his FBI supervisor and a positive force in the search for what had gone wrong. Caruso worked with us to a sufficient extent, although it was noticeably painful for him and he did not go beyond what he thought necessary.

The members of the ANLACE Task Force varied both in their CI abilities and their personal qualities. Barbara Campbell, Art McLendon, and Jim Holt, of whom more will be told later, were helpful additions. Caruso and Bob Wade proudly told us that all the members of ANLACE were special agents, not analysts. Obviously, they thought that this was a good thing; we did not, although we did not voice our opinion. Their statement was not quite true—although analyst Jim Milburn was associated with ANLACE, he was not allowed to join in the inter-Agency discussions. Milburn, like Holt, would play a prominent part in a later stage of the investigation.

The ANLACE Task Force interacted with CI/STF almost daily. CI/STF provided chronologies of all of the compromised cases, and answered numerous FBI requests for information. There were at least two overnight offsite conferences. The first was held at "the Farm" in December 1986, just as we were beginning to feel our way. The second was held at the Xerox training site near Leesburg in Virginia. There were also a couple of all-day conferences at our respective headquarters. NSA representatives attended at least one of these conferences, because of the continuing theory that our communications had been compromised.

Unfortunately, despite the efforts to coordinate our activities, there were barriers to full cooperation. First of all, we were not co-located. The

FBI was carrying out its research at FBI headquarters, and we were doing the same in Langley. More important, the FBI's mandate was to search for a possible mole in the FBI while we were taking a broader look for an explanation regarding what had gone wrong in 1985–86. A mole, whether in the CIA or FBI, was only one of the possible solutions.

The ANLACE Task Force did not come up with any leads to a current penetration as far as we know, although we were not privy to their final report. They did develop information on an old case, designated "unsub Dick."[1] They also produced a subsidiary report on the subject of FBI compartmentation of sensitive information, or lack thereof. Alas, the Hanssen case shows that management took little note of their recommendations.

In one area there was full cooperation between the FBI and the CIA. Someone had a smart idea that became known at the CIA as the RACKETEER program. The FBI had a more appropriate cryptonym: BUCKLURE. The idea was to use the lure of bucks to recruit a knowledgeable KGB officer. One million dollars was to be used in approaches to those KGB officers who might be aware of penetrations of the U.S. intelligence community. This program lasted for several years. The FBI approached KGB officers in the United States and the CIA approached their counterparts abroad. We realized that we were dealing with a subgroup of KGB officers who were probably the most dedicated and least likely to be suborned. However, we wanted to disseminate as broadly as possible the idea of a million dollars being available for the right person. Our hope was that there was someone out there who would want to take us up on our offer.

December 1986 saw the beginning of the Lonetree case, which was to have a major impact on the investigation of the 1985 compromises.[2] Sergeant Clayton Lonetree, a U.S. Marine guard who had been stationed in Moscow, walked in to our chief in Vienna, and confessed that he had been in unreported contact with a KGB officer. Lonetree explained that, while in Moscow, he became acquainted with a Russian woman named Violetta Seina, who worked at the U.S. embassy. They had fallen in love, but Lonetree knew this meant trouble because he was bound by antifraternization regulations. Violetta had suggested that perhaps her "Uncle Sasha" could help them, and introduced him to Lonetree at the end of 1985 or the beginning of 1986. Uncle Sasha in reality was a KGB officer named Aleksey Yegorov, who operated under the operational alias of

Aleksey Yefimov. He pretended to sympathize with the young couple but soon directed the conversation to the organizational makeup and personnel of the U.S. embassy. Lonetree, who had only limited access to Embassy secrets, provided what he knew in response to Uncle Sasha's questions.

Lonetree's love life and his relationship with Uncle Sasha was still inconclusive when he was transferred to Vienna. At that point the KGB made the mistake of trying to turn the case over to a KGB officer stationed in Austria named Yuriy Lysov. It was this attempted turnover, which seems to have been handled in a hamhanded manner, which made Lonetree recognize that he had no option but to turn himself in.

The investigation of the Lonetree case was handled by the Naval Investigative Service (NIS), which immediately pressed a large number of its personnel into service. Many U.S. Marine guards were interviewed in an attempt to determine the nature and scope of the security breach. Unfortunately, a large number of the interviewers were specialists in criminal cases and knew little about espionage in general, and nothing about the U.S. embassy in Moscow and how the KGB would go about penetrating it. Thus the interview reports left significant questions unanswered.

Our little task force in the CI staff immediately turned our attention to the Lonetree case, to the exclusion of almost everything else. We had always felt that Moscow Station might be the key to the problem of the 1985 losses, and our belief in this possibility was now strengthened. Our computer database had included a field that indicated whether Moscow was aware of each of the compromised cases. The initial Lonetree debriefings caused us to examine this question in more depth. Once again we checked the files on the compromised cases to determine just how much Moscow had been told, and when. This effort was somewhat duplicative of the SE Division research, described below, but the emphasis was different. We were trying to ascertain what Moscow Station personnel could have known, and when they learned it, while the SE Division task force was geared to investigating paper holdings.

In mid-March our investigation reached a new level of intensity. Corporal Arnold Bracy, a Marine guard who had served with Lonetree in Moscow, reportedly stated to an NIS interviewer that Lonetree had told him about having let the KGB into our embassy, including the CIA Station and the communications area. While Bracy soon recanted his confession, there was a good level of detail in it, and it was generally felt that the recantation could not be relied on.

The first question we in the CI staff asked ourselves was: If the KGB were going to mount a technical penetration of our embassy, how would they go about it? Dan N was given the unenviable task of obtaining copies of the duty schedules of the Marine guard detachment in Moscow, the hour-by-hour logs of the Marines who covered the various guard posts, and incident reports for the period that Lonetree was assigned there. This was an immense amount of material and Dan soon was surrounded by mounds of paper he untiringly shuffled as he tried to determine which Marine was on duty with which other Marine, at one of the posts that would give access to classified areas, late at night, or on a Sunday or holiday. We also consulted our in-house experts to get an idea of how long it might take to defeat alarms and combination locks, and how much time would be needed to photograph classified documents and return them to their original positions.

As it turned out, Dan's months of research did not produce any startling conclusions. He found a couple of instances where it just might have been possible for a disaffected Marine to allow the KGB entrance, but these instances were not very convincing. As he worked, Dan began drawing up a memorandum outlining what he had found. This memorandum went through many drafts. The first few stated our belief that the KGB had gotten into our premises. Later drafts increasingly hedged this conclusion. In the end, the memorandum was abandoned without being presented in final form.

The Bracy revelations, uncorroborated as they were, brought about a volcanic reaction in SE Division. When he heard the news, Redmond burst into Sandy's office, closed the door, and announced that we had a potential disaster of enormous proportions. He told her that as of that moment she was no longer chief of her branch, but was reporting to him. He then briefly described the situation and said that CIA had to assume a worst-case scenario. Sandy's job was to identify and inventory all official traffic that had Moscow as an addressee, digest its contents, and notify all affected CIA and other U.S. government organizations of the potential compromise of the contents. As an aside, the DDO, the DCI, the Director of NSA, and every other high-ranking government official wanted the information yesterday. Redmond left as quickly as he had arrived. Sandy took a deep breath, told members of her branch she had been reassigned effective immediately, picked up the "back room" files and a few personal belongings, and left.

The new SE Division project was officially known as the Moscow Task Force. Leningrad was later added to the title as the investigation expanded. As had been her habit when in trouble, the next morning Sandy asked for and received the assistance of Worthen. Within five days the two had located office space; staffed the task force with three additional officers; had desks, computers, and other necessary equipment installed; and were producing the infamous worst-case scenario memos.

Redmond and Sandy initially assumed that the task force would complete its review in four months. Six months was considered an unacceptable outside possibility. However, everyone was aghast to discover that Moscow Station paper holdings were enormous and the volume of daily electronic correspondence from the CIA and other U.S. government components was staggering. It took one year to collect, inventory, read, disseminate, and file over 60,000 pages of material sent to Moscow, approximately half of which they had retained. Gerber initially disputed the numbers in Sandy's final report on the conclusions and recommendations of the task force. The Moscow Station he had run in the early 1980s contained minimal files. However, the figures were clear-cut. Gerber ordered changes and Sandy finally completed the worst assignment of her career.

In August 1987, Lonetree was court-martialed in Quantico, Virginia. He was found guilty and sentenced to thirty-five years in prison. (His sentence was twice reduced. He received time off for good behavior and was released in 1996.) After the court-martial, Lonetree underwent a series of debriefings combined with frequent polygraphs. Most fortunately the debriefings were videotaped. We received copies of the tapes and were able to observe Lonetree's body language as he reacted to the questions posed to him while at the same time hearing his answers. After watching the tapes for several hours, we all became convinced that, as he had consistently maintained, he had never let the KGB into our embassy. Alas, this meant that we had spent almost an entire year following a path that led nowhere.

CHAPTER 11

CIC FORMATION

A T THE BEGINNING OF 1988, plans for the reorganization of the CIA's CI staff began to move into high gear. Various permutations and combinations were proposed and, as part of the front office, CI/STF inevitably became enmeshed in the lengthy discussions. The formal reorganization took place in April, when the old CI staff metamorphosed into the new Counterintelligence Center with the accompanying set of logistic and bureaucratic upheavals unavoidable in any large organization.

A certain amount of controversy surrounded the transformation. The preference was to have the center directly under the CIA director. However, the FBI protested that this would erode the FBI's charter for domestic counterintelligence. In the end the center was subordinated to the Directorate of Operations—a strange solution because it implied that the other CIA directorates had no counterintelligence problems and no need for counterintelligence awareness. It thus perpetuated one of the weakest aspects of the CI staff, even though the reorganization had been meant to overcome this shortcoming. Furthermore, although the FBI was invited to send a representative to the center, it declined.

As part of the transformation, Gus Hathaway would now wear two hats: Associate Deputy Director for Operations for Counterintelligence, and Chief of the Counterintelligence Center. Senior DO officer Ted Price was brought in and also wore two hats: Deputy Chief of the Center, and Chief of Operations for the Center.

Price was a Chinese-speaking officer who had served as a senior officer in Asia. No two people could have been less alike than Hathaway and Price, and they had problems co-existing. Hathaway ran his component by gathering around him a staff of people whom he liked and trusted, with little reference to organizational charts. Jeanne doubts whether he ever attended a management course, or read a book on the subject. Price, on the other hand, was the consummate modern bureaucrat who knew how the system worked and how to use it to achieve his goals. Before coming to the center, he had served as chief of the Career Management staff, a job that well suited his talents and interests.

The new center was divided into three groups: Operations, Analysis, and Security, plus the usual support elements. Our task force was subsumed into the Security Group, which had two branches: Investigations and Technical. We formed part of the Investigations Branch. Ray Reardon came over from the Office of Security to serve as group chief. Jeanne was appointed deputy chief, and also functioned as chief of the Investigations Branch. The branch was responsible for all investigations of penetrations of the Agency, not just those emanating from the KGB. Fran Smith came with Jeanne to this branch, filling the position of chief of the Soviet Section. Dan Payne joined the center and worked in Fran's section, with specific responsibility for continuing the investigation of the 1985 losses. Jeanne and Fran also worked on the problem, time permitting, but were often drawn away to concentrate on other matters.

As a consequence, the investigation became somewhat diffused. It also lost some of its priority, because SE Division was running successful operations against the Soviet target. Therefore, the 1985 losses came to be regarded by some as a historical problem that no longer existed. We were still learning about cases that had been compromised, but all of them were cases that had existed prior to 1985, and some of them stretched back many years. The heaviest blow was hearing that General Polyakov, who had retired some years earlier, had been arrested in July 1986. Another sobering arrest was that of Vladimir Mikhaylovich Vasilyev, the GRU officer who had worked with us in Budapest. A third arrest was that of Vladimir Mikhaylovich Piguzov, the KGB officer who had volunteered in Jakarta in the mid-1970s and who returned to Moscow in 1979. All three of these men were, like many of their colleagues, subsequently tried and executed.

Two other sources, although we did not know it at the time, were more lucky. Both of them served time in prison, but were eventually amnestied. One of them was Vladimir Viktorovich Potashov, a researcher at the Institute of the United States and Canada (IUSAC), a think tank in Moscow. A joint FBI-CIA asset, he was encrypted SUNDI PUNCH by the FBI and GTMEDIAN by CIA. He had volunteered in the United States in 1981 and later returned to the USSR where we lost touch with him. He was arrested in July 1986. Ames knew about this case, and presumably Hanssen and Pitts did also.

The other was Boris Nikolayevich Yuzhin, the KGB officer in San Francisco who had been recruited by the FBI. We had not been in touch with him since 1982. Betrayed by Howard, Ames, Hanssen, and Pitts, not to mention his own carelessness, he was arrested in December 1986.

While the CIA was rebuilding its agent stable in the second half of the 1980s, one major compromise took place. The CIA had identified a KGB illegal named Reino Gikman, who was living in Austria. Our coverage of Gikman indicated that he was in touch with a high-ranking U.S. State Department employee named Felix Bloch. We immediately informed the FBI. This notification took place on 28 April 1989. Less than two months later, on 22 June, Gikman telephoned Bloch to warn him that he was under suspicion. To a few, it was food for thought that the case had been compromised so soon after the FBI had learned about it. However, the prevailing view was that the French were to blame, because their internal security service, the DST, had surveilled Gikman, at our request, when he traveled to France to meet Bloch. As a result, while we did take this compromise into consideration during our investigation, we and the FBI perhaps did not award it sufficient attention. As we now know, Hanssen informed the KGB about this case within one month of the CIA telling the FBI about it.

It should be emphasized that, while some in management placed their main focus on other problems, not everyone took this relaxed view. Burton Gerber, Gus Hathaway, Paul Redmond, Sandy, Jeanne, Fran, Dan, and a few others still were determined to get to the bottom of the 1985 problem even if they were forced to spend part of their time following other threads, some of them justifiably awarded a higher priority.

An example is the 1989 Philip Agee "false flag" approach in Latin America. Agee, a former CIA officer who had left the Agency in 1968 and who had been working for the Cubans since 1973, approached a junior officer in our station. He identified himself as a CIA officer attached to the Inspector General's office and showed her a U.S. diplomatic passport, with his photograph, in an assumed name. He also showed her a letter, ostensibly from CIA Director William Webster, asking for her cooperation in an important investigation. Agee explained to our officer that he was looking into the misuse of Agency official pouches to bring narcotics into the United States. According to his fabricated story, it was possible that someone in our Latin American office was involved in this illegal activity, which is why he needed our officer's help. He added that she was to tell no one about his investigation because the perpetrator could be anyone in the office from the chief on down.

Agee looked the part of a senior Agency official and played his role with considerable skill. At first the junior officer had no reason to disbelieve his story, with its supporting evidence of a diplomatic passport and a letter from the director. He told her that he would be back in town in a few weeks to continue his investigation. During the pause in contact, the young officer began having doubts about his story. For instance, the letter from the director looked as if it had been typed on a typewriter, not a word processor. In general, it did not have the polished appearance that a communication from the director's office should have.

When Agee returned to town, he pushed his luck too far. He asked the junior officer to provide him with a list of all the office's clandestine sources, explaining that it was possible that one of these sources had ties to the world of narcotics and could have suborned his case officer. The young officer now decided that she had to report Agee's approach, which she did. When shown a photograph of Agee, she recognized him as the man with whom she had been dealing.

When this case broke, it caused a frenzy of activity. David Edger, a senior Latin America Division officer, and Jeanne were immediately dispatched to Latin America, where they interviewed all our personnel in an attempt to learn as much as possible about what had happened. Among the questions we asked ourselves were: Because Agee's approach was so smooth, was it possible that this was not his first attempt to play this role? Also, was it possible that he might strike again some day using a different scenario? And, were the Cubans, or the KGB, or both, orchestrating this plot? (Thanks to the FBI, we were eventually able to identify a Cuban hand in this approach. Agee had given our officer an address in New York to write to if she needed to get in touch with him. The FBI was able to connect this address with a Cuban intelligence officer.)

Given these unpleasant possibilities, it was decided to conduct CI compulsory awareness sessions for all Agency employees. Jeanne, who had the best grasp of the events in Latin America, participated in these sessions on many occasions for the next few years. This was necessary and inevitable, because it involved a counterintelligence problem legitimately being handled by Jeanne's component, but it took time away from the 1985 investigation.

A second digression taking up Jeanne's time is less justifiable in hindsight. A defector from the anti-government insurgency in El Salvador made some allegations about the behavior of our personnel assigned there. The defector had not made these accusations immediately upon escaping from El Salvador, but only after some months of being interviewed by various groups with their own political biases.

The accusations became a cause célèbre, and Jeanne was asked to conduct an investigation, presumably because senior management had been pleased with the way she had handled the Agee case. Looking back, it is clear that this was not a counterintelligence problem and that Jeanne had no special background to handle it. However, she saluted and did her best to look into it. This involved a somewhat nerve-wracking trip to El Salvador, because it took place shortly after insurgents had advanced close to the capital. The investigation cleared our personnel, at least to Jeanne's satisfaction. However, it was a detour and one less justifiable than the Agee case.

During this period SE Division's "back room" continued to handle an ever-expanding stable of sensitive Soviet and select East European intelligence sources. Always mindful that one of these sources might have the answer or hold a clue to the unsolved mystery of our 1985–86 compromises, Sandy and Diana worked closely with Jeanne as she pursued her formal investigation of the losses. The three were often in daily contact on issues, raw reporting was shared, and requirements for the sources on these sensitive CI matters were coordinated and frequently co-authored.

Due to the increase in new assets, the back room added personnel, each hand-picked by Sandy and Redmond. In addition to Worthen, two more luminaries were brought in—Sue Eckstein, a retired senior division officer on contract, and Myrna Fitzgerald, a superstar intelligence officer and Sandy's alter ego from their days in the Africa Branch. The office space itself was a vault within a vault, consisting of a maze of several small rooms in a far corner of the basement of the new headquarters building. The door was usually closed and only the senior leadership of the division and Jeanne were authorized entry to the space without the permission of a member of the group. It became an unspoken and inviolate rule that all other persons knocked on the door and then waited to enter until all papers and files were turned over or covered. Only one individual ever ignored the practice. That exception was Rick Ames, who one morning several months after his return from Rome simply opened the door and sauntered into the office to chitchat with Diana.

Fortunately for members of the unit, great progress had been made in computerization. We now had equipment that encrypted and decrypted electronic traffic quickly and without error, and the back room remained the only location where clear-text field and headquarters correspondence on the sensitive sources came together and source files resided.

That the back room handled the division's most important assets was not a secret within the corridors, but this fact did become a source of disquiet and resentment among a number of division employees. They came to recognize that correspondence concerning any significant Soviet volunteer in their geographic area of responsibility would immediately disappear into the bowels of the back room and that they would never hear of the case again, much less have any say in its handling. Although many of these employees were aware of the 1985–86 disasters and therefore the need for such severe security measures, they and others understandably took the division's policy on the handling of its crown jewels as a statement that they were less than trustworthy. Nevertheless, despite the rumblings in the hallways and the number of years that had passed since our spate of losses, the division was steadfast that the back room would continue to exist and carry out its charter.

The GTPROLOGUE case, which was to cause so much heartburn to Sandy and Jeanne, started in June 1988.[1] Aleksandr Vasilyevich Zhomov, a KGB internal CI officer, discreetly approached Jack Downing, at the time COS Moscow, on a Leningrad-bound train. Zhomov did not identify himself, but passed Downing an envelope and then disappeared. The contents of the envelope were internal KGB documents, plus a note explaining that the writer was from the department of the KGB's Second Chief Directorate, which was responsible for working against the CIA Station and outlining a plan by which he and Downing could communicate securely in the future. He said that he wanted to leave the USSR but would work for us until the time was ripe.

Among the documents was one of special significance to the investigation of the 1985 losses. It was a rundown of the activities of our Moscow Station in the 1984–86 period, and it indicated that those losses that had taken place in Moscow were the result of our poor tradecraft. Again—a benign explanation of what had gone wrong! This was enough to raise Sandy's and Jeanne's CI antennae.

Before too long, Jeanne wrote a memorandum to chief, SE Division, suggesting that GTPROLOGUE could be the son of Mister X—in other words, someone sent to deceive us on the subject of the 1985–86 compromises. Sandy also wrote a memorandum with very specific requirements to be covered with Zhomov when he and Downing were next in contact. His responses to the questions would establish whether he was a plant or a legitimate penetration of the Second Chief Directorate.

After reading Sandy's memorandum Jeanne telephoned the SE Division office directly responsible for running the case. She made a special plea that Sandy's requirements be an important order of business, because they could prove whether the case was good or bad. The reply was extremely disheartening. The SE front office had decided that "we don't want to make him mad." Therefore the new source would not be asked questions to determine his bona fides. In Jeanne and Sandy's opinion, this flew in the face of logic. When someone volunteered, it was up to that volunteer to provide evidence of his honesty, credibility, and value. Yet we were ignoring this normal and sensible procedure.

The case went on and on, and both Sandy and Jeanne freely expressed, both orally and in writing, the opinion that we were being taken in. And during this period we benefited from the reporting of defector Sergey Papushin who, like Zhomov, was an officer from the KGB's Second Chief Directorate and indeed was acquainted with him. Although the differences were not major, what Papushin said about Zhomov did not jibe with what Zhomov had told us about himself. For instance, Papushin told us that Zhomov was happily married and doted on his daughter. Zhomov said that his marriage was on the rocks, and this was one of the reasons he wanted to defect.

Eventually Zhomov was asked some of the questions that Sandy had compiled, but his answers were vague or improbable and did nothing to allay our doubts. Jeanne even wrote a second memorandum stating that after watching the case for more than a year she was still convinced that it was not valid. Sandy continued to insert the test questions in each cable to the field for presentation to Zhomov, only to have them deleted by the front office before transmission. Bearden was reported to have commented that these requirements were nonsense. He would soon learn how wrong he had been.

All of our efforts went for naught. In the end the CIA paid Zhomov a good deal of money, which served to sweeten the KGB's coffers, revealed to him our procedures for clandestinely exfiltrating our assets from the Soviet Union, provided him with a valid U.S. passport, and generally made fools of ourselves. He of course never went through with the exfiltration, claiming that our plan was too dangerous and that he would have to break contact. His message did not ring true, and finally the powers-that-be, including an unwilling Bearden, came to the conclusion that we had been duped all along.

Sandy and Jeanne, who had put their opinions on record long before, were in the position of being able to say, "I told you so," but that was scant comfort. The KGB must have had many a laugh at the CIA's expense, and this did not sit well with us. The only good that resulted from this mess was that it caused Sandy to abandon SE Division and its "new-think" flight from reality, and join in the revitalized hunt for the meaning of the 1985 disasters.

CHAPTER 12

BEGINNING OF THE FOCUS ON AMES

ONE MORNING IN EARLY NOVEMBER 1989 a breakthrough occurred, although we did not realize its full significance at the time. Diana Worthen approached Sandy Grimes in her office, obviously distressed and worried by the story she was about to recount. Worthen had been stationed in Mexico City during the same period as Rick Ames and had worked for him in the Soviet section. She and Rick became friends and this friendship was soon extended to Rosario Casas Dupuy, cultural attaché at the Colombian embassy. Rick and Rosario had started an affair, although Rick was still married to his first wife, Nan. He was a geographic bachelor because Nan had a good job in New York and refused to accompany him to Mexico.

Diana's friendship with Rick and Rosario continued over the years after they all had left Mexico. Rick divorced Nan and married Rosario in 1985. In 1986 they left for a three-year tour in Rome. While they were there, Diana sent Rosario a few small items in response to her requests for things not readily available in Rome. These included pantyhose and pregnancy vitamins. In return, Rosario sent Diana some expensive gifts, including a Gucci scarf worth at least two hundred dollars. Rosario's gifts to Diana were out of proportion with the small sums that Diana had expended.

When Rick and Rosario returned to Washington, Diana noticed a substantial change in their lifestyle. Before going to Rome they had lived in a rented apartment in a modest development in northern Virginia and

Rick drove an ancient Volvo. Now they were the owners of a large house in a posh section of North Arlington. Diana was astounded when Rosario told her that they had paid the asking price of $540,000 without trying to bargain. She was even more astounded when she learned that they were remodeling the kitchen, contracting for extensive landscaping, and ordering window treatments for every window, all at the same time. Additionally, Rick had purchased a new Jaguar for himself and a new Honda Accord for Rosario.

Diana could see that these expenditures amounted to a very large sum and she wondered where the money had come from. Neither Rick nor Rosario offered any explanation. In her musings, Diana was aware of a fact that most people did not know. When they were all in Mexico, Rosario had no extra money and lived from paycheck to paycheck.

After much soul-searching, Diana shared her observations with Sandy. Sandy immediately suggested to Diana that the information could be important, and that they should tell Redmond right away, which they did. Redmond impatiently listened to Diana's remarks, as Sandy reminded him that Rick knew about every case we had lost. He had access and now he apparently had money. Redmond was preoccupied with other matters and curtly told them to go to Jeanne. He then forgot about the conversation. On her own, Diana duly approached Jeanne to repeat her story once again. Unfortunately, the day she did so was within twenty-four hours of the surfacing of the Agee false flag operation. Jeanne told Diana to talk to Dan Payne, and almost immediately became immersed in the Agee problem to the exclusion of everything else.

At this point Diana felt exceedingly frayed, but she did not give up. She went to Dan Payne to tell her story for the fourth time. Dan was busy with a number of cases, but he listened to Diana and, more importantly, took preliminary action based on her account. He started by reviewing Rick's Office of Security and Office of Personnel files. These did not contain much of CI interest, although they revealed that in the distant past Rick had received two DUI citations. They also documented that, on two occasions in the 1970s, he had been drunk at an office Christmas party. (In those days, heavy drinking at CIA office festivities was not outside the norm. Christmas parties began in the afternoon and focused on alcohol, not food. The Office of Security had to maintain checkpoints at the various exits to the buildings, in an effort to ascertain who was too drunk to drive and to make arrangements to get them safely home. Those days are now long gone.) The security file also indicated that Rick had last been polygraphed in 1986, and that he was cleared in a single session.

Dan's next step was to read Rosario's operational, or 201, file. Diana had told him that Rosario had worked as a low-level agent for the CIA Station in Mexico City, both by occasionally making her apartment available for station officers to hold meetings in, and by reporting on individuals she met in the course of her duties as secretary of the local diplomatic association. More pertinent to Dan's interest at the time was information in the file disclosing that Rosario came from a politically connected family in Colombia. Her father was a former head of the Liberal Party. Rosario's assignment to the Colombian embassy in Mexico City was a direct appointment by Colombian president Turbay. Moreover, her father was also rector of a university, and had attended Princeton.

As part of his preliminary investigation, Dan went to the Arlington County courthouse to check on Rick's mortgage for his new residence, but could find no record of it. Eventually he had to make two more trips to the courthouse in order to convince Jeanne that he had checked in every possible way and that the mortgage really did not exist.

Dan also initiated a routine customs check. This turned up three currency transactions, as follows:

18 Oct 1985—deposits of $15,660 cash

18 Feb 1986—deposits of $13,500 cash

1 Aug 1989—$22,107 lira exchange

None of us knew what this meant, but Dan added the information to his growing file on Rick.

While all this was going on, a ghost from the past reappeared. His name was Sergey Petrovich Fedorenko. An academic researcher with the Soviet Institute of the United States and Canada (IUSAC), he had been recruited in New York back in 1973 and run in place by the CIA and FBI until his return to the Soviet Union in 1977. The CIA encrypted him GTPYRRHIC. His FBI cryptonym was MYRRH. One of his handlers was Rick, who traveled from Washington periodically to participate in the operation.

Fedorenko was not the only CIA or FBI agent who had escaped the 1985 destruction, but these "escapees" numbered fewer than ten and were therefore of major interest in our investigation. (Much later, when we reviewed these cases as a group, we estimated that they fit one of two categories: either they were minor players who did not have access to state secrets, and were therefore not dangerous to Soviet interests, or they had been dangles in the first place. All of the evidence is that Fedorenko belongs in the "minor player" category.)

Once Fedorenko arrived in the United States in late 1989, arrangements were made immediately to recontact him. The two people chosen to handle the debriefings were Pat Watson of the FBI and Rick from the CIA. Because we in the CI Investigations Branch were highly interested in hearing what Fedorenko had to say about the twelve years he had spent in Moscow out of touch with us, we asked Rick to come down and give us a rundown on Fedorenko's experiences. Unfortunately, what we learned did not really help. Fedorenko said that he believed he had been under suspicion, but that he had never been arrested.

The debriefings continued for some time, in a somewhat acrimonious atmosphere. Some in SE Division believed that Fedorenko was under KGB control, while others considered him a valid, if not particularly valuable, source. Jeanne and Sandy belonged to the second category. Eventually, Fedorenko settled in the United States, where he still lives today.

Throughout the affair, Rick defended Fedorenko, to the point of becoming obnoxious. Not only did he believe that Fedorenko was a bona fide asset, he also persisted in overestimating Fedorenko's access and reporting. This led to a minor hullabaloo. Zhomov had reported on a case that could have been that of Fedorenko, although it was not a close fit. A memorandum was prepared and placed in Fedorenko's file. The memorandum was sanitized so that no information regarding Zhomov's identity could be ascertained. With the exception of Jeanne and Sandy, the thinking at the time was the reverse of reality. Zhomov had to be protected because he was a bona fide volunteer with information of prospective great value. Fedorenko was a plant who had to be exposed. Anyway, Rick heard about the memorandum and learned that Fedorenko's file had been placed in a safe for which he did not have the combination. Thus Rick could not read the memorandum, even though it was pertinent to his case. This incensed Rick and he somehow managed to access the safe in question and read the report. He then wrote a rebuttal casting doubt on the theory that Zhomov's reporting pertained to Fedorenko.

That Rick entered the safe to read the memorandum was a breach of well-understood security practices and it further set some people against him. However, he was responsible for handling Fedorenko and, given his somewhat arrogant personality, it was not terribly surprising that he took this action. And he made no effort to conceal what he had done because he promptly wrote a refutation to Zhomov's supposed lead.

As it turned out, the CIA discarded Fedorenko based partly on SE Division management's mistaken assessment of Zhomov's report and partly on Fedorenko's troubles with a polygraph examination. The FBI, on the other hand, continued to believe in Fedorenko and kept in contact with him.

While all this was going on, Dan had been diverted from his preliminary investigation of Rick. The fast-changing scene in Eastern Europe had resulted in the CIA's recruitment of a number of new sources, some of whom provided information possibly related to penetrations of the CIA. One case that absorbed Dan's time involved an Eastern Bloc service's knowledge of personal details about one of our officers. How had the service in question learned this information? After an exhaustive investigation, Dan deduced that the officer in question had a relative who was working for the Eastern Bloc service and had supplied the information.

Another case concerned Karel Koecher. Koecher, a Czech national, had been recruited by his country's intelligence service in the early 1960s. He immigrated to the United States in 1965, and became a U.S. citizen. After he received his citizenship he applied to the CIA, and was hired as a translator/transcriber with SE Division after successfully completing a polygraph. He later left the CIA because of dissatisfaction with his position, which was not commensurate with his educational background.

In November 1984, based on defector reporting, the FBI arrested Koecher. He was exchanged in February 1986 and sent back to Czechoslovakia. After the Czech Velvet Revolution in 1989 he visited the West. Dan contacted him and talked to him at some length. Dan's interest in Koecher revolved around the period that Koecher had been assigned to SE Division. Although he worked in a building outside CIA headquarters, he interacted with his fellow transcribers at the same outlying location. Some of them had subsequently moved to sensitive jobs in headquarters. The thinking was that Koecher could have supplied assessment and vulnerability information about his co-workers and that this information could subsequently have been used in a recruitment approach. Further, the Czechs might have shared this information with the KGB.[1]

After dealing with these diversions, Dan got back to his investigation of Rick. In January 1991 he did a credit check and found nothing unusual. (We learned later that, as luck would have it, the month that Dan chose for his check was the only month of the year that did not include any extravagant spending.) He also looked into Rick's CIA credit union account. This also did not turn up anything out of the ordinary. What it did reveal lulled us into a false sense of security. Rick had taken out a $25,000 new car loan for his $43,000 Jaguar and was paying it off on a regular basis in amounts commensurate with his CIA salary. Presumably Rick thought that it would be easy for us to check this account so he deliberately made it look innocuous. In fact it took a National Security Letter, signed by the Director of Security, to gain access. At the time this was a very unusual step to take.

As part of his scrutiny, in December 1990 Dan asked the Office of Security to initiate a background investigation of Rick, with a subsequent polygraph. We deliberately delayed requesting this reinvestigation until January 1991 because employees were on a five-year schedule at that time. Had an investigation been launched earlier, it might have aroused Rick's suspicions. Dan also wrote a memorandum to the Office of Security suggesting that the reinvestigation concentrate on Rick's financial situation and spending habits. A personal history form was sent to Rick on 22 January 1991, with a request for updating. He returned it sometime in March.

The Office of Security background investigation was completed on 12 April 1991. It revealed that numerous people knew about Rick's lavish lifestyle. All of those interviewed attributed his wealth to his spouse and her Colombian family. The comments on Rick were generally favorable, and everyone recommended him for continued access to classified information. Some noted that he occasionally drank to excess, but no one saw this as a serious problem. One person did comment that he thought Rick might be a spy, but when asked to explain this statement backed off and said "no, the profile is not right for that." This particular individual had tangled with Rick over the value and validity of Fedorenko.

Rick was polygraphed in mid-April. Regrettably, the process was flawed in that the polygrapher did not have access to the full memorandum that Dan had written but only to a summary. Also, the background investigation results had not yet made it into Rick's security file. During the polygraph examination, Rick freely discussed his finances. He admitted his wealth, and attributed it to his mother-in-law. He stated that he was the part owner of two pieces of land in Colombia, and was considering going into the import-export business there after retirement. He even cockily said that he was getting a "free ride" on his wife's money.

After the first session, the polygrapher was not quite satisfied with the results pertaining to the question about Rick's foreign contacts. Therefore, he was promptly scheduled for a follow-up session and the subject of his foreign contacts was reviewed with him. Rick explained that he had been introduced to numerous people in Colombia when he and his wife visited her family. He added that he had no idea whether any of them were employed by the Colombian security services, and suggested to the polygrapher that this might explain his reaction to the question. The polygrapher accepted this explanation and Rick was allowed to go. The question of Rick's finances was not explored in any great depth.

In July 1991 we took a new tack. We dispatched an officer to Bogota to brief our chief there and ask him to use his stable of assets to gain further information on Rosario's family. Bogota did what we asked, tasking one of its Colombian agents to find out what he could. A month or so later the agent reported back that the family was indeed wealthy and well connected politically. According to the agent, the family once donated land worth several million dollars for the construction of a soccer field in central Bogota. Furthermore, the extended family was involved in real estate development, and owned a chain of popular ice cream parlors.

Based on the successful polygraph and the seeming corroboration from Bogota that Rosario's family was indeed wealthy, the Office of Security closed its file on Rick. We in the Counterintelligence Center did not follow suit because we still had our suspicions. However, he was only one of the individuals we were looking at closely.

The CIA mole-hunting team (left to right): Sandy Grimes, Paul Redmond, Jeanne Vertefeuille, Diana Worthen, and Dan Payne. (Authors' collections)

Paul Redmond, Deputy Chief of SE Division, later Deputy Chief of the Counterintelligence Center and senior member of the mole-hunting team, Washington, DC, 1988. (Courtesy of Paul Redmond)

Diana Worthen with a photo spread of some of the CIA and FBI sources who were executed as a result of Ames' treachery. (Authors' collections)

Dan Payne with his chart of Ames' monthly bank deposits from unidentified sources during 1985–91. That income totaled $1,326,310. (Authors' collections)

Rick and Rosario Ames on vacation in Puerto Vallarta, Mexico, 1984. (Courtesy of Diana Worthen)

Walt Lomac, SE Division branch chief, making the most out of his exile to Africa for his defense of General Polyakov, 1969. (Courtesy of Walter Lomac)

Walt Lomac is finally recognized for his stand in the Polyakov case in a 1979 medal presentation ceremony. George Kalaris, Chief of the Counterintelligence Staff 1974–76 and Chief of SE Division 1976–79, is the presenter. (Courtesy of Walter Lomac)

In retirement, SE Division officers Dick and Louise C with "friends," Montana, 2006. (Courtesy of Louise and Dick C)

Burton Gerber, Chief of SE Division, 1984–89, and wife Rosalie, Washington, DC, 1988. (Courtesy of Burton Gerber)

GRU General-Mayor Dmitriy Fedorovich Polyakov, the highest-ranking Soviet intelligence officer ever to spy for the United States during the Cold War. Ames' treason in 1985 led to Polyakov's arrest in 1986, execution in 1988, and burial in an unmarked, unknown grave. (Authors' collections)

GRU General Polyakov and wife Nina at a diplomatic reception, New Delhi, India, 1970s. (Authors' collections)

*Ever the avid sportsman, General Polyakov proudly displays the meal of the day,
ca. 1970–80. (Authors' collections)*

Polyakov family, Moscow, mid-1960s (left to right): son Aleksandr, father Dmitriy, son Peter, and mother Nina. The Polyakovs' first child, also a son, died in the early 1960s. (Authors' collections)

General Polyakov and wife Nina (far right) during a gathering with neighbors at their dacha—a peaceful, retired life outside of Moscow, 1980s. (Authors' collections)

KGB officer Leonid Georgiyevich Poleshchuk and wife Lyudmila, Kathmandu, Nepal, ca. 1973. Poleshchuk was executed in 1986 after Ames named him as a CIA agent. (Courtesy of Andrei Poleshchuk)

Leonid and Lyudmila Poleshchuk with son Andrei at the Kievski Railroad Station, Moscow, September 1983. (Courtesy of Andrei Poleshchuk)

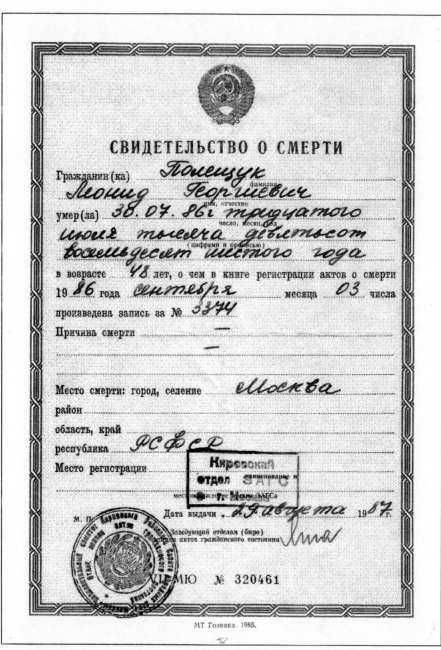

СВИДЕТЕЛЬСТВО О СМЕРТИ

Гражданин (ка) *Полещук*

Леонид Георгиевич
фамилия

имя, отчество

умер(ла) *30.07.86г тридцатого*
число, месяц, год

июля тысяча девятьсот

восемьдесят шестого года
(цифрами и прописью)

в возрасте *48* лет, о чем в книге регистрации актов о смерти

19 *86* года *сентября* месяца *03* числа

произведена запись за № *5374*

Причина смерти —

—

Место смерти: город, селение *Москва*

район

область, край

республика *РСФСР*

Место регистрации

Кировский
отдел ЗАГС
наименование и
местонахождение органа ЗАГСа

Дата выдачи *29 августа* 19 *87* г.

м. п.
Заведующий отделом (бюро)
записи актов гражданского состояния

VII-МЮ № 320461

МТ Гознака. 1985.

Official Soviet death certificate for KGB officer Leonid Georgiyevich Poleshchuk.
Date and place of death are given as 30 July 1986, Moscow. The space on the form
for cause of death is left blank. (Courtesy of Andrei Poleshchuk)

CHAPTER 13

THE INVESTIGATION GETS NEW LIFE

I N EARLY 1991 JEANNE HAD TO FACE that her career was beginning to wind down. She was scheduled for mandatory retirement at the end of 1992. The Counter-espionage Group of CIC was about to get a new chief. Ray Reardon, with whom she had worked productively for more than four years, was returning to the Office of Security to fill a senior position. Jeanne did not want to continue as deputy chief under a new chief, and was not eligible for the chief's position because the slot was "owned" by Security. Considering her options, and plagued by a sense of guilt that she had not solved the problem of the 1985 losses, she approached the head of CIC, Jim Olson, and asked him if she could spend the time remaining before her retirement taking another look at what had gone wrong. Jeanne envisioned working as a singleton, with an emphasis on analysis. This was soon to change.

Paul Redmond joined CIC in April 1991, as deputy to Olson. On one of his first days in the center, he and Jeanne went down to the FBI to deliver a sensitive memorandum to Ray Mislock, chief of the Soviet section of the intelligence division, and his deputy, Bob Wade. During the course of conversation, Paul mentioned that Jeanne was planning to revisit the 1985 problem, with the hope of gaining new insights. Wade immediately remarked that they—the FBI—would like to buy into this project. Shortly thereafter it was agreed that the FBI would designate a special agent, Jim Holt, and a senior analyst, Jim Milburn, to work on the undertaking.

Holt and Milburn were excellent choices. Both were serious, low-key individuals with whom it was easy to work and to share cramped spaces, and neither seemed to have an ingrained dislike of the CIA. Jim Holt had been the case agent for Martynov, and had a visceral interest in trying to find out who had betrayed him. Jim Milburn was the FBI's top analyst on the Soviet target. Unfortunately, while he was respected for his knowledge, his system did not adequately reward him because he was an analyst, not a special agent, and therefore a second-class citizen. (Even as of 2006, this appeared to be a continuing problem in the FBI bureaucracy. Serious efforts have been made to upgrade the role of analytical personnel but one does not yet find them in major managerial positions. This being the case, it is easy for management to disregard their findings when these findings are inconvenient.)

At the same time, Paul telephoned Sandy and asked her to participate in the project. He was aware of her intention to resign from the Agency and knew that only an opportunity to determine how and why we lost General Polyakov and the others would keep her working. She arrived in late May 1991 and the two Jims came in June to complete the group, which we named the Special Investigations Unit of the Counterintelligence Center, or CIC/SIU, which reported directly to the CIC front office, specifically Paul Redmond. For all practical purposes, Dan Payne was also a member of our little coterie, although on paper he still belonged to the Counter-espionage Group. More and more of his tasking came from us as time went on.

Our spaces were cramped, and not conducive to free conversation because we were located in the middle of the Counter-espionage Group, which was not privy to our investigation. Jeanne had a real office, with a door and floor-to-ceiling walls, but it was only ten feet or so square. It contained a desk with a computer workstation, three chairs, a credenza with a small printer, and a two-drawer safe. We had to crowd ourselves in any time we wanted to have a discussion, and the last person had to sit on the safe. If Redmond joined us, an inverted wastepaper basket functioned as an additional seat. Sandy and the two Jims had workstations in adjoining cubicles outside.

As a security measure, our computers were connected to a private local area network, not to the CIA mainframe. We did, however, have one computer nearby that we could use to access the CIA network in order to send and receive e-mail, do name traces, etc.

Although other possibilities still had not been ruled out, the group decided to concentrate its efforts on trying to identify a human penetration of CIA. As a first matter of business, we asked the Office of Security to draw up a list of Agency personnel who, by virtue of their positions in 1985, could be expected to know about the CIA's operations against the Soviet target. This was simply a mechanical effort, based on manning tables, and the list at its most extensive totaled 198 persons. However, once Sandy and Jeanne took a look at it they realized that they could do some immediate paring. Because of their knowledge of who was who and what was what in SE Division at the time, they were able to identify those who, although they were slotted in key jobs, actually were elsewhere. Also, numerous individuals from the Reports Group were listed. A little checking revealed that these individuals could not have been privy to information about the sourcing of the reports they handled. In this way the list was whittled down to about 160 Agency employees who, at first glance, had at least some access to information about one or more of the sources who had been compromised.

Because it is of course impossible to investigate 160 people without an army to do the job, it was necessary to effect some stringent prioritization. The method Jeanne developed has received a substantial amount of criticism, although no one has been able to articulate a better solution. First of all, Jeanne and Sandy did some further paring, removing from the list a few people whom they subjectively believed were unlikely to betray their country. Then they submitted the new, smaller list to a vote. Those who voted included Sandy, Jeanne, the two Jims, Paul Redmond, Jim Olson, Fran Smith, John O'Reilly (who at the time was the CI chief in SE Division), and Wade and Mislock. We asked them to list five or six individuals who needed to have a hard look taken at them—people who made them uneasy for one reason or another. Further, they were asked to list the one they worried about most first, and to rank the others in descending order. Wade and Mislock were asked to vote simply as a public relations overture. We realized that they did not have enough information about the individuals on the list to enable them to make reasonable choices.

When the lists were all received, Jeanne and Sandy weighted them numerically, giving six points for every time a name was mentioned first, five points for every name that was mentioned second, and so on. They then added up the numbers accorded to each person and, lo and behold, Rick Ames' name led the list. He received twenty-one points. However, the compilation also showed that several individuals had received fifteen, sixteen, or seventeen points. Our consensus was that we should start our investigation by concentrating on all of those who received fifteen points or more. We reasoned that if we concentrated just on Ames and he turned out not to be the mole we would have wasted a substantial amount of time. Anyway, it was far too early to narrow our options that much.

Of those who voted, only Sandy gets the gold star. She listed Ames first. Redmond also listed him first but, in his typical anarchic way, prefaced his contribution by saying that it was in no particular order. Jim Olson had Ames in second place while Jeanne had him only in fourth. The FBI votes did not match closely with those of the CIA participants, but this is understandable given their lack of background at this point. Somewhat later, the four of us in CIC/SIU voted again. All of us listed Rick as one of our candidates, and he again led the list numerically. Jeanne was beginning to see the light, because she moved him from fourth to second in priority.

While we had culled our first-cut list to a manageable few, we did not forget all the other employees who had had some access. We asked the Office of Security to have their personnel read all 160 security files and notify us if any contained information of CI significance. Further, we requested that those on the list who had not been polygraphed since the beginning of 1985 be subjected to such an examination. Eventually this project was completed, although a few people were never polygraphed because they were overseas, or retired, or had resigned.

We gave personal attention to the individuals on our short list, starting with their Office of Personnel and Office of Security files. Much of this review was carried out by Jim Holt, who also conducted FBI traces. Eventually, we also had the resident psychologist in CIC review the Office of Medical Services holdings on these individuals.

As a matter of policy, employees have medical confidentiality. We could not examine these files ourselves, and we were only provided oral briefings on the results of the reviews. For some arcane reason, the FBI was not allowed to be present at the psychologist's briefings, which were attended only by Sandy and Jeanne. However, we were permitted to brief our FBI colleagues on what the psychologist had told us, and indeed did so. Also, the psychologist was not allowed to tell us what the files contained unless the information was pertinent to our CI investigation.

Fortunately, the review did include results of psychological testing, and some of the findings were of decided interest. The reviewer made use of what is known as the Project SLAMMER profile. Project SLAMMER was an inter-Agency effort to develop a profile of those U.S. citizens who have committed espionage. Those who had been convicted of this crime were subjected to in-depth psychological interviews in prison, if they were willing, as most were.

The results of the file review did not reveal Ames to be the person who fit the SLAMMER profile better than anyone else. However, there were some interesting items that added to our holdings on him. The psychologist who interviewed him in 1967, at the time when he was applying for the Career Training Program, characterized him as "sheepish" and unsure of himself. He was not highly recommended for the program. After additional testing several years later, he was described as having undergone some changes. According to the test results, he had learned to put up a front and hide his thoughts.

Concurrently, Jim Milburn started a review of the compromised cases. Although the FBI knew about these compromises, and had been given summaries and chronologies of them starting in 1986, they had not previously had access to the files themselves. Now these were made available to them. In return, Sandy and Jeanne were invited to go to FBI headquarters and review any of their files that might be germane to the investigation. However, we were inundated with work at the time and never got around to doing so. In any event, these files had already been reviewed once by the two Jims and we trusted their thoroughness.

One of the criticisms leveled at Jeanne after the wrap-up of the Ames case was that she did not want to provide information to the FBI. That is certainly not true. Jeanne does plead guilty to not wanting to lose control, however. She and her group strongly believed that CIA experts were in a better position to uncover a traitor within their own organization than FBI outsiders would be. (By the same token, they realized that the FBI would be in a better position to identify a spy in their midst than would Jeanne, Sandy, or any CIA CI officer.) We were afraid that the FBI would gallop off in the wrong direction and we would not be able to influence their activity. Thus we were content with the way the situation evolved during the next eighteen months.

As part of our many-pronged investigation, we drew up a list of those KGB officers who we believed might have knowledge of a human penetration of the CIA, either because they were in key positions in 1985 or because they were experienced CI officers with a good command of English. This list eventually comprised some 60–70 names. We then started to review their operational (201) files. Our review was mainly geared to compiling information on any foreign travel, whether for temporary duty or permanent assignment.

As part of the review, we tried to identify any aliases the selected KGB officers may have used in their operations, plus any awards or out-of-cycle promotions they might have received. We hoped that, when we had settled on a small number of suspects, we might be able to match travel of one of these suspects to travel of someone on our KGB list. Jeanne was always skeptical of the utility of this endeavor because we had been able to collect only a very few of the aliases used by this target group. She and Sandy believed that a KGB officer who traveled on such an operational mission would do so in alias. If we did not have the alias, we could not match up the travel with that of a CIA officer. We further believed that a CIA officer traveling to meet his KGB handler would make a serious effort to conceal his itinerary.

As it turned out, however, Jeanne and Sandy were wrong. The KGB, and later SVR, officers who traveled to meet Ames generally did so in alias, but for some reason one of them used his true name on a trip to Bogota. We were able to ascertain that he was there at the same time as Rick because Rick had not tried to conceal his travel, merely providing an innocuous explanation by saying he had to help his mother-in-law with some problem. This concurrent travel was another item that increased our suspicions of him, although of course it did not prove conclusively that he was a spy. The search for travel patterns was one aspect of the investigation in which we asked, and received, NSA assistance.

While we were drawing up the list of key KGB officers, we became more and more frustrated by the changes that were taking place in SE Division operational conceptions and the deleterious effect they might have on our investigation. Under the overly rosy assumption that the KGB was no longer an important adversary and that our future friendly relations with Russia would include a productive liaison relationship with the KGB's successor, the division began to send out messages to our overseas stations downplaying the importance of the KGB target. Stations were told that, if a KGB officer approached them and during the first contact appeared to have information of significant interest to the U.S. government, it was all right to debrief the volunteer on a "cash-and-carry" basis before showing him the door. Long-term relationships were discouraged, and asylum would not be considered. The message was clear: running well-thought-out operations against the KGB target was no longer a career-enhancing activity. Stations reacted accordingly. (The author of two of the guidance messages was Rick Ames. However, Sandy and Jeanne do not see anything sinister about this. He was told to write the cables by Division Chief Milt Bearden, and the content reflected the current operating philosophy as determined by Bearden.)

One salient example of the results of this doctrine was described by Paul Redmond in his unclassified book review of *The Sword and the Shield: The Mitrokhin Archive and the Secret History of the KGB,* by Christopher Andrew and Vasili Mitrokhin.[1] Mitrokhin was a KGB archivist who brought thousands of pages of valuable notes to the West. He volunteered twice to the Americans, was turned away, and then went to the British who recognized him for the gold mine that he was.

Another list we compiled was a combined FBI-CIA rundown of all reporting from any source since the 1970s on the subject of possible penetrations of the CIA. This compilation ran to some twenty pages. While this had to be done, it was not very useful in the overall scheme of things. Most of the reporting was vague, or was provided by sources who did not know what they were talking about. They did not have direct access to this type of information, or were prone to embellishment, or simply wanted to please their debriefers.

As a follow-on to this compilation, the two Jims began a series of re-briefings of defectors and in-place sources. All of them had been asked when we first got in touch with them, whether they knew about any penetrations of the U.S. government. Now they were debriefed in more detail, and with more subtle questions about awards, promotions, alias travel, etc. This turned up some intriguing tidbits, but nothing that aided us substantially in our search.

Another failed avenue of investigation involved Rosario's father's will. It will be recalled that Diana Worthen had told us that Rosario did not appear to have any money except for her salary in 1983, when she was stationed in Mexico City. Yet, according to Rick, it was his wife's money that enabled him to lead a cushy lifestyle. We discussed this anomaly several times. One theory we developed was that perhaps Rosario's father had kept a tight grip on the family purse strings. When he died, which we knew had occurred at the end of 1983, Rosario's mother probably gained control of the family wealth and may have had more liberal views of sharing it with Rosario.

To test this theory, we needed to gain access to the father's will. Unfortunately, as we learned, wills in Colombia are not public documents and are not available in a central location. They are deposited with a notary. Bogota was believed to have more than two hundred notaries. We made a conscious decision not to follow this investigative trail any further. We reasoned as follows: Rosario's family, whatever its financial status, was prominent in Bogota and had a certain amount of name recognition. Further, an individual sometimes chooses a notary the way he chooses a lawyer. That is, one goes to a relative, a college friend, or someone else with whom he has at least a nodding acquaintance. If the news ever got back to Rosario's family—and subsequently to Rick—that we were trying to hunt down the will, it might totally sink our efforts. At this point, there was no warrant out for Rick's arrest. He had two valid passports. If he got wind of what we were doing, he would simply flee the United States for Colombia, and laugh at us from his comfortable condominium in Cartagena. Anyway, this is one of the points Congress freely criticized us about, but we would make the same decision today given the same choices.

One of the most fruitful, if lengthy and time-consuming, projects was that of interviewing a number of CIA employees who had been in key positions as of 1985. This project made the FBI somewhat nervous because the term "interview" means something specific to them as an investigative technique. To assuage their uneasiness, Jeanne and Sandy promised that, should any interviewee begin to make incriminating statements, they would immediately leave the room and the FBI could take over the conversation. What we had in mind, however, was merely to ask these people if they could help us in our research. We asked all the interviewees the same questions, covering such mundane things as: Who picked up the sensitive Restricted Handling cables from the front office each morning? Who had access to which safes? Could conversations be heard between cubicles? Were they aware of any security violations during the period?

We never tried to keep our investigation a secret. Indeed, we hoped that someone would come to us with helpful information. However, only two people did—Diana and a person who had pertinent information about one of the other people who could have been the mole. This latter individual turned out to be guilty of various forms of misbehavior that in a more tightly run Directorate of Operations would have led to his dismissal. He also had money beyond his salary, and owned at least three expensive cars. However, as far as we could determine, he was not a spy.

In the end, we interviewed some forty people. They included both persons about whom we had not the slightest suspicion, and people who were on one of our lists. Among those we interviewed was Rick Ames. It would have raised suspicions not to interview him because he had been in a key position in the 1983–85 period. Two things stood out about this interview. First, when Rick was asked about security violations, he mentioned that he had left his safe open one night. We already knew this because the violation was a matter of record in his security file. He pointed out that the safe in question had contained paper on many of the cases that had been compromised and the combinations for all the safes in his branch. It was normal for him to mention this event, because this was the sort of thing we were asking about. However, he brought up the subject again later in the interview, somewhat out of the blue. This caught Sandy and Jeanne's attention and they regarded it as overkill. He seemed to be hinting that perhaps some unidentified individual had gotten into the safe, and that that someone was the mole.

The second thing that stood out in this interview was Rick's reaction to the next-to-last question. We asked everyone: If you were going to betray CIA secrets to the KGB, how would you go about it? We also included subsidiary questions, such as: Would you identify yourself? Would you prefer a one-shot deal or a continuing relationship? Would you be deterred by the knowledge that you are subject to periodic polygraphs? While the main purpose of this series of questions was to get additional ideas about possible scenarios, the secondary aim was to help educate our FBI colleagues as to how the mind of a CIA officer was likely to work.

Many of the people we posed our questions to were case officers, adept in role playing. They entered into what was to them a game, coming up with a variety of imaginative stratagems. One told us that he would go to a sub-Saharan capital he was familiar with. He said he knew the local service had an observation post across the street from the Soviet embassy, but they were only interested in identifying their own citizens who entered the embassy. Being Caucasian, he thought that he could enter the embassy and no one would think twice about it. Another officer told about how he had previously been stationed in the Far East and knew one of the local KGB officers from the diplomatic social circuit. This particular KGB representative had impressed our officer by seeming to be intelligent, open-minded, and not a drinker in the Soviet sense. Our officer knew that this Russian was again overseas and he thought that, given his favorable past impression, he would make his approach to him.

Both Sandy and Jeanne thought that Rick's response to the question was out of character. Rick can be quite articulate when engaged, and he can think on his feet. However, he hemmed and hawed, providing a somewhat hesitant and lukewarm response. In retrospect, he was melding some things he actually had done with others that he had not. To him, unlike to the others, this was more than a game. For instance, he said that he would make his approach overseas whereas in reality he had dealt directly with the Soviet embassy in Washington. On the other hand, he said that he would identify himself, and this is indeed what he had done. He further stated that he would not be deterred by the polygraph, and this turned out to be the case.

The last question we asked everyone was: What do you think happened in 1985? Some thought that there had been a human penetration of the CIA, some thought our problem had been technical, and others came up with various permutations and combinations. Rick, when asked for his opinion, mentioned Ed Howard, and then posed the rhetorical question: How long is the arm of coincidence?

At one point in this phase of the investigation, we became seriously sidetracked for a while. We received a report from an officer in one of our overseas stations that he had been in contact with a KGB officer, and that this KGB officer had told him that the KGB was running a mole inside the

CIA. As the story was told to us, the mole was an ethnic Russian who had served in Moscow. Based on this report, we began to concentrate on CIA employees who fit the parameters of this lead, although we did not completely discontinue examining information on those employees, such as Rick Ames, who did not. Eventually we discovered that there were major flaws in this story, and that it probably was a total fabrication.

During this same period we also received some misleading reporting from Sergey Papushin, the defector from the KGB's internal CI component, to the effect that this component was running a CIA officer who had been assigned to Moscow. In other words, there was some similarity between Papushin's statements and those recounted in the above statement. Unfortunately, Papushin had a severe alcohol problem, which shortly thereafter caused his death. We ultimately decided that his reporting could not be relied upon. We then started to refocus on our short list as originally compiled. However, we had lost valuable time.

CHAPTER 14

AMES EMERGES AS A MAJOR FOCUS

I**T IS HARD TO ISOLATE A SPECIFIC TIME FRAME** when we became more and more focused on Ames. This was a gradual development. To the end, we never lost sight of the other individuals on our short list. However, as time passed Ames began to consume more of our daily attention. For easy reference, Dan Payne christened him with the informal cryptonym JOYRIDE, chosen because of the remark that Rick had made during his polygraph to the effect that his wife had money and he was getting a free ride.

A salient activity in our hard look at Ames was Sandy's creation of a chronology of his whereabouts and activities. This started as an informal reference, listing a few facts of Rick's career just for convenience. It ended up as a text-searchable word-processing document more than five hundred pages long, mind-numbing to compile and even more mind-numbing to read, but of high value to the investigation as it unfolded. Indeed it directly led to the major breakthrough in the case in August 1992.

The chronology included information from Ames' official Office of Security and Office of Personnel files plus other available material. The greatest volume of input came from an electronic search. It is possible to capture text from the CIA's electronic files going back many years. We asked that all these files be searched for Ames' true name and aliases, and that we receive the output in printed form. (Officers in the Directorate of Operations are assigned pseudonyms, always consisting of a first name, middle initial, and last name, for use in Agency traffic. This system was originally developed so that employees would not know each other's identities, which added a degree of security to our operations. However, in practice most DO personnel know both the true name and pseudonym of their colleagues.)

We no longer remember how many thousands of documents resulted from this search, but Sandy had stacks and stacks of paper to wade through. The search produced not only pertinent and peripheral documents about Rick Ames, but also any communication naming any other Agency employee whose first, middle, or last name was Ames, any reference to Ames, Iowa, plus all mentions of the Ames Building, a complex in Roslyn, Virginia where the Agency had office space. In between other projects, Sandy spent months reading through this material and adding anything to her chronology that she thought might be useful.

Another large block of data that was added to the chronology consisted of Ames' badge ins and outs. Agency personnel are all issued plastic badges and have to insert them into a machine at building exits and entrances. For many years it has been possible to print out all the comings and goings of any employee. We got such a list from the Office of Security, and more months were spent by Sandy inputting Ames' exits and entrances. This produced a picture of Ames' daily habits. He rarely came to the office on time, he rarely stayed late, and even more rarely worked on a Saturday. Unfortunately for Sandy, he was a heavy smoker and during the later part of the period under review employees were not allowed to smoke in the building. Therefore many of the exits and entrances in Sandy's rundown were nothing more than cigarette breaks.

As it happened, however, one part of Ames' pattern turned out to be of great importance to the FBI after they took over the investigation. It was obvious that Ames was not a morning person and usually did not show up at the office on time. This pattern was occasionally broken and Ames would show up at perhaps 0730. When the FBI was trying to ascertain on which days Ames had had indirect contact with his KGB handlers, by loading or unloading a dead drop or by making or observing a signal, they eventually deduced that he did so early in the morning. There was a correlation between Ames' early arrivals and his operational activities as detailed in the CIA's chronology.

When Sandy went through Ames' personnel file early in her project, she found references in his 1984–85 annual evaluation (called a PAR, or Performance Appraisal Report) to a sanctioned contact he had with two Soviet diplomats in Washington, DC. This was not surprising because in those days it was common for SE Division officers assigned to headquarters to conduct assessments of local Soviet officials. This was done under the watchful eye of the FBI, which simply did not have the manpower to cover everyone at the Soviet embassy and ancillary offices. The FBI therefore allowed, and sometimes encouraged, CIA officers, usually in alias and with a fictional persona, to fill the gap by building up social relationships with these targets. As is normally the case, for legitimate security reasons the PAR was not very specific.

When Sandy started processing the electronic search of official traffic, she was able to fill in some of the particulars and, of key importance, to identify the two Soviets with whom Ames had been in contact. Their names were Sergey Ivanovich Divilkovskiy, a press counselor at the embassy, and Sergey Dmitriyevich Chuvakhin, an arms control specialist. Considerable details, some of which were quite startling, emerged when Sandy pulled their operational files. (It should be remembered that most of what was in these files was derived from Ames' reporting, and is not necessarily accurate or complete. In a later chapter, we will outline what really happened between Ames and the Soviets, as opposed to what we learned from the files.) The FBI suspected Divilkovskiy of being affiliated with the KGB. Further, some vulnerabilities had surfaced in his family life. Therefore, he was of interest to the FBI as a possible recruitment target or as a CI threat to be countered.

Ames had a few lunch or drink contacts with Divilkovskiy before the latter returned to Moscow at the end of 1984. According to the file, Ames asked Divilkovskiy if he knew a Soviet colleague who would like to meet an American businessman to exchange ideas now that Divilkovskiy was leaving. Divilkovskiy gave Ames Chuvakhin's name and Ames duly reported to the CIA and FBI that he intended to call Chuvakhin in an effort to develop a relationship. Because Chuvakhin was not a KGB or GRU officer, and nothing in his personal life seemed to offer a "hook," the FBI did not pay particular attention to him. He was a natural object of interest to the CIA, however, because he presumably possessed information of importance to our government.

Ames, in the alias he had used with Divilkovsky and the same story about being an out-of-town businessman, first tried to set up a meeting with Chuvakhin in early 1985. Chuvakhin did not seem to be very interested in contact with Ames, but he agreed to a get-together for drinks at the Mayflower Hotel on 16 April 1985. However, Chuvakhin did not show up. According to the file, Ames went to the nearby Soviet embassy to ask Chuvakhin if there had been some mix-up. He had a short chat with Chuvakhin and then left. CIA officers were not supposed to visit the Soviet embassy for any reason without first informing the FBI, because the FBI had an observation post covering the entrance and tried to identify all unknown visitors. However, Ames did call the FBI later that day to apologize and explain that he had gone in on the spur of the moment because he was frustrated by his unsuccessful efforts to touch base with Chuvakhin.

The next contacts between Ames and Chuvakhin, duly reported by Ames, took place in May. They consisted of a meeting at the embassy for drinks on the fifteenth and a lunch on the seventeenth. Further contacts continued in June and July. Then Ames' reporting ceased, although there were indications that the relationship continued and the FBI had asked more than once for updates. One possible explanation that occurred to us was that Ames, caught up in the time-consuming and high-priority task of debriefing Yurchenko and writing up his notes for impatient consumers, plus making last-minute preparations for his wedding to Rosario, and processing for his overseas assignment to Rome all at the same time, had just not had time to file his accounts of his meetings with Chuvakhin. This was not out of line with Ames' usual practices. He had been chastised in the past for being delinquent in submitting required reporting. Yet it was an oddity worth noting. The last relevant item in Chuvakhin's file was a cable to Rome that reached there just as Ames arrived in July 1986, almost a year after the non-reported meetings had started. The cable asked once again for Ames' account of any contacts with Chuvakhin, but it was never answered.

Sandy further discovered that Ames had followed somewhat the same pattern in Rome. He had some contacts with a Soviet embassy official named Aleksey Khrenkov. These contacts were spread over the three years of Ames' tour, but the reporting was desultory and contained gaps.

Concurrent with Sandy's compilation of Ames' daily activities, Dan Payne, urged on by Paul Redmond who let his impatience boil over because he believed that we were not proceeding with sufficient speed, had started spending almost full time pulling together information on Ames' finances. Using National Security Letters, which were signed by the Director of Security and which requested the addressees to provide information on Ames without disclosing to him that this was being done, Dan contacted the banking and credit card institutions where Ames had accounts. The institutions complied with the letters and Dan soon had great masses of financial details to organize into a coherent picture. Unfortunately, as the law read at the time, brokerage houses were not mentioned. Although Dan made a determined effort, he was never able to convince Merrill Lynch, Morgan Stanley, and others to give him their records. He also never got a list of Ames' foreign dealings, although we knew that he had an Italian bank account while stationed in Rome and that during the same period he had opened an account with Credit Suisse in Switzerland. He was also believed to have bought property in Colombia.

Dan entered his collection of Ames' financial records into a computer spreadsheet. Like Sandy's endeavors, this was a tedious job because he had acquired not just monthly statements but all the supporting minutia such as canceled checks, deposit slips, and credit card slips. It soon became clear that, even though some of the puzzle pieces were missing, extremely large sums of money were passing through Ames' hands.

Dan sat behind Sandy in an adjoining cubicle. After he finished putting his data into the spreadsheet, he passed the accumulated bits of paper across the high barrier separating their desks. Sandy would then look over the collection of bank and credit card statements to decide which items warranted inclusion in her chronology. Not wanting to make her compilation more unwieldy than it already was, she decided not to input the more humdrum items such as grocery bills and other routine purchases. What she was looking for were any indications of travel or activity outside his routine, any purchases of computer equipment, and any big-ticket or unusual expenditures.

In August 1992 Sandy hit pay dirt. Dan had been logging deposits into Ames' checking account and that of his wife. As he finished with the slips, he passed them to Sandy as was their practice. When Sandy input the deposits into her chronology, she discovered three correlations between meetings with Chuvakhin and subsequent deposits, as follows:

17 May 1985—Ames lunches with Chuvakhin
18 May 1985—Ames deposits $9,000
2 Jul 1985—Ames lunches with Chuvakhin
5 Jul 1985—Ames deposits $5,000
31 Jul 1985—Ames lunches with Chuvakhin
31 Jul 1985—Ames deposits $8,500

To Sandy this was an epiphany. She told us what she had found, then sped to Redmond to fill him in. Her excited announcement to him was: "It doesn't take a rocket scientist to tell what is going on here. Rick is a goddamn Russian spy."

As for the rest of us, it took some time for the significance of Sandy's discovery to set in. The FBI especially had another mole candidate whom they favored. However, gradually we began to understand that we had found the first link that would eventually lead to Ames' arrest and conviction. (Much later in the investigation several other deposits, suggesting further correlations, were found. Unfortunately, we did not have the full picture in the fall of 1992. We had asked the FBI to search their files for information on any contacts between Ames and Chuvakhin, and also to review the telephone tap coverage of the Soviet embassy. The first part of this tasking was accomplished but FBI headquarters balked at the review of the telephone coverage, explaining that this would be a very labor-intensive undertaking and that they could not justify it unless they opened up a formal investigation.)

Not long after Sandy's epiphany, Dan completed his financial research. Even without counting the assets for which we had been unable to obtain records, from 1985 to 1991 Ames had a total income of more than one million dollars from unidentified sources. To be precise, the figure amounted to $1,326,310.

By now 1992 was drawing to a close and so was the five-person SIU investigation. Jim Milburn began to draft a final report. This was an official FBI document and, although we had a say in the draft stages, the final wording was not under our control. The report was issued in March 1993. As we understand it, it did not pinpoint Ames as the primary suspect, but included a short list on which Ames' name appeared. It was formatted this way because Milburn and his colleagues did not want to place FBI investigators in a box where they would have to devote all their attention to Ames without considering the other most likely "possibles."

Professionally and personally for Jeanne and Sandy, this was one of the darkest times in the entire mole hunt. They were totally convinced that Ames was the traitor the team had spent two years looking for and that analysis proved the case. They also knew that the FBI did not share their conviction and would continue to focus on other persons on the short list. They could envisage the possibility that Ames would fall into a bureaucratic black hole and never have to face the criminal justice system. Rather, he would retire from the CIA at his convenience, and spend the rest of his life enjoying an opulent lifestyle paid for with the blood money he had earned.

Luckily, in 1993 additional information became available. This new information, while it did not identify Ames, pointed in his direction. It added to the comfort level of those who had not been convinced by the results of our analytic efforts and forced the FBI to open a full-scale investigation of Ames, as outlined in the next chapter.

CHAPTER 15

THE FBI TAKES OVER

ON 12 MAY 1993, THE FBI OPENED a full investigation of Ames. The operation was code-named NIGHTMOVER and run out of the Washington Metropolitan Field Office, then located in a rundown section of town called Buzzard's Point. Les Wiser Jr. was chosen to be the FBI supervisory special agent in charge of the case. Wiser, a quick and imaginative thinker with a law degree and counterintelligence experience, was a good choice. Whatever may have been his feelings about the CIA, he was open with us and pragmatic enough to ask for our help when necessary to get the job done. We also had a collegial relationship with three of his top aides, Rudy Guerin, Mike Donner, and Del Spry, and of course the two Jims continued to be active in the investigation as it unfolded. On the analytic side, Danielle Lunden served as a valuable member of the team.

At the FBI headquarters level, our cool but correct contacts with Tim Caruso continued. A veteran of the FBI's unsuccessful ANLACE probe, he was assigned to head up what was called PLAYACTOR, the FBI's independent look at the 1985 compromises, which was being carried on at the same time as CIC/SIU's scouring of the same evidence. The only upside to PLAYACTOR was that we became acquainted with Mike Anderson, Caruso's deputy, who understood counterintelligence and who was a team player. When possible, we preferred to deal with him rather than with Caruso.

PLAYACTOR was more of a hindrance than a help. Its salient achievement, a monstrous wall chart, was a source of mirth and annoyance to Sandy and Jeanne. Mirth because it was a wonder to behold, and annoyance because we were constantly being asked for information to feed into it, tasking we considered a waste of valuable time because the information was often irrelevant to the problem at hand. The best description is from Peter Maas' *Killer Spy*:

> The chart Tim Caruso had drawn up covered an entire wall filled with cross-indexed squares. Across the top were all the known compromises. There was a dateline for them that began in 1955. Color-coded leads were at the bottom. The different colors depicted which sources they had come from. . . . In the center of the chart, also color-coded, were not only the details of past FBI operations, but all the details of CIA operations that were kept from the FBI until Jim Holt and Jim Milburn took up residence at Langley. Looking at the chart, you saw the entire history of compromises, suspected or real, the seismic moments, where the hot spots were in both time and place.[1]

In other words, it was the well-known mixture of apples and oranges, with some cherries, bananas, and a kumquat or two thrown in for good measure.

Unlike PLAYACTOR, Wiser's NIGHTMOVER investigation moved along at a fast clip, employing all the means and techniques of a major FBI investigation. The CIA provided support to important aspects of the probe. When the FBI wanted to place a beacon in Ames' car to track his movements, Dan Payne designed a scenario to deliver the car to the FBI technicians so that they could implant the beacon under controlled and relatively safe circumstances. He suggested that Ames be invited to a counternarcotics conference at FBI headquarters along with his supervisor, Dave Edger. We then primed Edger to ask Ames to drive, knowing that Ames would acquiesce in order to please his boss. While the conference was being held, the technicians moved the car from its parking space, successfully inserted the beacon, and returned the car to its slot without anyone being the wiser.

When the FBI first placed Ames under surveillance, they did so without closely coordinating with us. This turned out to be a mistake because when the FBI surveillants wanted to follow Ames onto the CIA compound, they approached the unwitting guards for assistance. This approach stirred up a spate of rumors that reached as far as Director of Security. In order to calm the situation, we caused a notice to be disseminated informing our security officers that the FBI and CIA were conducting some joint exercises and that once the FBI surveillance teams identified themselves they were not to be subjected to further interference.

One of the most time-consuming projects for us as well as for the FBI was the placement of cameras and phone taps in Ames' CIA premises. First, we managed via Edger to get him moved to an office suitable for the FBI's purposes. Next we facilitated the presence of the FBI's specialists. All of the entries took place at night, after most CIA personnel had gone home. We obtained the combination to the vault in which Ames' office was located, and one of us was always present when the FBI was at work, should it be necessary to deal with security guards or employees working at odd hours. Luckily it never was. In practice, on occasion many of us spent half the night in this endeavor, but had to disguise our moonlighting. This meant appearing the next morning on time and putting in a regular day's work. Don Robinson, a security officer then in charge of CIC's Counter-espionage Group, volunteered for much of this support duty.

After the camera was in place, we concocted another scenario in the hope of filming Ames purloining a top secret document. We chose a document we thought would interest Ames, but which the U.S. government could afford to lose. Again thanks to Edger, we had a copy of this document routed to Ames. We hoped that he would cut off the classification and identifying data, or stuff it into his shirt or take some other compromising action. However, it must have been one of Ames' lazy days. He merely glanced at the document and tossed it into his out box!

Another major part of the investigation was the surveillance of Ames in Bogota. Unfortunately, our teams never did see Ames meeting his SVR case officer, although meetings did indeed take place.

Our cooperation continued to the end. When the FBI decided the time had come to arrest Ames, we produced yet another scenario for Edger to carry out. He and Ames were supposed to go on an overseas trip together. On Monday 21 February 1994, Presidents' Day holiday, Edger called Ames in the morning. Following his script, he advised Ames that a cable had arrived that affected their trip and that needed an immediate response. Could Ames come to the office and deal with the problem?

Ames trustingly left his residence. The FBI was waiting around the corner and arrested him without incident.

The FBI's plan was to take Ames and his wife, who was arrested shortly after her husband was placed in custody, to the FBI office at Tysons Corner in northern Virginia and, dealing with them separately, induce them to confess. Sandy and Jeanne had been requested to await events at their CIA office, which was otherwise empty because of the holiday. Dan Payne was to fulfill the role of courier between Tysons Corner and CIA headquarters if needed. The FBI wanted them in position to provide instant research and expertise in case one of the Ameses began to confess. As it happened, Mrs. Ames made a few incriminating statements but Ames himself refused to cooperate.

Until the very end, Ames was totally complacent. He never had an idea that the arrest was imminent and did not attempt to keep a low profile. While the FBI's net was closing around him, he was drawing attention to himself by approaching SE Division management in an effort to sell himself for the position of deputy chief of Moscow Station.

CHAPTER 16

REACTIONS TO THE ARREST OF AMES

ALL OF US, BOTH CIA AND FBI, who had worked so hard to bring Ames to justice felt a sense of relief once we knew he was under lock and key. Of course, we were aware that there was more labor ahead to produce a conviction and a sentence of life without parole. (This was the most that could be expected, because the death penalty for espionage in peacetime did not exist at the time. It has since been reinstated.) All our self-gratification began to dissipate almost immediately, however.

The FBI drafted a public statement concerning the arrest that gave the impression that they had done all the real work, while we had merely provided cooperation and support. The draft incensed the CIA, which produced its own drafts, which the FBI refused to accept. Finally, the FBI's version was issued by the attorney general. We also issued one. There would be no joint statement. (Retired FBI Special Agent I. C. Smith has described the atmosphere at FBI headquarters on this occasion, characterizing it as an "attempt to jab a stick in the CIA's eye."[1]) Of greater significance, news of the arrest brought Congressional wrath on the CIA and, to a lesser extent, the FBI. The investigation that led to Ames had been ongoing for years as a major effort and Congress had not been kept advised. In retrospect, this is perhaps the greatest "lesson learned" from the whole case. As one consequence, the atmosphere of CIA–FBI cooperation that had dominated the investigative phase quickly dissipated as senior managers on both sides tried to deflect criticism from the

Congressional oversight committees and their own inspector general staff by shifting blame to the rival organization.

During the last year or two before the arrest, the CIA's senior management held discussions about the advisability of notifying the majority and minority leaders of the two intelligence oversight committees, the Senate Select Committee on Intelligence (SSCI) and the House Permanent Select Committee on Intelligence (HPSCI). Jeanne was responsible for drawing up talking points. She produced numerous drafts that were sent up the line for approval. They were returned with major revisions. Some in senior management were in favor of giving Congress ample debriefings, some wanted to provide only the bare minimum, and some did not want to tell Congress anything at all. The proponents of this last position won the day because it was never possible to fashion a draft that satisfied everybody.

Beginning the day after the arrest, CIA and FBI representatives were called to Capitol Hill to explain themselves to a largely hostile audience. Jeanne was summoned several times. In general, the SSCI was more thoughtful, or better controlled by its chairman, Senator Dennis DeConcini of Arizona. Requests for explanations, while often cold, were generally polite. The situation degenerated only when CIA Director James Woolsey was present. He and DeConcini had long engaged in mutual animosity and this affected the exchanges when they were in the same room.

HPSCI was not so restrained. On one occasion, Jeanne was the sole witness, or sacrificial lamb. This was a closed session, with no media representatives present. However, it appeared that the members of the committee were so accustomed to posturing for the press that they could not turn it off. The tone of the questions was accusatory, and the mantra was "What took you so long?" Jeanne felt like she was being cross-examined by a hostile attorney trying to make a point with a jury, rather than being asked in temperate terms to explain what she had done or not done in the investigation, and why. Representatives Dicks, Dixon, and Torricelli were especially vociferous. Representative Dan Glickman chaired the session, but did not have full control because members freely interrupted each other in their efforts to be heard. Glickman did, however, get at least one question in to Jeanne in a rather sneering tone: "What makes you think that you were capable of leading a CI investigation?" This was typical of the questioning. Jeanne left not only furious but downhearted, having lost whatever respect she might have had for our legislative branch, at least as exemplified by its lower house.

Eventually, both the SSCI and HPSCI produced reports.[2] The bulk of the SSCI report consists of a case summary and was thoroughly reviewed with the CIA in draft. This was succeeded by conclusions and recommendations, some of which have been implemented. The HPSCI report also came up with a number of findings, with one of which Jeanne and Sandy take particular issue. This is the finding that the CIA personnel involved in the investigation failed to keep senior management advised in a timely manner. We suggest that, in part, this misunderstanding is due to statements made after the arrest by senior managers who wished to elude criticism, on the theme of "If I had known about it, I would have fixed it." Senior managers were kept advised, at least in general terms, of the seriousness of the problem, the nature of the investigation, and the progress we were making. Indeed, Jeanne personally briefed two CIA directors— Judge Webster and Robert Gates. She always started her briefing with a statement about the executions of the Soviet officials who had worked for us, and she does not believe they could have missed the tenor of what she was saying. She continued by outlining what was being done to solve the problem, but accepts that they may not have absorbed the details because, after all, they had a great many knotty situations, some of extremely high priority, to contend with.

One aspect of the SSCI and HPSCI probes was particularly outrageous. Chairman Glickman and Congressman Combest of HPSCI and Chairman DeConcini of the SSCI conducted personal interviews with Ames. The only real result, as we see it, was to inflate Ames' ego. If these officials did not trust the FBI/CIA debriefings, or had some questions we had not covered, there is no reason why they could not have sent one of their trusted staff members instead of traipsing down themselves to drink in what Ames had to say. "Disgusting" and "obscene" were words used by CIA employees when they heard of these interviews.

In the meantime, as mandated by Congress, the inspector general's office at the CIA, under the aegis of Inspector General Frederick P. Hitz, was conducting its own investigation. This was a mammoth effort, yet a flawed one. Many of the investigators lacked knowledge of the Directorate of Operations as an entity, much less how it carried out its day-to-day business in the world of espionage. Moreover, the investigative techniques employed left much to be desired. The interviewers held long sessions with each individual who had taken part in the Ames case. These interviewers took notes, but the interviews were not recorded. At first, the IG staff did not want the interviewees to have access to the results of the interviews because this was their normal Star Chamber procedure. However, a flood of impassioned protests caused them to change the ground rules for this particular investigation.

Once the interviews had been typed, which sometimes took place only after a long delay, the interviewees could review them for accuracy. When Jeanne did just that, she was stunned by the inaccuracies. For instance, at one point she said that someone's reappearance was fortuitous. This came out, the individual's "report" was fortuitous. At another point she said that someone was a valid asset. The report of the interview erroneously reflects that she called the individual a "valued" asset. (In reality, in this particular case the asset was valid but not valuable!) Sloppy drafting had Jeanne stating that she did not remember having briefed DCI Casey. Obviously, if she had done so it would not be the sort of thing that she would have forgotten!

The IG team was in haste to prepare their report before Congress reconvened. They produced an unwieldy and unpolished draft that was parceled out to all who had played a significant role in the Ames case for comments. (Unfortunately this draft also contained some sensitive material that should never have had such wide distribution.) Jeanne's were lengthy and critical. To give the IG credit, many of the changes she and others suggested were made and the final product, while by no means perfect, is reasonably accurate.[3] In looking over this abstract now, however, Jeanne and Sandy notice one glaring omission. The report makes no mention of CIA management's failure to keep Congress informed. As noted separately, this was one of the strongest lessons learned in their opinion. Another point not covered was the lack of a formal, written agreement with the FBI when Jim Holt and Jim Milburn came over to the CIA in the summer of 1991. The four of us did not need such an agreement in order to co-exist productively, but in the furor after the arrest, and attempts to play the blame game, it would have been useful for all to have such a document to point to.

Almost one year after Ames' arrest, CIA management scheduled an awards ceremony to honor those who had participated in the investigation. As is traditional, the reception was to include family members. Sandy's family had traveled from North Carolina; Dan Payne's sister had come, or was coming, from Chicago. At the last minute the invitations were withdrawn. The word we heard was that DDCI Studeman had decided to cancel the event because the press might hear about it and "Congress wouldn't like it." This despite the fact that many of the honorees had played no role in deciding how the investigation should proceed. They were the loyal workers who had done a good job in such necessary areas as locating files for us, checking Ames' time and attendance records, and helping the FBI bug his telephones.

The event was later rescheduled more than one year after Ames' arrest. However, because of CIA management's pusillanimity, the revised-version ceremony was limited to the actual awardees. No one else was allowed to be present, nor was the ceremony publicized in any way. Further, the designation of who was to receive which medal particularly offended Jeanne. Redmond got the most prestigious one; Jeanne and Dave Edger were awarded medals at the next level; and a medal one step further down was awarded to Sandy. Jeanne thought this was singularly unfair because she and Sandy had worked as a team and, after all, it was Sandy who was convinced throughout that Ames was a spy and who discovered the correlation that broke the case. Sandy was affronted also. This was a team effort and each played a significant role. Ames might never have been discovered without the participation of all the major players, from Worthen to Redmond. As she sees it, it should have been the same medal for all. Moreover, the fact that Dan and Diana did not receive medals at all was even more egregious. They received monetary awards. While money is always pleasant, it was not their primary motivation, and they were left without a permanent memento of their achievement.

In any event, the recognition was too little and too late for the dedicated employees who had been so helpful to us, the core team, in our efforts. Given their feelings, both Sandy and Jeanne boycotted the ceremony and neither has ever displayed the medals they were awarded.

By the way, Wiser, Holt, and Milburn of the FBI were also given awards at this ceremony. No official recognition from the FBI was ever received, except that Jeanne and Dan got letters from Director Freeh thanking them for their contribution. By this time Jeanne may have been a little thin-skinned because of the criticism she had received, but it sounded condescending to her—as if she were being thanked for holding the FBI's coats while they did the real work. Paul, Sandy, and Diana did not even receive a letter.

Not everything was this downbeat, however. After Ames was arrested, the Department of Justice officials who had been involved in his prosecution, headed by U.S. Attorney Helen Fahey and prosecutor Mark Hulkower, hosted a relaxing private party at a tavern in Alexandria for the CIA and FBI. During the latter part of the Ames investigation, the CIA's legal advisers had opened up a direct channel to the lawyers who would be responsible for the prosecution. We soon became close colleagues, bypassing the FBI. Indeed it was decided that Jeanne, instead of anyone from the FBI, would testify at the trial as the expert on the KGB. During the party, they gave us all framed certificates, plus some joke gifts. Ms. Fahey made a speech in which she pointed out that this sort of recognition was given only rarely to those outside the DOJ community. All in all, this was a very pleasant evening and Sandy and Jeanne are proud of their certificates.

Jeanne was present at one other noteworthy event. A day or two after Ames' arrest, there was a meeting at the White House between Clinton/Gore and congressional leaders to discuss whether Ames' activities would or should have any impact on our relations with Russia. (It was agreed that they should not.) Woolsey was invited to attend. He asked Jeanne and Ted Price, who by that time was DDO, to accompany him, in case he needed our expertise to answer a question. We sat behind him in the chairs reserved for various staffers. Before the meeting got under way, when everyone was milling around, Woolsey went up to Clinton and told him who Jeanne was. Clinton came over, shook hands, and then gave his famous "thumbs-up" signal. Gore also came over later and shook her hand. When Clinton said "Congratulations" or some such word, Jeanne told him that she would take his message back to our team.

While all this was going on, the wheels of justice were turning. On 28 April 1994, in the Alexandria Federal Courthouse, Ames and his wife, both dressed in jailhouse olive drab, pleaded guilty to conspiracy to commit espionage. The small courtroom was packed. Sandy was out of town, but Jeanne was there, as were Diana Worthen, Dan Payne, and numerous other representatives from the CIA and FBI. Rosario spoke first. She looked as if she had not slept in weeks, and she was clutching a large, stagy crucifix more suited to warding off vampires than providing solace in a difficult moment. About the only thing that Jeanne remembers from her statement was her reference to her intellectual attainments. She had it put into the record that she was a PhD candidate at Georgetown. Her sentencing was delayed until Ames' debriefings had been completed.

When it was Ames' turn, he rose in a dignified manner. True to form, he pontificated at great length. What he said perhaps sounded convincing to the uninitiated. Parts of his speech were attempts at self-justification, characterizing espionage as a sham and saying that the Soviet officials he had betrayed had made "similar choices and suffered similar consequences." He omitted to point out that many of them were executed, while he did not face the death penalty. His bitter reaction to the way that the government had treated Rosario seemed to be sincere. He had seemingly blanked out of his mind that, for the last year at least, she had known that he was committing espionage on behalf of the Russians and had greedily shopped away the profits. After he had his say, Ames was sentenced to life imprisonment.

The debriefings of Ames began the day after his conviction. They were managed by the FBI, and at first they did not want anyone from the CIA present. After some high-level negotiations it was agreed that Jeanne could represent the CIA. She was thus present at the first thirteen sessions. Initially it was awkward. None of the FBI debriefers had any prior professional relationship with Ames, but Jeanne had known him at least casually since the 1970s. They had been colleagues working against the Soviet target, and in 1983 were fellow branch chiefs located only a few doors away from each other.

Ames was told on the way to the first debriefing session that Jeanne would be there. He responded by muttering "Oh, shit!" (Perhaps he said something stronger, but this is what Jeanne was told.) When he first entered the debriefing room, and his shackles were removed, the FBI shook hands with him. Jeanne felt she could not do the same, so she kept somewhat in the background and merely said "Hi, Rick!"

As a rule, we debriefed three days a week, for most of the day with a break for lunch. The venues varied. Sometimes we met at the Alexandria City Jail, but Ames disliked this because he could not smoke. On other occasions we met at the FBI's Washington Field Office at Buzzard's Point. At first, Ames was shackled whenever we took a break. However, the FBI soon relaxed and only chained him up at the end of the day. Ames seemed not to be embarrassed by this. When it was time to go, he just held out his arms for the cuffs. For Ames, lunch was the high point of the day. The Alexandria City Jail did not employ a cook. The inmates cooked for themselves, with generally dismal results. On debriefing days, Ames got to enjoy a pizza of his selection, a meatball submarine, or some other tasty dish. And he smoked like a chimney all day, with little concern for the non-smokers in the room.

The debriefings covered a lot of ground, some of it only superficially because we were aware that a damage assessment team would take over when we had gone over the FBI's and CIA's priority requirements. Jeanne was always allotted time to ask Ames about some of the Directorate of Operations cases that he might have compromised. This was a somewhat frustrating exercise because generally the requirements she received from the various DO components were organized by cryptonym. Ames did not do well in remembering cryptonyms. One had to tell him something about a case before he could remember if he had told his Soviet handlers about it. Naturally, the people preparing the requirements did not always want to reveal this sort of sensitive information, fearing that someday Ames might be exchanged for some U.S. spy held by the Soviets, or might find some way of communicating with them from his jail cell. However, we did manage to clarify a number of points. In general, Ames appeared cooperative. He only expressed significant anger on one occasion, in relation to what he had heard about Rosario's travails at the hands of the prosecution, particularly leading attorney Mark Hulkower.

Did Ames tell the truth during the debriefings? Jeanne believes that he did for the most part. He knew that if he were caught in a lie it would affect Rosario's sentence. He had not had access to sensitive Soviet operations for some years and he had no way of determining what knowledgeable sources we had acquired in the KGB and GRU during the interim, and what they had told us. Therefore, he could not know when it was safe to lie and when it was not.

In one area, however, he was less than forthcoming. This was his description, or lack thereof, of his KGB handlers and his relationship with them. For instance, he said he could not positively identify a photograph of Viktor Cherkashin, the KGB CI chief in Washington whom he had met in the embassy on at least one occasion. ("Oh, yeah . . . it sort of looks like him . . . could be . . . maybe.")[4] He was also very vague when it came to his two regular contacts, Yuriy Karetkin and Vladimir Mechulayev, obfuscating which one was present at which meeting. Further, when asked about the details of the meetings, and what they discussed, he would say that he had been drinking and could not remember much. It was plain that his loyalties were to them, and he did not want to do anything to cause them trouble. Moreover, it was no doubt in the back of his mind at the time that perhaps at some future date he would be swapped for a U.S. spy in Russian hands.

All this meant a heavy workload for Jeanne. It takes at least one day of writing to cover one day's debriefing. The pressure for rapid processing of the reporting was intense at first. All the CIA powers-that-be wanted to be the first to have it. And the FBI could not write up their notes with such speed. The sessions were taped, but the FBI took notes longhand while Jeanne used a laptop. Therefore they depended on Jeanne's reports to brief their own management. Probably the biggest drawback to Jeanne's notes was that they were arranged strictly in the order of discussion. Jeanne did it this way as an aid to the transcriber of the tapes, because the transcriptions would be the formal record. However, the notes would probably have been more useful to management had they been arranged in some other fashion.

While their relationship had always been casual, Jeanne rather liked Ames back in the days when they were fellow officers working against the Soviet target. To some extent this bled over during the debriefings. When they were discussing a topic of mutual interest, Jeanne would sometimes forget that she was dealing with a convicted felon who had no conscience and who was responsible for many deaths. He would just be good old Rick. Part of this was because the debriefings frequently turned into dialogues between the two about cases or programs known to both of them but with which the FBI was not familiar. Sometimes Jeanne would consciously have to pull back and regain her distance and objectivity.

One event at the beginning of the debriefings has attracted a certain amount of attention and become part of the lore of this case. At the first session, Ames was asked if he had given any names of CIA or FBI personnel to the KGB. The intent of the question was to determine if he had signaled anyone who might have some vulnerability, which would make him or her an attractive recruitment target. Ames mentioned a couple of names and then told Jeanne offhandedly that he had also given her name to his KGB handlers. Jeanne absorbed this, but was not particularly surprised. During the early days of Ames' contacts with the KGB, she had been a single female stationed in a remote African outpost and she knew that the misogynist KGB considered single women tempting targets, vulnerable to the wiles of a strong and handsome male. Indeed, during this tour she had sometimes wondered why the local Soviet contingent treated her with marked coolness.

At this point, debriefing time ran out but we returned to the subject the next day. We soon learned that we had been misinterpreting what Ames had to say. He had given the KGB the names of persons he thought could be the scapegoats for his treasonous activities. In other words, the suggestion was that the KGB could mount a disinformation operation pointing to someone other than Ames as the traitor, somewhat along the lines of the Mister X case discussed in Chapter 10.

Ames made no apology to Jeanne when describing how he had tried to set her up in this manner. Her first instinct was to leap across the table and strangle him, but almost immediately she saw how ironic and even humorous it was. Here he was sentenced to life without parole, the object of great opprobrium from his colleagues and the nation at large. He would have to put on his chains and go back to his cell and his bologna sandwich when the day was over, while she was free to go where she wanted, and do what she wanted. Her evening might be spent with a gourmet meal at a restaurant, including a glass or two of wine, or watching an episode of Masterpiece Theater. For the rest of his life, his choices would be severely limited. He would never go to the theater again, never eat in a restaurant, or sip vintage wine, and if he had access to a group television set, he would have to watch what his generally lowbrow prison mates wanted to watch, which surely did not include the intellectually stimulating programs he would prefer. For a moment, but a moment only, she almost felt sorry for him.

The FBI team plus Jeanne spent one session talking to Rosario. Jeanne had never met her, but had heard a great deal—almost all of it unfavorable—from the FBI. She was described as totally self-centered, controlling, obsessed by money and material acquisitions, and psychologically abusive to her son Pablo.[5] Our meeting certainly did nothing to dispel this impression. Her lawyer, William B. Cummings, a southern gentleman, was present. As she entered the room, she kissed him and whined that she did not know why we wanted to badger her. If we asked a question that she did not want to answer, she would break into tears and exclaim to Cummings, "Bill, they're being mean to me!" When given a chance, she would expound on how much better Colombia was than the United States, to include her judgment that there were no good universities in the United States—not like they have in Colombia. Also, she characterized American women as peasants. It was obvious to her that we were uncultured because we went to the supermarket in jeans and sneakers while she, being a lady, always dressed in a pants suit. Little useful information was obtained from the session.

Overall during this period Jeanne, Sandy, and the other investigators realized that there was a certain amount of ambivalence regarding them. Were they villains or heroes? Jeanne's treatment by HPSCI clearly showed her that there were those who, with a less than complete grasp of the facts, put them in the former camp, invoking the theme that if the investigation had been undertaken by more competent people Ames would have been arrested in no time flat. The IG report has it both ways, saying that the investigation was inadequate but placing most of the blame on senior management. As described, both Jeanne and Sandy were given medals but under circumstances that led them to view the medals with a jaundiced eye. On a more positive note, however, Sandy and Jeanne always felt that they had the support and approval of their peers and colleagues, and these are expressed even to the present day. And they are in demand on the lecture circuit, presenting their story to a wide variety of television and live audiences. This was strange to them at first because CIA officials are taught to avoid publicity at all costs and indeed a person who needs outside appreciation would probably not be happy in the CIA. Yet in time they became used to the limelight and frankly admit that the ego gratification they receive is not unpleasing.

In addition to the television interviews, there have been five books written about the Ames case so far. Only three of them are worth mentioning. By far the most complete coverage comes from Pete Earley in *Confessions of a Spy*. This is the only book that we, Redmond, Worthen, Payne, and others cooperated with, having been asked to do so by senior CIA management. This book appeared about a year after other publications, and Earley used the time to do a lot of digging and interviewing, including a trip to Moscow, to round out the story.

David Wise's *Nightmover* contains some interesting material, and he obviously has some good sources among present and former CIA officers. He does, however, make one major error in postulating that Ames' espionage began in Mexico City in the early 1980s, orchestrated by a KGB officer named Igor Shurygin. We and the FBI accept the statements by Ames and Cherkashin that Ames volunteered in April 1985. This coordinates with the facts as we know them. Ames first got access to information on sensitive Soviet cases in September 1983, yet these cases continued to run successfully and productively until the summer of 1985, when they began disappearing at an alarming rate. Furthermore, during the period September 1983 to April 1985 Ames sank deeper and deeper into debt, while in the summer of 1985 his situation markedly improved.

A third book of some interest is Peter Maas' *Killer Spy*. This was written with FBI cooperation and is mainly a blow-by-blow account of the FBI's role in the investigation. As an insider description, it contains material not found elsewhere.

One made-for-television movie also exists. This is *Aldrich Ames: The Spy Within*, with Timothy Hutton playing Ames. It has some value as a psychological study because Hutton does a good job of portraying Ames as a person. However, from a factual viewpoint, it leaves a great deal to be desired. It is decidedly off base when attempting to portray the inner workings of the CIA and the individuals who worked there, as well as some basic facts of the case. This movie was produced by a man who was a friend of Ames' during his youthful University of Chicago phase. He telephoned Jeanne in an effort to get her to cooperate with his project, but she declined.

AMES THE PERSON, AMES THE SPY

ALDRICH HAZEN AMES IS AN ALL-AMERICAN BOY, born in River Falls, Wisconsin on 26 May 1941, the son of a minor academic and a high school English teacher. In 1947 the CIA was founded, with one of its main tasks the collection of foreign intelligence. Casting around for people who might be of use in this endeavor, the CIA's attention was drawn to Rick's father, Carleton Ames, who had received a PhD in Burmese history in 1949. Carleton was recruited into the Agency, and the family, consisting of wife Rachel Ames, Rick, and two younger sisters, moved to Washington.

In 1953, Carleton was sent to Rangoon, and his family accompanied him. Unfortunately, aside from his linguistic abilities Carleton had no talents that would make him a success as an operations officer. His tour lasted the minimum two years, after which he returned to Washington, never to serve overseas again. He was assigned to the recently established Counterintelligence Staff and remained there in an analytical position until his retirement.

When the family returned from Rangoon, Rick became a freshman at McLean High School, where he was active in the drama and debating clubs. His mother was a popular English teacher at the high school. After he turned sixteen, he applied for a summer job at the CIA. He worked there for two summers in lowly clerical and maintenance jobs. It was, and is, the practice in the CIA to employ teenage children of its employees for summer work. They are already vetted to some degree because of their parents' clearances. However, due to their youth they are not polygraphed and do not have access to sensitive information.

In the fall of 1959, Rick matriculated at the University of Chicago. This was his first time away from home and he did not have the self-discipline to study and attend class regularly. As in high school, he was active in a drama group. Eventually he was dismissed from the university, but did not return home right away. Instead he worked temporarily in a local theater.

By early 1962 Rick was back in McLean and applied once again to the CIA. He was hired in June as a full-time clerical employee, assigned to a position in the Directorate of Operations as a document analyst. At the same time he was accepted at George Washington University, and continued his studies part time, graduating in 1967 with a bachelor's degree in history and a fairly decent grade-point average.

After graduation, Rick applied for officer status through the Career Training Program (CTP). Candidates have to pass intelligence tests, tests on current events, personal interviews, and psychological screening. Rick was successful, although not highly recommended. These were the days of the Vietnam War, and the CIA was pressed to build up its cadres. Perhaps under other circumstances he might not have made the cut. This same year his father retired from the Agency.

Rick was in training from December 1967 to September 1968. Having successfully completed the course for DO operations officers, he was assigned to the then–Soviet Bloc (SB) Division. This is where we first crossed paths with him. He was promoted to GS-09 in June 1968, to GS-10 in June 1969, and to GS-11 in October 1970. (These promotions were non-competitive. All CTP graduates were routinely promoted as far as GS-11 unless they made some serious misstep. After GS-11, their promotions had to be earned.)

In May 1969 Rick married Nancy Jane Segebarth, also a CIA officer. She had joined the Agency in 1964 after graduation from Denison University, and had completed the Career Training Program some time before Rick did. She subsequently worked as an analyst in the Directorate of Intelligence.

In September, Rick, accompanied by his new wife, arrived in Ankara, Turkey to serve as a junior officer in the CIA Station. The Deputy Chief of

Station was Duane R. "Dewey" Clarridge, who had transferred from Istanbul to Ankara a year after Rick's arrival. In his memoir, *A Spy for All Seasons: My Life in the CIA*, Clarridge's assessment of Rick, while somewhat overdone, is not far off the mark: "He lacked the necessary, fundamental personality skills. . . . He was in the wrong business or, at least, the wrong side of the intelligence trade. He was introverted and devoid of interpersonal skills. He was never going to be effective with foreigners, as he was unable to relate to them, much less bring them along toward recruitment. . . . Perhaps because of all this and his concurrent frustration, Ames had developed an indifferent attitude toward his work." In his final written review of Ames' performance, Clarridge recommended that Ames be assigned to analytical work.[1]

Ames and his wife left Ankara in January 1972. During their tour, she had resigned from the Agency. In those days wives took second place to their husbands when it came to careers. Although she had a higher grade than her husband, she had been assigned to a routine job that did not match her talents and that she did not find acceptable. She never returned to the Agency and indeed always regarded it with a jaundiced view.

After home leave, Ames took a position in SB Division until starting full-time Russian language training in January 1973. He completed the training but never really had a good grasp on the language. Before starting the course he took a language aptitude test and was judged to be somewhere in the middle. However, it is difficult to imagine him spending many hours memorizing declensions, conjugations, vocabulary lists, and stress patterns.

Ames spent the next two and a half years at headquarters in the newly named Soviet and East European Division. Among other things, he served as the desk officer for the operation involving Aleksandr Dmitriyevich Ogorodnik, who was encrypted as AEKNIGHT and later CKTRIGON. Ogorodnik was a Soviet Ministry of Foreign Affairs (MFA) officer stationed in Bogota, Colombia, where he was recruited by the CIA in 1974. Ames supported this phase of the operation. Later, Ogorodnik returned to Moscow, where he remained in touch through our station there. In the summer of 1977 he was arrested by the KGB but before he could be interrogated he committed suicide with a cyanide pill that we had supplied to him. Although there are some who disagree, it is generally thought that Karel Koecher, who had been infiltrated into the CIA by the Czech intelligence service and who was involved in the translation of some of the audio coverage of the AEKNIGHT operation, was responsible for providing the lead to Ogorodnik that the KGB was able to capitalize on.

Rick enjoyed his work on this case, particularly one task that took a lot of time and that most desk officers would have shunned. Ogorodnik asked for help in fulfilling his MFA collection requirements. Rick would research and write unclassified responses for passage to Ogorodnik, who in turn provided them to his supervisors for transmittal to Moscow. For his work on the headquarters desk, Ames was promoted to GS-12 in November 1974.

In August 1976 Ames was transferred to New York City. This was his most successful tour. He was not required to spot, assess, develop, and recruit sources of intelligence for the U.S. government. Rather he was assigned to participate in the handling of two important Soviet cases, in close cooperation with the FBI. One of the cases was that of Ambassador and Under-Secretary-General at the United Nations Arkadiy Nikolayevich Shevchenko (CKDYNAMITE). Shevchenko worked in-place for the FBI and CIA before his 1978 defection.[2] The other case was think-tank researcher Sergey Fedorenko, discussed in Chapter 12 above.

An incident in connection with this case received a certain amount of attention after Ames' arrest although it was not considered highly remarkable at the time, and Ames did not receive any official reprimand. Ames was returning from a meeting with Fedorenko and was traveling by subway. He dozed off or got distracted. Right after leaving the train at his stop he realized that he had left his attaché case behind, and that the case contained notes from the meeting. He immediately called one of his FBI contacts, who managed to retrieve the briefcase in short order. Fortunately, no harm was done.

Ames spent five years in New York, a longer-than-usual tour, and a sign that his supervisors were pleased with his work. In January 1979 he was promoted to GS-13.

By the summer of 1981, it was time for Ames to move on. After having turned down some other possibilities, he accepted a direct transfer to Mexico City to head the branch that worked against the Soviet target. His wife did not accompany him because she did not want to give up her prospering business career. This decision marked the beginning of the end of their marriage.

Now a geographical bachelor in Mexico, Ames was free to follow his own inclinations. It appears that he increased his alcohol consumption during this period. He became friendly with a group of embassy officers who enjoyed indulging in long, liquid lunches. Also, there was no one to inhibit his after-hours drinking because he occupied an apartment by himself. Moreover, he was again in a position where he was expected to do his share of spotting, assessing, and development of foreigners toward eventual recruitment. Not unexpectedly, he followed his Ankara pattern of doing little in this arena although he was facile in developing ideas for others to execute.

While it may appear surprising to the outsider, in May 1982 Ames was promoted to GS-14. This was his last promotion, and he received it for the work he had done in New York. The CIA bureaucracy creates substantial time lags between an individual's achievements and recognition thereof. Performance appraisal reports are normally prepared only once per year. They are then followed by lengthy panels comparing the accomplishments of all officers in a certain grade with the same specialty. The panel's recommendations are next reviewed and the number of promotions available is established. Lastly, the promotions are finalized and announced.

During his tour in Mexico, Ames had a fateful encounter. He met Maria del Rosario Casas Dupuy, Cultural Attaché at the Colombian embassy. Rosario was already known to the CIA Station. She had been recruited by case officer David S to serve in two roles. First, she agreed to allow her apartment to be used for case officer meetings with agents while she was at work. Secondly, she functioned as what is called an "access agent." That is, she reported to the CIA on individuals of interest with whom she came into contact. She served as secretary of the local diplomats' association, known as AMCOSAD, and therefore met representatives from numerous countries. However, according to extant records, she did not do much for the CIA and was paid only the nominal sum of one hundred dollars per month.

Soon after Rick met Rosario, romance began to bloom. Intellectually, they were well suited, although Rosario's scholarly attainments far outweighed his. Possibly, Rosario was thinking in terms of marrying an American diplomat who would be an ambassador some day. At this point she did not know about his CIA affiliation and, indeed, was very unhappy when she learned the truth.

Although Rick tried to keep the relationship somewhat discreet because people knew that he was married, they did go places together and Rick took her to at least one office party. By the end of his tour, the romance had become quite serious.

Rick left Mexico City after serving a minimum tour of two years. Among other shortcomings, he never obtained a useful grasp of Spanish, and he never brought any of his contacts to operational fruition. Leaving Rosario behind, he headed for Washington and a job at CIA headquarters.

Again, we see the hand of fate. Many have asked why Rick, after a lackluster performance in Mexico, was chosen to head up one of the most sensitive branches in SE Division. Rod Carlson was the group chief in SE who was responsible for three branches. One branch, headed by Jeanne at this time, was responsible for all CI production from defectors and in-place Soviet and East European sources. The second branch was responsible for monitoring all East European developmental operations and recruited sources from a CI point of view. The third, now headed by Rick, had the same responsibilities for Soviet cases. Jobs in these branches, important though they were in the overall scheme of things, were more geared to persons with an analytical or research bent. Therefore they were not always highly popular with operations officers who liked on-the-street work and often there were few applicants for vacant positions. As an officer with overseas operational experience against the Soviet target and observable intellectual capabilities, Rick was a strong candidate and thus got the job.

Not long after Rick had settled into his Washington job, he was joined by Rosario. The precipitating event was the death of her father in December 1983. Rosario had been close to her father, and his death deeply affected her. Rick did his best to console her long distance, but she soon gave up her job and moved in with him in his rented apartment in the Virginia suburb of Pimmit Hills. His wife Nan was still in New York and, for all practical purposes, their marriage was over.

Now Rosario no longer had an income. In her defense, it should be pointed out that she was in the United States on a visitor's visa, which would have limited her job opportunities. She also had to return to Colombia every few months to renew her visa. However, it seems that she spent her ample free time spending Rick's money. For a time, Rosario's mother visited them and joined in the spending spree. As always, Rosario wanted only the best for herself. One cannot imagine her shopping at Wal-Mart. Nordstrom and Nieman-Marcus were more her style. The same applied to dining out. No McDonald's, but evenings spent at the Palm, Galileo, and other upscale restaurants.

As time went on, Rick could see himself falling ever more deeply into debt as a result of Rosario's extravagances. Moreover, he was still married to Nan and knew he would have to make some sort of financial settlement with her. She held pension rights to his salary and they owned a townhouse together in Reston, a middle-class Virginia suburb. Along with all this, he could see that he might have reached an impasse in his career. It was still not clear that he had seen his last promotion; however, it was evident that he was not a candidate for fast-track advancement.

Whether there were any precipitating factors is not known, but by the early spring of 1985 Ames had decided that the soundest way out of his financial difficulties was to commit espionage. It is difficult to comprehend that a person would take this drastic step, but the psychological studies of Americans who have committed this crime show that they have one factor in common: narcissism. In their minds, what is important is self-gratification or self-interest. In order to achieve their selfish goals, they generally require substantial sums of money. That they are betraying their colleagues, their organization, the lives of other people, and their country as a whole seems not to weigh in the balance. From what we know, this appears to be true of most of the important American spies of the past thirty years, although revenge can also be a factor, as in the case of Edward Lee Howard, and the rare ideological spy, such as Cuban spy Ana Montes, still exists.

As outlined in Chapter 14, on 16 April 1985, Ames had scheduled a meeting with Soviet embassy arms control specialist Sergey Dmitriyevich Chuvakhin. This was a sanctioned contact, and the planned meeting was known to the FBI and CIA. However, Ames intended to use this contact as a cover for making his approach to the KGB. Ames had suggested to Chuvakhin that they get together for drinks at the Mayflower Hotel, a short distance from the Soviet embassy, and Chuvakhin had agreed. Ames showed up on time, but Chuvakhin never appeared.

Fortified by several vodka martinis while waiting for Chuvakhin, Ames eventually strolled over to the embassy. He knew that the receptionist at the entrance would be a KGB employee and he handed this individual an envelope he had intended to pass to Chuvakhin at the Mayflower. The outer envelope was addressed to the local KGB chief in true name. Inside was a second envelope, this time addressed to the same KGB chief by his operational pseudonym. This was designed to get the KGB's attention because no one outside the KGB would be privy to this name. Ames had of course gotten it from the CIA/FBI debriefing of either Sergey Motorin or Valeriy Martynov, the two penetrations of the KGB in Washington. (Throughout, we provide the story of these events as Ames told them to the FBI after his sentencing, supplemented by other information on Chuvakhin and local KGB CI chief Cherkashin compiled by the FBI at the time. The version given by Cherkashin in his recent book varies considerably in the details. According to his own statement, Cherkashin retired in 1991, and subsequently had no access to KGB records. Therefore, while the broad outline of events is correct, his recollection of individual episodes may be faulty.)[3]

The double-wrapped envelope contained a message. According to Ames, he provided information on two or three cases that the CIA Station in Moscow was handling. He says he believed that these cases were being run against us by the KGB, and that he was not giving information that would harm anyone. They would, however, help to establish his bona fides as a CIA insider. Also included in the envelope was a two-page telephone list, containing the names of all SE Division management personnel down to the deputy branch chief level. He says that he underlined his own name because he had no intention of concealing his identity. The message asked for fifty thousand dollars in recompense for the information he had provided. He had chosen this sum because, while he was in Mexico, the KGB had made a recruitment approach to a CIA transcriber/translator, and had offered him that amount. Ames thought therefore that this would sound like a reasonable offer to them. He also suggested that Chuvakhin be used as a go-between because they already had an overt relationship that, halting as it was, had been approved by the FBI and CIA.

Having made his overture, Ames settled down to wait. He knew that no decision could be made locally; the facts would be sent to Moscow, and Moscow would determine what to do next. From time to time, Ames called Chuvakhin with an innocuous-sounding suggestion that they get together, knowing that if the decision had not yet been made, Chuvakhin would put off meeting with him. Then, in mid-May, the breakthrough came. Chuvakhin, who had previously never taken any initiative in the relationship, called Ames and suggested that they get together for a drink at the Soviet embassy and then proceed to lunch at a local restaurant.

On 15 May, Ames showed up at the Soviet embassy as scheduled. There Chuvakhin turned him over to Cherkashin. Because Cherkashin was afraid that the FBI could have bugged the room in which they met, or possibly that Ames was a provocation and had come to the meeting wearing a recording device, they merely exchanged written messages and did not speak out loud to each other. Cherkashin informed Ames that the KGB accepted his offer and that he would be paid the fifty thousand dollars he had requested. Further, they agreed that Chuvakhin could be used as the go-between for the time being.

There was no lunch with Chuvakhin that noon. It was postponed for two days. Then the routine was established. Ames and Chuvakhin would lunch periodically. Each would carry a shopping bag to the lunch, and the bags would be exchanged. Ames' bag would contain classified documents and perhaps an operational message for the KGB; Chuvakhin's bag would contain press handouts from the Soviet embassy, plus perhaps money, Russian vodka, and a message from the KGB. After each lunch, Ames would write up an official CIA communication for the FBI and for CIA's Washington Station, with a ho-hum account of the non-operational aspects of the meeting. His aim was to make the contact seem mildly worthwhile, so that he would not be told to break it off, while at the same time not making it sound so promising that it would attract undue interest.

According to our best calculations, Ames passed Chuvakhin what has become known subsequently as the "big dump" on 13 June. This was a collection of documents that provided information on all of the major cases that the CIA and FBI were running against the Soviet target—information that directly led to the deaths of a number of these assets. The KGB appreciated the value of Ames' offering because a few months later he received an operational message from them stating: "Congratulations, you are now a millionaire!" The KGB had set aside two million dollars for him.

If we accept Ames' statements that the big dump took place on 13 June, then we have a puzzle. Oleg Gordievsky, the deputy KGB resident in London and a longtime British source, was recalled to Moscow on 17 May and interrogated, although not arrested. Either Ames has, innocently or deliberately, given the wrong date, or Gordievsky was betrayed by someone or something else.

To deepen the mystery, Cherkashin tells a hard-to-swallow story about a "Washington-based British journalist" providing the KGB with information that tipped Cherkashin off that Gordievsky was working for the British, and Cherkashin told his KGB boss about this case personally during a visit to Moscow in the spring of 1985.[4] This simply does not fit with reality. First of all, as far as the FBI has ever been able to determine, Cherkashin did not leave for Moscow until 20 May, while Gordievsky was recalled three days earlier. Secondly, the Washington-based British journalist has all the earmarks of being a false lead planted by Russian intelligence to cover up the real story. Surely Cherkashin had to submit his manuscript to the SVR for approval before he published it, just as we have to do.

One could speculate that the real story of Gordievsky's downfall has not yet come out, and that the Russians have some good reason for obfuscating. One plausible explanation is that Ames gave up Gordievsky in April when he made his first approach. However, in that event, why are the Russians trying to fool us more than ten years later? Ames readily admits that he gave up Gordievsky, but believes that it took place in June, at the time of the big dump. Surely the date is not important enough to warrant concocting a false scenario. As far as the two of us are concerned, Gordievsky's compromise still remains a mystery.

On 31 July, Ames and Chuvakhin had a planned lunch meeting at Chadwick's in Georgetown. To Ames' surprise and consternation, they were joined by other Soviet officials, including Cherkashin. One reason for placing the two in the same place at the same time had to do with KGB worries about the CIA's polygraph requirements and their unfortunate attempts to solve the problem. If asked during a polygraph examination whether he had met any KGB officer in Washington, Ames could reply in the affirmative and point to this luncheon. However, despite the KGB's best efforts, Ames was faced with a dilemma. Up to now he had been dutifully reporting each outing with Chuvakhin, who was not an intelligence officer and not of high interest to the FBI. If he reported this contact honestly, to include Cherkashin's presence, it would shine a spotlight on him, something he needed to avoid. If he reported the meeting but stated that only he and Chuvakhin were present, he had to consider that Cherkashin was the focus of intense FBI coverage. What if the FBI had him under surveillance that day, and tracked him to Chadwick's?

When faced with this knotty problem, Ames did what he often did—he procrastinated. Indeed, he never wrote a report on this meeting. He had good excuses for getting behind in his write-ups, because on 1 August KGB CI officer Vitaliy Yurchenko defected and Ames was chosen to be one of his debriefers. Also, he was deep in wedding plans. Thus, despite repeated requests he managed to avoid putting anything on paper. And soon he was in full-time Italian language training, away from the headquarters building except on Fridays and hard to reach by telephone, because he was in class.

Some have tried to give a sinister cast to the connection between Ames and Yurchenko. However, Ames did not choose himself for the job of debriefer; it was chosen for him by division management, probably because he was knowledgeable about the KGB, had some Russian, and was available. Furthermore, he was only one of a team of three CIA debriefers, with the FBI fielding its own team. To cap it off, Yurchenko had round-the-clock guards from the CIA's Office of Security. (As it happened, Dan Payne, a prominent figure in this book, was one of them.) In sum, before his defection Yurchenko could not know the circumstances he would be held under, and Ames only knew after the event that he would be involved in the debriefing. The two did have one or two semi-private conversations at an early point but there's no reason to think they touched on Ames' espionage activities. And in September Ames left his debriefing activities to start Italian language lessons and had no further contact with Yurchenko.

Rick and Rosario's wedding celebration was a low-key affair, although he now had enough money to allow for more of a splash. It took place on 10 August, not long after his divorce was finalized. The ceremony was held in a Unitarian Church. It was attended only by family members and a few close friends, including Diana Worthen. Rosario was a Roman Catholic but the Unitarian Church was selected because of Rick's divorce. Rick himself is not known to have been a churchgoer, or to have had any particular interest in organized religion once he reached adulthood. By this time, Rosario had become a U.S. citizen, which was required by CIA regulations. She had also successfully completed a CIA polygraph.

Ames' first face-to-face meeting with Vladimir Mechulayev, the KGB officer who was to become his primary handler for the next few years, took place in Bogota in December 1985. As previously agreed in operational notes, Ames waited for his Soviet contact in a Bogota shopping mall. His handler approached him with the proper password or parole. They then proceeded to a Soviet embassy vehicle and drove away to the Soviet compound. Once inside, in a room set aside for the purpose, the two men began to get to know one another. They had a lot to discuss, with emphasis on making arrangements for communications during Ames' upcoming tour in Rome. The meeting lasted a long time. Ames' excuse for leaving Rosario and her family was that he wanted to do some Christmas shopping. However, when he did not return in good time, they began to worry about his safety. Luckily, Ames did return before they called the police, but it was a close shave.

In July 1986 Rick and Rosario left for Rome, where Rick was assigned as chief of the Enemy Targets Branch. This meant that he had responsibility for operations not only against the Soviet target, but also against the East Europeans, the Chinese, and the North Koreans.

As far as his espionage activities were concerned, they followed more or less the same pattern that had been developed in Washington. Again, a go-between was employed. This time it was a Soviet diplomat named Aleksey Khrenkov. However, the relationship between Ames and Khrenkov was somewhat different from that between Ames and Chuvakhin. Chuvakhin had always been a reluctant player, and he and Ames never had any conversations relative to the clandestine aspects of their lunch dates. Khrenkov, on the other hand, seemed to enjoy Ames' company and from time to time stated that it was an honor to be dealing with him. We do not know whether Khrenkov was a deep-cover KGB officer. The CIA had no previous traces on him, but it is certainly possible. It is also possible that he was someone known to us, serving abroad in alias.

The procedure of exchanging shopping bags continued, with Ames handing over large volumes of Rome Station traffic and receiving money, vodka, and innocuous unclassified Soviet embassy handouts in return. It had been arranged with Mechulayev during the Bogota meeting that Khrenkov would be at a certain diplomatic reception in Rome and that Ames should be there too. They would meet casually in the course of the party and strike up a light conversation. Eventually, one or the other would extend an invitation for drinks or lunch. This charade was employed so that Ames would have a cover reason for his acquaintance with Khrenkov. Indeed, as had been the practice with Chuvakhin, at least at first, Ames duly reported each meeting with Khrenkov, describing it as low-key developmental activity. Because the CIA file on Khrenkov contains only three cables, some of this reporting must have consisted only of comments to Station management on the order of "By the way, I ran into Khrenkov the other day, but he didn't have anything noteworthy to say." Ames was faced with the same dilemma as in Washington. He wanted to cover himself by reporting his contacts, but he did not want to say anything that would cause anyone to pay particular attention to them. As it happened, he was lucky because senior Station management did not seem overly interested in the Soviet target and he was able to take advantage of this lack of attention.

The meetings with Khrenkov were supplemented by annual visits from Moscow by Mechulayev. After a clandestine car pickup, Khrenkov would drive Ames to the Soviet housing complex where Mechulayev would be waiting for him in a private room. As before, they would have a long sit-down meeting, discussing events so far and making plans for the future. During one of these meetings, Ames told Mechulayev about two cases that he had not included in the big dump. One was Sergey Fedorenko, the think-tank researcher who was run by the FBI and CIA in New York in the 1970s. The other was a Soviet academic whom Rick had also known in New York. It appears that Rick had some residual feeling for these individuals, because of his personal encounters with them, and was somewhat reluctant to betray them. However, by 1986 his loyalty to his KGB handlers overrode these qualms.

It was during one of these Rome meetings that Rick struck a new financial agreement with the KGB. It appears that, having promised him two million dollars in late 1985, there were no plans to pass him additional funds. However, Ames wanted a regular income so it was finally decided to pay him ten thousand dollars per month. He also received a bonus at the time of his son's birth in November 1988.

Because he was always paid in cash, Ames began to have a money-laundering problem. To alleviate his situation, he opened two accounts at the Credit Suisse in Zurich and traveled there from time to time to make deposits. He would usually drive and take Rosario with him, because

Zurich was her kind of town. Ames had bought a second-hand Jaguar and, as he drove over the Alps, he pictured himself as the new James Bond. At least that is what he told his debriefers after he had been convicted and sentenced.

In July 1989 Ames and his family left Rome. They took some vacation time, and then proceeded to buy a home in North Arlington and decorate it to their liking. Before leaving Europe, Ames went to Switzerland to withdraw most of his ill-gotten gains from his bank accounts. It was this money that was used to buy the house.

After tending to his personal affairs, Ames reported for duty at CIA headquarters in September 1989. He was assigned as chief of the European Branch in the External Operations Group of the Soviet and East European Division. In this position he had access to information on all developmental cases and recruited assets run by the CIA against the Soviet and East European target in the European area. This was a position that must have been of high interest to his KGB handlers, but he held it for only a few months. In the wake of the upheavals in Eastern Europe he was transferred to be Chief of the Czechoslovak Operations Branch in January 1990, to manage the new opportunities now available in that country. In this position he had much less access to information of value to the KGB.

Another reassignment took place in August. Ames was chosen to serve on a promotion panel, ranking GS-12 officers and evaluating their eligibility for promotion to GS-13. He was now almost completely divorced from regular access to operational information, but no doubt gleaned some juicy personnel tidbits that could be of value to his handlers, should they ever decide to use them. Specifically, he reviewed the files of our officers under non-official cover, our most vulnerable employees. How much of this information he gave to the KGB is unknown. Ames says that he did not supply them with most of what was available to him, at least in any systematic way.

The panel lasted about two months. Ames did not return to SE Division, but moved to the Analysis Group of the Counterintelligence Center for a one-year rotational assignment. There his job was to provide analysis on the KGB. It was in this position that he got access to CIA holdings on the double agents being run by the U.S. military and the FBI against the KGB and GRU. He periodically copied this information from a computer database and passed it to the KGB, thereby compromising pretty much the entire program. He also had access to historical information on some of our most important Cold War cases. This too was passed. Professionally, he wrote a paper on the internal KGB, with emphasis on its regional offices, and one on the KGB's relationship with Cuban intelligence.

Once his tour in the Analytic Group was at an end, Ames returned to SE Division for a short time. He was assigned to the "KGB Working Group," and worked closely with the new division chief, Milt Bearden. His job was to think strategically about how the CIA should manage its dealings with the KGB in the future. This effort has been described as "placing a stake in the heart of the KGB," but the evidence does not support that view. Indeed, as outlined in Chapter 13, the KGB was no longer considered a major adversary and Ames, as instructed by Bearden, wrote short conceptual reports about the new outlook.

Once his temporary assignment to the KGB Working Group was finished, Ames was transferred to the Counternarcotics Center, where he served as the officer responsible for Central Eurasia in the Regional Programs Branch of the International Counternarcotics Group (CNC/ICGRP). He remained in CNC until his arrest in February 1994.

We cannot take credit for assigning Ames to CNC, although it was an ideal place to put him as our suspicions continued to grow, and we kept him there as part of a conscious effort. Indeed we got him promoted to a more prestigious position in 1993. This served two purposes. First, he was required to serve in CNC for another year as part of his enhanced status. Secondly, he now had a private office. This permitted the FBI additional opportunities for video coverage of his activities.

Our interests in the counternarcotics arena are similar to those of Russia, and we have developed a cooperative relationship. Therefore Ames had little access to specific operational endeavors that would have been of use to his SVR handlers. (As previously noted, the foreign operations element of the KGB had metamorphosed into the SVR in December 1991.) However, he was still privy to such CIA matters as personnel assignments, policy and guidance directives, technical developments, and changes in our methods of operation.

Before Ames returned to the United States in the summer of 1989, he and his handlers had worked out a system of two-way dead drops in the

Washington area. Ames would put down a package in a pre-arranged location. One drop site was located under a bridge. The package would be covered in dark plastic, such as is used for garbage bags, and would contain classified documents. Ames would then signal to the KGB that he had loaded the drop by making a mark. One such signal was a chalk mark on a mailbox in Georgetown. The KGB followed a reverse procedure. They would load a drop containing money and perhaps an operational note with questions for Ames or directions for future communications. Once they had loaded their drop they would signal to Ames and he would pick it up.

The above procedures worked successfully, but were only carried out a few times a year. Just as had been done with Walker in the past, and was being done with Hanssen concurrently, it was possible for the KGB to circumvent FBI coverage. However, each exchange had its risks, and because they were infrequent Ames was limited in the amount of classified materials he could pass.

The drop system was supplemented by annual meetings either in South America or in Europe. As always, Ames preferred Bogota because he had a reason to go there. However, the KGB sometimes insisted on meeting in other venues, to include Vienna and Caracas. There were some hitches in the procedure, with Ames not always showing up where he was supposed to at the scheduled time, because of either his drinking or simple carelessness. At some point Mechulayev was taken off the case. He was replaced by Yuriy Karetkin. We do not know why the change was made, but it may have been caused by KGB management's concerns over Rick's undisciplined behavior and their lack of control over him.

Throughout the operation, the KGB and SVR generally paid Ames in non-sequential U.S. hundred-dollar bills but at least once during the Roman phase in Swiss francs or German deutsche marks. During his yearly meetings, he was handed $100,000 to $150,000 in currency. The procedure was for Ames to bring a stash of classified documents from the United States to each overseas meeting. Generally, he placed these in his carry-on luggage or in an empty computer carrying case. When he got his bundle of cash in return, he again used his hand luggage for transportation. In those pre-9/11 days, he relied on the fact that he was traveling as a U.S. official and that he did not fit the profile of a terrorist. Therefore he thought it unlikely that his luggage would be searched.

Not surprisingly, Ames had an ever-growing cash flow problem. His solution was to dribble his currency into the economy in relatively small amounts. He made cash deposits to his various bank accounts, and he paid Rosario's credit card bills at local upscale department stores and boutiques the same way. Sometimes he had a cash backlog so he hid stacks of bills in his garage, where Rosario had access to them if needed.

We are often asked about Rosario's role in Ames' espionage career. As described in Chapter 16, some have concocted a theory that his espionage started in Mexico City in the early 1980s and that Rosario played a significant role from the beginning. However, this theory does not seem to be tenable.

According to stories told separately by Rick and Rosario after their arrest, in 1985 or 1986, when the money started to roll in, Rick explained to Rosario that the new income came from a friend named Bob in Chicago. When Rick was at the University of Chicago back in the 1960s, he had done Bob a favor by arranging an abortion for Bob's girlfriend. In the intervening years Bob had become wealthy and when he heard that Rick was going to Rome, he asked Rick to take care of his European investments. This was a pretty unbelievable story because Bob did not manifest his existence in any way. He did not send a Christmas card, did not write or phone, and never visited the Washington area. Furthermore, as Rosario should have been aware, Rick had absolutely no qualifications to serve as anyone's financial counselor.

In any event, Rosario must have known that Rick was up to something illegal because she co-signed his income tax returns each year. These were filled out as if Rick's only substantial income was from his GS-14 salary, as reflected on his W-2 forms. On the other hand, we tend to believe that Rosario did not know that he was involved in espionage on behalf of the Russians until a year or so before their 1994 arrest. They both told a somewhat muddled story about her having found an operational message in one of Rick's old wallets. She was upset for two reasons. First of all, this was serious business and could incur severe penalties. Secondly, she did not like Russians, believing them to be uncultured peasants.

All of this did not stop her from enjoying the ill-gotten gains, however. Before Rick made his last trip to Bogota, he and she had a conversation that was recorded by the FBI in which she discussed the money that he was going to get. And when he reached Bogota they had another conversation, this time on their tapped telephone, which indicated that she was anxious that everything would go smoothly and successfully. These conversations, plus her signature on the IRS forms, earned her a five-year prison sentence. After she finished serving it, she left immediately for Colombia, where she still lives today with her family. The family had cared for her son while she was incarcerated. Typically, she accepts no responsibility for what happened, blaming everything on Rick.

●—●—●

What was Rick like as a person? Sandy first met Rick in the early 1970s when they were in the early stages of their careers as SE Division officers. Although they did not socialize outside the office, they came to know one another fairly well in 1975, when they, along with two other Division officers, carpooled. The rides to and from work were enjoyable, consisting of friendly banter and discussions of hypothetical operational scenarios. To Sandy the Rick Ames of the 1970s and early 1980s was simply a nice guy—easygoing, a good conversationalist, and comfortable to be around. Like an absent-minded professor, he was unpretentious in dress and manner. His hair was unkempt, his sock colors often did not match, his shirts were rarely pressed, and he was always late for the carpool whether he was the driver or the rider. However, none of that really mattered to his contemporaries at the office. Rick was just Rick—a gentle sort whose company his fellow officers enjoyed while silently laughing at his goofy physical appearance. This is not to say that he was always happy-go-lucky. Occasionally he became irritated, particularly if his operational judgment was questioned by those at his level. They might be equals, but he was a greater equal. Nevertheless, to this day Sandy insists that there was no way the Rick of those early years could have ever betrayed his colleagues and his country to become one of the most famous traitors of our time. He had neither the anger, the courage, nor the soul to commit such an act.

Jeanne's contacts with Rick covered the same period, but were more casual. Like Sandy, she remembers him as being mildly unkempt, with hair that badly needed styling, teeth stained from his cigarette habit, and outmoded frames for his eyeglasses. On the other hand, she found him an interesting conversationalist, full of ideas. He was not the sort of person who bored his listener with descriptions of the traffic on his way to work or comments about the cafeteria menu. Like many who knew him superficially in the office, Jeanne as well as Sandy had no idea that his alcohol consumption was anything but normal.

In retrospect, there are some aspects of Rick's background and persona that warrant comment. First of all, his father's CIA career was a relative failure, a fact he must have known. Indeed, Rick has stated that he read his father's personnel file. This is somewhat baffling because he should not have had access to this restricted record. Rick could not or would not explain how it happened. Yet it was important enough for him to have remembered it and mentioned it during his 1994 debriefings.

Rick's mother, on the other hand, was a popular teacher at McLean High. In contrast to his father, his mother was successful in the career path she had chosen. It must not have been comfortable for Rick to be a student at a school where his mother was a teacher, but we do not know how he dealt with this situation.

Many have commented on Rick's lack of self-discipline and tendency to procrastination. His unsuccessful career at the University of Chicago is an early example. Certainly he had the intelligence to succeed but, away from home for the first time, he failed to study or attend classes regularly. Throughout his career his managers recorded his inattention to submitting his financial accountings on time. And there was one fairly egregious instance where he neglected to submit a performance appraisal report (PAR) for one of his employees on time, finally handing in a sloppy, superficial product. It was so far below standards that, when the promotion panel convened to review all PARs for the year it was singled out for criticism and a formal memorandum was sent to Rick outlining his deficiency in the matter.

Along with his lack of self-discipline, Rick had a habit of doing only what interested him, and letting other things slide. As someone said, he "never had a boss." When intellectually engaged, he could do a superior job and could articulate why a certain project was important or why it was necessary to make a specific decision. His work in the counternarcotics center in developing coordination between the countries bordering the Black Sea is an example. Even after his sentencing, he was still interested in how this initiative was faring.

Another example is his behavior vis-à-vis the GTWEIGH case in the summer of 1985. He had an advisory role in operational decisions involving Division sources and developmental cases outside the Soviet Union. For the first time in Sandy's experience in the Africa Branch, Rick not only exercised his role on one of her cases, but did so forcefully. He was adamant in his disagreement with Sandy on the passage of funds in Moscow and repeatedly argued that the potential risk of compromise to Poleshchuk was too great.

What is of particular interest here, of course, is whether Rick was making this argument because he really believed it, even though he was working for the KGB and the position he was advocating worked against KGB interests. Jeanne believes that Rick was able to compartmentalize. Sometimes he was a straightforward, concerned CIA officer, with no heed to the fact that he was also a KGB spy.

Sandy disagrees with this interpretation. She contends that Rick wasn't arguing his course of action because he really believed it was correct, even though it worked against KGB interests. She sees his action as a combination of guilt and self-preservation. Even Rick has some soul and it must have been almost unbearable waiting for his actions to culminate in the various arrests. Conversely, in his arrogant mind he could make himself look good by advocating the proper decision. He was in a position to say: "I told you all it was too dangerous. See how smart I am." Lastly, his advocacy made him an unlikely suspect should GTWEIGH's compromise lead to an immediate mole hunt.

Along with all this, as Sandy has noted, Rick had some of the attributes of an absent-minded professor. The most famous example of this trait is his behavior in New York, as recounted earlier. After meeting a sensitive asset, Rick took the subway to a rendezvous with the FBI. He got off the train, leaving his briefcase, which contained debriefing notes, behind. Luckily the FBI safely retrieved the briefcase for him.

While Rick would vehemently deny it, both Jeanne and Sandy sensed that, with the exception of his wives, he had a somewhat condescending attitude toward women. Although his first wife Nan outranked him and made more money than he did, which was unusual in those days, he remained extremely proud of her intellectual abilities and achievements. Moreover, after she left the Agency he often spoke glowingly of her work on the 1972 congressional campaign of Democrat Joe Fischer, who ran against and defeated a well-known incumbent Republican. The same can be said of Rick's respect for Rosario and her academic accomplishments.

However, outside the house Rick's offhand comments and demeanor left a different impression regarding his views on the ability of women in the workplace. Also, we had the distinct feeling that he was pleased to know that it was two women that were heading up the investigation of the 1985 compromises, because it would be easier to outwit us.

In the later days of his career, after he had become comfortable with his espionage activities, Rick exuded self-confidence, as if he was certain that he would never be caught. Whether this had anything to do with his attitude toward women, or whether it was associated with his long-held inability to face unpleasant facts, is moot, but it certainly existed. On Sandy's first morning in the Counterintelligence Center, Rick nonchalantly walked into her work area to welcome her. After some small talk he casually asked about her new assignment. When told that she and Jeanne and two FBI representatives were going to try to find answers to our 1985 compromises, Rick immediately began a lecture on the most basic tenets of a counterintelligence investigation. "Sandy, the first thing you should do is look for differences between the cases we lost and the new sources we are currently and successfully running." He added that he would be more than happy to offer any assistance. A few months later, Jeanne had a similar experience. The day after Rick had been interviewed by the task force, Jeanne and he happened to be waiting for an elevator at the same time. Rick mentioned the interview, said that he had given the problem some thought and, like he had with Sandy, offered his assistance.

Much has been made of Ames' alcohol use. As we see it, he certainly abused alcohol on occasion and is best described as a binge drinker. Yet he could use alcohol normally on social occasions and he was not alcohol-dependent in the sense that he slipped some vodka into his orange juice every morning. Interestingly, neither of his two wives, when interviewed after the arrests, considered him a true alcoholic.

Rick probably began drinking early in adulthood. As noted in Chapter 12, there were two DUI incidents at the outset of his career, and he overindulged at two Christmas parties. The only time that his management took official notice of his drinking was in Mexico City. When Rick came back to headquarters after this assignment, he was called in by the Office of Medical Services for an interview. He admitted that he had been drinking too much, but attributed it to the breakup of his first marriage and the subsequent stress. He added that he was now on an even keel and alcohol was no longer a problem.

This was not the truth, however, because on one occasion in Rome he got dead drunk and was picked up by the police. Significantly, this happened while Rosario was away in Bogota visiting her family. She herself drank very little and did her best to limit his consumption when she was on the scene. For whatever reason, Station management never reported this lapse to CIA headquarters. Another binge took place not too long before his arrest. Once again he was out of Rosario's control, on a trip to meet his KGB handler in Europe. He spent the night in a Zurich hotel. Rosario knew where he was and telephoned him. She got a thoroughly incoherent response when she reached him.

There were also occasions, both in Rome and at headquarters where Rick went out for lunch, had too much to drink, and came back and took a nap at his desk. These cannot have been too frequent, however, because most of his colleagues were not aware of any problem. In general, it appears that overindulgence in alcohol was a solitary pastime. When in company, he drank normally but, as he himself stated during his debriefings, sometimes he felt he "owed it to himself" to go to a bar and knock back a few vodkas.

18

HANSSEN AND AMES—
A COMPARISON

A FTER AMES' ARREST AND CONVICTION, Sandy and Jeanne bowed
out of the "mole-hunting" business. Jeanne continued to work at the
CIA part-time. She spent one year writing a classified study of the
Ames case, then moved to a counterintelligence job that involved operations, not personnel. Sandy meantime devoted herself to her family and
private life. However both were peripherally involved in what became,
after many false starts, the Hanssen case. Both of them knew that there
were several loose ends after Ames was arrested. Some CI leads that indicated a KGB penetration of the U.S. intelligence community just could
not be made to fit with Ames' access, no matter how hard the FBI tried.

First and foremost was the Felix Bloch case. As recounted earlier,
Bloch was a U.S. State Department officer. In the spring of 1989, when
the CIA got wind that he might be cooperating with the KGB, the FBI
was immediately informed. Less than two months later, the KGB warned
Bloch that he was under suspicion. Ames could not have known about
this case. He was in Rome at the time and there was no Italian connection. One theory was that the French DST, which had helped with the
surveillance of Bloch, could be responsible for the leak, but there was no
evidence that this was so. Thus the case remained a question mark, and a
burning one, in the minds of many.

Another operation involved an FBI technical penetration of a Soviet
establishment in the United States. KGB technicians removed the FBI's

device and it looked as if they had known exactly where to search for it. The CIA was aware of the technical capability involved, but despite an intensive investigation, the FBI never could ascertain that anyone in the CIA knew about the specific device and its location.

Yet another operation concerned the FBI's recruitment of a Soviet official in New York and his subsequent compromise. The CIA had been informed of the case because it had important implications for the collection of intelligence. However, after the compromise it appeared as if the KGB had information about the case not available in the CIA.

The investigation of non-Ames-related indications that there was a penetration of the U.S. intelligence community started in 1994, soon after Ames' arrest. The FBI was the lead agency, and was convinced that the spy was to be found in the CIA. Eventually CIA officer Brian Kelley became the focus of suspicion and a broad array of the tools and techniques of an espionage investigation were employed over a period of years to prove that he was guilty. All of this was to no avail, however, because Kelley was innocent.

The FBI had made the mistake of narrowing their focus to one single person too early and ignoring the bits and pieces that did not fit. Not until late 2000 was the Bureau forced to admit that they had been wrong all along. The spy was one of their own: Robert Philip Hanssen. He had been working for the Soviets, first the GRU and later the KGB and its successor agency the SVR, since 1979. We find it ironic that the mantra of those criticizing our investigation of Ames was "What took you so long?" Yet, of the 1980s cases that caused major damage, Ames represents one of the fastest roll-ups. Hanssen spied successfully for more than twenty years. John Walker's espionage career lasted some eighteen years. The Clyde Conrad ring operated for almost as long. It is also interesting to note that in these cases the CIA provided leads that helped in their denouement.

A comparison between Ames and Hanssen provides food for thought. Both were born in the United States as were their parents, and from the heartland. Hanssen's father was controlling and abusive. Ames' father appears to have been more of a withdrawn, passive type. Hanssen's father was reasonably successful in his career on the Chicago police force, although there is some reporting that he retired under a cloud. Ames' father, on the other hand, was something of a failure in his career.

Hanssen's mother deferred to her husband, as well she might. Ames' mother was more assertive and outgoing.

Both Hanssen and Ames followed in their fathers' footsteps. Hanssen joined the Chicago police force in 1972 and worked there for three years before obtaining FBI employment in 1976. As has been recounted, Ames started his CIA career as a teenager, and never worked anyplace else except for a short period in Chicago.

Both Hanssen and Ames are intelligent. They had IQs higher than most of those around them. But neither had a stellar academic career. Hanssen was a somewhat better scholar. He had poor undergraduate grades but managed to get an advanced degree in accounting. Ames flunked out of the University of Chicago. He then redeemed himself by managing to get a BA degree in history at George Washington University, with reasonably good grades, especially in the subjects that most interested him.

In matters of religion, Hanssen and Ames were at different ends of the pole. Ames never showed any interest in organized religion in adulthood, and is probably best described as an agnostic or even an atheist. His second wife was a Roman Catholic, but he did not join her church. Hanssen also married a Roman Catholic, but the results were very different. He converted from the Lutheranism of his youth and became a super-devout Catholic, often attending daily mass. He also joined the conservative Opus Dei movement and was given to proselytizing.

When it comes to personal lifestyle, there are obvious differences. As far as alcohol consumption is concerned, Hanssen drank little; Ames drank a lot on occasion and could not control his binges. They also diverged in their attitudes toward pornography. Hanssen was interested in pornography, and surfed the Internet in support of this interest. He even involved his wife though she was unwitting. He described her in sexual terms on the net, going so far as to use her real first name. In this same vein, he allowed his friend Jack Hoschouer to view the two of them having sex, which again she did not know. Ames on the other hand was not very interested in sex, and was impotent at times. In any event, it is difficult to imagine him treating his wife with the disrespect that Hanssen showed his.

In 1985 both Hanssen and Ames volunteered separately to the KGB in Washington, DC. It was their idea. Both were in it at least partly for the money and neither was ideologically attracted to the USSR. However, both were interested in the Soviet Union and knew a fair amount about the country and its intelligence structure.

This was not Hanssen's first experience as a Soviet spy. He had previously volunteered to the GRU in 1979 but his wife found out about his activities in 1980 and persuaded him to cut off contact.

Ames, who preceded Hanssen by several months in 1985, identified himself but Hanssen did not. Indeed, Hanssen never met any of his handlers while Ames had personal contacts with Washington CI chief Viktor Cherkashin, who managed both cases in the early years. It must have been comforting to Cherkashin when he discovered that there was such an overlap in their access and knowledge. Otherwise the reporting from Hanssen, the unknown quantity, would have been highly suspect. And, as the cases developed, Ames established close relations with his KGB handlers and admired them.

The timing is noteworthy. Ames worked for the CIA for more than twenty years before volunteering; Hanssen volunteered after three years. He made his approach to the GRU almost as soon as he got access to information that would interest the Soviet Union. Ames had had at least some access for many years, and broad access starting in the fall of 1983. Possibly there was some trigger, such as an especially hefty Nordstrom bill or unpalatable feedback from an Agency guidance counselor, which took him across the line in April 1985.

Both Ames and Hanssen communicated with their Soviet handlers via dead drops in the Washington area. Hanssen had no other form of communication, but Ames also had personal meetings via a go-between in Washington and Rome, and direct personal meetings with his Moscow-based handlers in Europe and South America.

Ames was polygraphed twice after he began his espionage career. In both instances he managed to satisfy the operators that he was leveling with them. The polygraph was not an issue in the Hanssen case because he was never subjected to this kind of examination.

While Ames may have been nervous at the outset of his espionage activities, it seems that he gained confidence as time passed and he perceived no signs that he was under suspicion. When the SIU team interviewed him in 1992, he gave Sandy and Jeanne the impression that he thought that he was smarter than we were, and that he would have no trouble pulling the wool over our eyes. As we used to say at the time, he viewed us as "two dumb broads." According to the FBI, when he was finally arrested he was dumbfounded. He did not see it coming. Hanssen, on the other hand, became more and more uneasy in the final months of his treason. His last written message to the SVR showed that he knew that his activities were bound to end in a highly unpleasant way.

CHAPTER 19

FINAL THOUGHTS

W E HAVE OFTEN BEEN ASKED TWO QUESTIONS about the Ames case. One is what were the lessons learned and the other is whether there are any basic tenets of a successful CI investigation. Beginning with the lessons learned, they were few in number, and none was edifying. In retrospect, we should have done more in the way of documenting our progress by preparing periodic progress reports for the official record. Moreover, every time we or our FBI colleagues briefed our respective managements, we should have written a memorandum recording the occasion, the names of those briefed, and the contents of the briefing. If we had done this, we would have been spared some of the attempts by those who knew better to minimize their knowledge and thus their responsibility for what was judged at the time to be an investigation that had taken too long. When the joint unit first went into business in the summer of 1991, Jeanne did set up a log of "things to do." The log included notations of what had already been done. However, Jeanne abandoned this log after a while because it appeared to be unnecessary, and just one more thing to slow us down. In retrospect, this was a mistake. In this same vein, we should have written a separate final report in 1992, or at least a CIA addendum to the FBI's assessment, stating our conclusions as to who the spy was and who the spy was not and detailing the information that led us to that judgment.

Secondly, from the beginning we should have paid more attention to the dictum "follow the money." We of course knew that the majority of spies were motivated by financial profit, and that it was usual for them to spend some of their ill-gotten gains instead of putting them away for a retirement nest egg. Yet it had never been the practice to pay special attention to sudden affluence. As a matter of fact, the Office of Security background investigations were aimed more at discovering who was in debt than to discovering who was in the clover. Such an approach made sense if one were trying to identify employees with potential vulnerabilities, but it was not likely to uncover someone who had already begun to profit from espionage. Luckily, we had Dan Payne as a member of our team. Thanks to his initiative and perseverance the right steps were taken to pin down the sources of Ames' substantial income.

As covered at length in earlier chapters, one of the most important mistakes made was the failure to inform Congress of the investigation, with periodic updates as to the progress being made. This was not the team's responsibility, but the failure to take these steps led to general Congressional animosity and suspicion of CIA's professionalism, which in turn led to subsequent overmanagement of espionage investigations by the legislative branch.

CI investigation is an art form carried out by experts. It is not a science, and throwing money and unqualified personnel or helpers at such a problem does not guarantee or even improve the chances of success. In many cases, quite the opposite result is achieved—analytical chaos with no resolution. Luck is involved—both in what you learn during the investigation and what you don't learn until the damage assessment is done— but in a wide-ranging and lengthy probe it probably does not play the defining role.

While there are several "must haves" for a successful CI investigation, knowledge of the target organization, in this case the KGB, is paramount. We had to be experts on the personnel, organization, tradecraft, and operational philosophy of the KGB to have a chance of success. Luckily, our previous assignments had allowed us to acquire the necessary expertise.

Personal knowledge of the personnel, organization, and methods of operation of the penetrated organization, in this case the CIA, is equally important. We had to educate our FBI colleagues on how CIA case officers thought and operated. Also, as we have always said, we would have a difficult time finding a spy in the Department of Defense, or any organization other than our own, simply because we don't know the players or how the game is played.

Scattered throughout this book is a large amount of material concerning the relations between the CIA and FBI. This subject has been the theme of many books, most of them fairly nonsensical. They describe the exchanges between the two services in a fairly stark and negative fashion, often attributing many of the ills of the intelligence world to failures in cooperation. In fact, the relationship is much more nuanced and has varied from time to time and from target to target. Certainly it is partly personality-driven and turf-driven. In a general sense, differences are perhaps more acute at the upper levels. Those actually involved in the various cases have often been more attuned to getting the job done than trying to grab all the credit even when they didn't necessarily see eye to eye. The cooperation between Les Wiser's squad and our little group in the CIA was, as we see it, exemplary. Despite a few disagreements, some caused by stress and some by interference from management, we managed to keep our eye on the prize: getting Aldrich Ames arrested under circumstances that would leave no doubt as to his guilt and eligibility for the most severe punishment legally permissible.

Further examples can be found in past Soviet cases. When Piguzov produced information in 1978 to the effect that former CIA officer David Barnett had volunteered to the KGB, the FBI was informed, and was given access to the pertinent Directorate of Operations files. This lead from a CIA operation resulted in Barnett's 1980 arrest, conviction, and sentencing to eighteen years in prison, as described above.

In the late 1970s and early 1980s, cooperation reached a new high. An integrated FBI/CIA unit called COURTSHIP was set up in the Washington, DC, area. It was this unit that was responsible for the recruitment in 1982 of KGB officer Valeriy Martynov, who was run jointly thereafter. Additionally, the FBI allowed CIA officers to participate in the debriefings of KGB officers who were under control of the Bureau. Examples are Boris Yuzhin and Sergey Motorin. From an earlier period there is of course the Polyakov case, recounted in detail in earlier chapters. Of course, less collegial inter-relationships also existed, as can be seen from the Kulak case and the sparring for credit in the wake of Ames' arrest.

Returning to the positive side, it is not generally known that the FBI let the CIA disseminate reporting from FBI cases to the U.S. intelligence community. Those with a jaundiced view of the FBI might emphasize that the FBI is not an intelligence organization and has never been able to produce polished reporting to pertinent U.S. customers so they had no choice. Those with a more charitable outlook would focus on the fact that the FBI was thereby losing credit for its operational successes, but that in so doing it was adding to the security of its sensitive assets. Although there were a few notable exceptions, in the main the CIA disseminated all of the counterintelligence reporting from both its own and the FBI's sources. With all the reporting lumped together this way, it was much easier to disguise how many sources existed and just what their access was.

On another level, there is a final but difficult story that must be told. Ames has acknowledged the impact of his crime on his own family, and has spoken candidly about his other direct victims including those who lost their lives or were imprisoned. However, there exists yet another group of innocents whose personal losses were enormous and whose futures were irrevocably changed because of Ames' treachery. Who were these people? They were, first of all, the spouses of the condemned, their parents, and their sons and daughters. As is only right, the CIA has made every effort to resettle the families in the United States when they have so wished. We have met some of the sons and daughters. While each victim's story is unique to his father's case, many shared common tragic elements. In several cases their mothers died prematurely and as one son has so poignantly described it, "After the arrest of my father, my mother never smiled again." Yet some of the younger generation have not only survived, but because of their courage and strength of character have succeeded in their new lives to an astonishing extent.

In the course of the post-arrest investigations, immediate family members were separately interrogated for extended periods at Lefortovo prison. KGB surveillance teams were assigned to each. The KGB conducted numerous and lengthy searches of their homes and apartments. Personal belongings were confiscated and never returned. Repeated requests for visitation were repeatedly denied or were put off for extended periods. Family members were not permitted to attend the trials and were denied any details of the case against their loved one. No pardons were granted. The families were unaware that sentencing had been carried out until a notice of death arrived in the mailbox. The men were buried in unmarked graves whose location is unknown. One family member was told to consider changing his last name and warned that his life would never be the same. "Some important people will never, ever trust you. Like father, like son, you know."

The Ames story is only a part of this book. In a broader sense, we feel that we were lucky in that we lived and worked in a simpler world. In the Cold War environment, there was only one main enemy who could harm us—the Soviet Union. Moral ambiguities as to the necessity of neutralizing the USSR to the best of our ability simply did not exist. The target was not amorphous, discrete, or widely scattered. We could concentrate our efforts on one country and one government. Alas, the colleagues who have come after us do not have that luxury.

HONOR ROLL

T HE FOLLOWING IS OUR HONOR ROLL of Agency employees either with whom we worked closely over the years or who had a significant impact on our careers. We would like to acknowledge publicly their commitment to the mission. Some rose to high-level positions; some did not; some were maligned; some left the Agency under a cloud; and some died before they could bring their careers to fruition. Some were more intellectually gifted than others; some had more common sense; some were better case officers; some were better analysts; some were better leaders; and some were better teachers. But they all had one thing in common. They were men and women of honor, courage, integrity, and talent. Their names are presented alphabetically. Unfortunately, a few retired under cover or are still active in the Agency. We have had to omit those names.

Pauline Brown	Walt Lomac
Dick Corbin	Len McCoy
Cleve Cram	John McMahon
Paul D	Ruth Olsen
John Winthrop Edwards	Dan Payne
Jim F	Ben Pepper
Joe F	Paul Redmond
Jack Fieldhouse	Sheri Riedl
Myrna Fitzgerald	Fran Smith
Frank Friberg	Dick Stolz
Burton Gerber	Ruth Ellen Thomas
Dottie Hanson	Don Vogel
Gus Hathaway	Freddie Woodruff
Dick Kovich	Diana Worthen

SELECTED CHRONOLOGY

26 May 1941—Aldrich Hazen "Rick" Ames born in River Falls, Wisconsin

18 Apr 1944—Robert Philip Hanssen born in Chicago, Illinois

Dec 1954—James Jesus Angleton becomes chief of CIA's newly created Counterintelligence Staff

Nov 1961—GRU officer Dmitriy Fedorovich Polyakov volunteers to the U.S. military in New York City. Later backs off, but is brought to recruitment by the FBI.

Dec 1961—KGB CI officer Anatoliy Mikhaylovich Golitsyn defects to CIA in Helsinki

Mar 1962—KGB S&T specialist Aleksey Isidorovich Kulak volunteers to the FBI in New York

Jun 1962—Ames joins the CIA, works part time while completing his college education at George Washington University

Jun 1962—KGB Second Chief Directorate (internal CI) officer Yuriy Ivanovich Nosenko, while on a trip to Bern, makes his first contact with the CIA

Early 1960s—GRU photo technician Nikolay Chernov volunteers to the FBI in New York. Shortly thereafter returns to the USSR. One further contact takes place in the early 1970s while he is on a short trip to the United States.

22 Nov 1963—assassination of U.S. president John F. Kennedy

Feb 1964—defection of Nosenko

Nov 1965—SB reports officer Len McCoy writes his paper defending Nosenko

May 1966—the East European (EE) Division and the Soviet Russian (SR) Division of the CIA's Directorate of Operations are combined into the Soviet Bloc (SB) Division

Dec 1967—after completing college, Ames applies for the CIA Officer Training Program and is accepted

Summer 1968—Rolfe Kingsley becomes chief, SB, replacing David Murphy

Sep 1969—Ames is assigned to Ankara

May/Jun 1970—Richard Stolz becomes chief, SB/CI

Jul 1970—Burton Gerber becomes chief, SB/CI/I. Cynthia Haussmann is his deputy.

Late spring 1971—David Blee becomes chief, SB, replacing Deputy Chief Stacy Hulse, who served for a short period as acting chief following the departure of Kingsley

Apr 1972—Ames leaves Ankara, is assigned to SE Division

1 May 1972—death of J. Edgar Hoover

1973—academic researcher Sergey Petrovich Fedorenko recruited by the FBI/CIA in New York City. Ames later becomes one of his handlers, traveling from CIA headquarters.

Jan 1973—Ames begins a year of full-time Russian language studies

Summer 1973—John Horton becomes chief of SB Division, changes the name to the Soviet and East European (SE) Division

Dec 1973—Ames finishes Russian language studies, returns to SE Division

1974—Soviet Ministry of Foreign Affairs official Aleksandr Dmitriyevich Ogorodnik recruited by CIA in Bogota. (Ames was the desk officer responsible for this case.)

1974—KGB officer Leonid Georgiyevich Poleshchuk recruited by CIA in Kathmandu

1974—KGB officer Oleg Antonovich Gordievsky recruited by the British SIS in Copenhagen

31 Dec 1974—Angleton fired from his position as chief of the CI staff by DCI William Colby. Replaced by George Kalaris.

1975—Poleshchuk returns to Moscow with a communications plan, which he never implements

Spring 1975—Stolz becomes chief, SE Division, replacing Horton

12 Jan 1976—Hanssen joins the FBI. After training, he is assigned to Indianapolis/Gary, where he serves on a white-collar crime squad.

Spring 1976—GRU officer Sergey Ivanovich Bokhan recruited by CIA in Athens

Aug 1976—Ames is assigned to New York City. He continues to handle Fedorenko; also is one of the handlers for Soviet UN ambassador Arkadiy Nikolayevich Shevchenko.

Aug 1976—after spending two separate tours in New York, Kulak returns to Moscow preparatory to retirement

1977—Fedorenko returns to the USSR

Jan 1977—Adolf Grigoryevich Tolkachev, a scientific worker in an R&D institution, volunteers to the CIA in Moscow. Regular communications not established until 1979.

Mar 1977—Admiral Stansfield Turner becomes CIA director, replacing George H. W. Bush

Jun 1977—CIA officer Gardner "Gus" Hathaway becomes COS, Moscow, replacing Robert Fulton

Summer 1977—Ogorodnik arrested in Moscow and commits suicide

1978—Shevchenko defects

1978—KGB officer Vladimir Mikhaylovich Piguzov volunteers to the CIA in Jakarta. The same year he returns to Moscow and we lose contact with him.

2 Aug 1978—Hanssen is transferred to New York, where he initially works on accounting matters in the criminal division

Late summer 1978—Bokhan returns to Moscow. He makes one "sign of life" signal, but otherwise we do not hear from him.

Mar 1979—Hanssen is transferred to New York's intelligence division to help establish the office's automated CI database. This was a classified database of information about foreign officials, including intelligence officers, assigned to the United States.

31 Oct 1979—KGB communications specialist Viktor Ivanovich Sheymov volunteers to the CIA in Warsaw

Nov 1979—Hanssen volunteers (anonymously) to the GRU

1979—KGB officer Boris Nikolayevich Yuzhin recruited by the FBI in San Francisco

1980—beginning of the GTTAW technical operation in Moscow. This operation involved CIA officers going down a manhole to tap into classified communications.

Jan 1980—Burton Gerber becomes COS, Moscow, replacing Gus Hathaway

Spring 1980—Sheymov is exfiltrated from the Soviet Union

May 1980—Polyakov summoned to Moscow from New Delhi, ostensibly to attend a conference. He does not return to India and we never have contact with him again.

20 Oct 1980—Harold James Nicholson joins the CIA

Nov 1980—KGB S&T officer Vladimir Ippolitovich Vetrov ("Farewell") makes his first overtures to a French businessman

Early 1980s—Kulak dies of natural causes

1981—IUSAC official Vladimir Viktorovich Potashov volunteers to the U.S. defense secretary in Washington. Subsequently handled by the CIA and FBI.

Jan 1981—Edward Lee Howard joins the CIA

12 Jan 1981—Hanssen is transferred to FBI headquarters. At first he is assigned to the budget unit of the intelligence division, which, per the affidavit issued at the time of his arrest, "had access to the full range of information concerning intelligence and counterintelligence activities involving FBI resources."

28 Jan 1981—William J. Casey becomes CIA director, replacing Turner

Spring 1981—Hanssen drops contact with the GRU

14 Jul 1981—John H. Stein becomes DDO, replacing Max Hugel

Sep 1981—Ames transfers from New York to Mexico City

1982—GRU officer Vladimir Mikhaylovich Vasilyev volunteers to the U.S. military in Budapest. Subsequently handled by the CIA.

1982—Yuzhin returns to Moscow

1982—Bokhan returns to Athens for a second tour and resumes contact with the CIA

Feb 1982—Howard begins to work in SE Division

Early 1982—KGB officer Valeriy Fedorovich Martynov recruited by an FBI officer in Washington, DC. Subsequently handled as a joint FBI/CIA asset.

Sep 1982—CIA officer Carl G becomes COS, Moscow, replacing Burton Gerber

1983—the GTABSORB technical operation is run by the CIA in the USSR. This operation involved the shipment of concealed sensors on the Trans-Siberian railroad.

Jan 1983—KGB officer Sergey Mikhaylovich Motorin recruited by the FBI in Washington, DC. The CIA apprised and disseminates his CI production.

Early 1983—Vetrov tried for espionage and executed

2 May 1983—Howard is forced out of the CIA

Aug 1983—Hanssen is transferred to the Soviet analytical unit, which supported FBI operations and investigations involving the Soviet intelligence services and provided analytical support to senior FBI management and the intelligence community. He also serves on the FBI's foreign CI technical committee, which was responsible for coordinating technical projects relating to FCI (foreign counterintelligence) operations.

Summer 1983—Rod Carlson becomes chief of SE/ORP

Sep 1983—Ames leaves Mexico City and is assigned to SE/ORP Soviet Branch at headquarters, where his job is to monitor worldwide CIA operations against the Soviet target from a CI viewpoint

18 Sep 1983—Earl Edwin Pitts joins the FBI

Late 1983—GRU officer Gennadiy Aleksandrovich Smetanin volunteers to the CIA in Lisbon

1984—Moscow City Directorate KGB officer Sergey Yuryevich Vorontsov volunteers to the CIA in Moscow

1984—USMC sergeant Clayton Lonetree arrives in Moscow to serve as a Marine guard at the U.S. embassy

1 Jul 1984—Clair George becomes DDO, replacing Stein

16 Jul 1984—Burton Gerber becomes chief of SE Division, replacing Dave Forden. Gerber's deputy is Ken Wesolik.

Sep 1984—Paul Redmond becomes chief of SE/USSR

ca. Sep 1984—Murat N becomes COS, Moscow, replacing Carl G

ca. Sep 1984—probably Howard's first substantive personal contact with the KGB

2 Oct 1984—FBI agent Richard Miller arrested for espionage on behalf of the Soviet Union. Tried three times, finally convicted in Oct 1990, but released in May 1994.

Nov 1984—former CIA contract employee Karel Koecher arrested for espionage on behalf of Czechoslovakia

Early Jan 1985—Motorin returns to Moscow

Jan 1985—Poleshchuk assigned to the KGB residency in Lagos, resumes contact with the CIA

Mar 1985—KGB illegals support officer Gennadiy Grigoryevich Varenik volunteers to the CIA in Bonn

Mar 1985—Konstantin Chernenko dies and Mikhail Gorbachev becomes CPSU general secretary

16 Apr 1985—Ames volunteers to the KGB in Washington, DC. Provides information and asks for fifty thousand dollars.

Spring 1985—Hathaway becomes chief of the CI staff, replacing David Blee who retires

15 May 1985—Ames has a face-to-face meeting with KGB line KR (counterintelligence) chief Viktor Ivanovich Cherkashin at the Soviet embassy in Washington

17 May 1985—Gordievsky is recalled from London. After arrival in Moscow, he is drugged and interrogated, but not arrested. In July SIS exfiltrates him from Moscow.

20 May 1985—Cherkashin makes a clandestine trip back to Moscow, which was not detected by the FBI at the time. He returns to Washington on 31 May.

24 May 1985—former Navy enlisted man John Walker arrested for espionage on behalf of the USSR. He had provided the KGB with cryptographic materials and other intelligence for approximately twenty years.

Late May 1985—in accordance with CIA advice, Bokhan defects to the United States. He had been recalled to Moscow to take care of a problem involving his son, and the CIA suspected that he was under suspicion.

9 Jun 1985—Tolkachev is arrested in Moscow, subsequently tried and executed

13 Jun 1985—probable date of the "big dump." Ames betrays numerous CIA/FBI assets to the KGB.

13 Jun 1985—Moscow Station CIA officer Paul Stombaugh arrested by the KGB trying to meet Tolkachev

Jul 1985—Milt Bearden assigned as deputy chief of SE, replacing Wesolik

19 Jul 1985—exfiltration of Gordievsky from Moscow

1 Aug 1985—defection of KGB CI officer Vitaliy Sergeyevich Yurchenko to the CIA in Rome. Immediately brought to the United States, where Ames becomes one of his debriefers.

Early Aug 1985—based on Yurchenko's reporting of Howard's cooperation with the KGB, we assume that the GTTAW technical operation in Moscow has been compromised. Howard was trained to service the device.

Early Aug 1985—Poleshchuk, on home leave in Moscow, is arrested when he attempts to pick up a dead drop put down by Moscow Station. Subsequently tried and executed.

Late Aug 1985—Smetanin is arrested while on home leave in Moscow. Subsequently tried and executed. His wife is given a five-year sentence for aiding him.

Sep 1985—Lonetree's first private meeting with Violetta Seina, local employee of the U.S. embassy in Moscow

19 Sep 1985—the FBI interviews Howard based on Yurchenko's reporting

21 Sep 1985—Howard evades FBI surveillance and flees the United States. Probably arrives in the USSR a day or so later.

23 Sep 1985—Hanssen is transferred to New York, where he serves as supervisor of a technical surveillance squad

Fall 1985—Redmond becomes chief of SE CI (formerly SE/ORP), replacing Carlson

2 Oct 1985—we learn that Poleshchuk has been arrested

4 Oct 1985—Hanssen volunteers (anonymously) to the KGB

4 Oct 1985—Smetanin does not show up for a post-home-leave meeting. We never have contact with him again.

8 Oct 1985—Ames begins full-time Italian language training

6 Nov 1985—Yurchenko re-defects. Martynov is one of his escorts back to Moscow.

ca. 7 Nov 1985—Martynov is arrested, subsequently tried and executed

9 Nov 1985—Varenik is lured to East Berlin, where he is arrested. Subsequently tried and executed.

25 Nov 1985—NSA employee Ronald Pelton is arrested for espionage for the USSR. The arrest was based on a lead from Yurchenko.

11 Dec 1985—last contact with Vasilyev, who dead-drops materials to us in Moscow

Mid-Dec 1985—we learn that Smetanin has been arrested

Late 1985—Casey first briefed on the compromised Soviet operations

Dec 1985–Jan 1986—we conduct probes in Nairobi and Moscow to see if the KGB is reading our communications. Results are negative.

Dec 1985–Feb 1986—sometime in this period, Lonetree has his first meeting with "Uncle Sasha" (KGB officer Aleksey Yefimov/Yegorov)

Jan 1986—SE Division begins stricter compartmentation of its cases. A super-encipherment system is instituted.

Mid-Jan 1986—Mister X "volunteers" to the CIA via an anonymous letter in Bonn. Claims to be a KGB officer. Tells us that we have a mole in Warrenton, and that Varenik was caught because his father found his spy gear. Sends a total of six letters, through summer 1986.

Mid-Jan 1986—Motorin arrested in Moscow, subsequently tried and executed

Late Jan 1986—KGB opens a GTABSORB shipment in the USSR

Early 1986—former DDO, and later IG, John Stein prepares a report for DCI Casey. Reportedly it is his conclusion that there is no connection between the compromised cases.

Feb 1986—Vorontsov arrested in Moscow, subsequently tried and executed

Mar 1986—Lonetree transferred to Vienna

10 Mar 1986—Moscow station officer Mike Sellers arrested by the KGB trying to meet Vorontsov

4 Apr 1986—last phone call from Motorin to his girlfriend in Washington. Calls give the impression that Motorin is not in any trouble.

16 Apr 1986—Robert M. Gates becomes DDCI, replacing John McMahon

Apr 1986—Ames finishes Italian language training, works temporarily on the Italian desk while preparing for his overseas assignment to Rome

2 May 1986—Ames is polygraphed. Clears out after only one session.

7 May 1986—Moscow Station officer Erik Sites is arrested by the KGB trying to meet with GTEASTBOUND, later identified as a dangle

May 1986—Bearden assigned to Afghanistan. Replaced as deputy chief, SE, by Bill Piekney.

Early Jun 1986—Vasilyev arrested in Moscow, subsequently tried and executed

1 Jul 1986—Potashov arrested in Moscow. Subsequently tried and sentenced to prison, but amnestied in 1992.

7 Jul 1986—Polyakov arrested in Moscow, subsequently tried and executed

21 Jul 1986—Ames leaves for Rome, where he heads the Hard Targets Branch

7 Aug 1986—Howard surfaces publicly in Moscow

23 Aug 1986—FBI arrests Soviet scientist and KGB officer Gennadiy Zakharov, as the result of a "sting"

30 Aug 1986—the Soviets arrest U.S. journalist Nicholas Daniloff in retaliation

17 Sep 1986—the United States expels twenty-five named Soviets; the Soviets retaliate by expelling five Americans. The numbers then escalate until mid-October.

30 Sep 1986—both Daniloff and Zakharov are released

Oct 1986—we learn of the arrests of Motorin and Martynov

27 Oct 1986—beginning of the CI/STF investigation in the CIA

4 Nov 1986—beginning of the ANLACE investigation in the FBI

14 Dec 1986—Lonetree begins confession to COS Vienna

23 Dec 1986—Yuzhin arrested in Moscow. Tried and convicted of espionage and sentenced to fifteen years, amnestied in 1992.

3 Jan 1987—Pitts is assigned to New York

29 Jan 1987—Casey resigns after suffering a stroke, dies 6 May

Feb 1987—Piguzov, with whom we had been out of contact since 1979, is arrested in Moscow. Subsequently tried and executed.

Mid-Mar 1987—U.S. Marine corporal Arnold Bracy reportedly confesses that he helped Lonetree let the KGB into the U.S. embassy in Moscow. Confession later retracted.

May 1987—beginning of the RACKETEER/BUCKLURE program, designed to tempt KGB officers into cooperating with the United States

26 May 1987—Judge William H. Webster becomes DCI, replacing Casey

12 Jun 1987—charges against Bracy dropped

Summer 1987—Redmond becomes deputy chief, SE Division, replacing Piekney

15 Jul 1987—Pitts volunteers to the KGB in New York

3 Aug 1987—Hanssen is transferred back to FBI headquarters, where he serves as a supervisory special agent in the intelligence division's Soviet analytical unit

13 Aug 1987—Lonetree found guilty by a military court-martial and sentenced to twenty-five years. He is freed in February 1996.

4 Jan 1988—Richard F. Stolz becomes DDO, replacing George

Apr 1988—the CI staff is reorganized and becomes the Counterintelligence Center. Hathaway now wears two hats: chief of the CI Center and a new position, ADDO for Counterintelligence

Jun 1988—beginning of the GTPROLOGUE dangle case in Moscow

28 Apr 1989—The CIA informs the FBI that State Department officer Felix Bloch may be working for the KGB

22 May 1989—Hanssen informs the KGB via dead drop about the Bloch case

22 Jun 1989—Bloch is warned by the KGB that he is under suspicion. An FBI technical operation picks up the message. The FBI immediately interviews Bloch, but he refuses to confess and is never arrested.

Jul 1989—Ames leaves Rome

Jul 1989—Bearden returns to SE Division, replacing Gerber

Aug 1989—Pitts is transferred to FBI headquarters in Washington

Sep 1989—after home leave, Ames becomes chief of the SE component that follows Soviet and East European cases in Europe

Early Nov 1989—Diana Worthen brings Ames' wealth to CIC's attention

Nov 1989—Fedorenko travels to the United States. The FBI and CIA (in the person of Ames) resume contact with him. Fedorenko, who was never arrested, eventually resettles in the West.

Dec 1989—Ames becomes chief of the Czech Branch

Mar 1990—Hathaway retires and is replaced by Hugh E. "Ted" Price

25 Jun 1990—Hanssen assigned to the FBI's inspection staff as an inspector's aide. Travels to FBI offices in the United States and abroad.

Aug 1990—Ames serves on the GS-12 promotion panel

Oct 1990—Ames assigned to CIC/AG, where he works on KGB-related matters

Jan 1991—Thomas A. Twetten becomes DDO, replacing Stolz

Early 1991—Price becomes ADDO, is replaced as chief, CIC by James Olson, who previously was deputy chief

May 1991—Redmond becomes deputy chief of CIC

Jun 1991—CIC/SIU set up

1 Jul 1991—Hanssen returns to the intelligence division at FBI headquarters and serves as a program manager in the Soviet operations section. He is in the unit responsible for countering efforts by the Soviets to acquire U.S. S&T intelligence.

31 Aug 1991—Webster resigns

Late Aug 1991—Ames returns to SE Division to serve on the "KGB working group"

6 Nov 1991—Robert M. Gates becomes DCI, replacing Webster

Dec 1991—the KGB First Chief Directorate becomes the SVR

Dec 1991—Ames transferred to the counternarcotics center, where he remains until his arrest

16 Dec 1991—Hanssen and the KGB/SVR have a dead-drop exchange. Hanssen then breaks off contact.

End Dec 1991—the Soviet and East European (SE) Division is renamed the Central Eurasian (CE) Division

Early 1990s—Chernov, who had not been in touch with the FBI since the early 1970s, is arrested in Moscow, tried, and sentenced to eight years. However, he is amnestied after six months.

1992—Nicholson assigned to Kuala Lumpur

6 Jan 1992—Hanssen serves as chief of the national security threat list (NSTL) unit. He focuses the unit's efforts on economic espionage.

18 Oct 1992—Pitts becomes dormant

5 Feb 1993—R. James Woolsey becomes DCI, replacing Gates

Jul 1993—Hanssen makes an unsuccessful approach to the GRU, again anonymously. The event results in a Russian protest to the USG, and the FBI opens an investigation.

Jan 1994—Price becomes DDO, replacing Twetten

21 Feb 1994—Ames arrested for espionage, with attendant publicity

Apr 1994—Hanssen is temporarily assigned to the Washington metropolitan field office

28 Apr 1994—Ames pleads guilty to espionage

ca. May 1994—Nicholson volunteers to the SVR in Kuala Lumpur. Leaves post shortly thereafter.

Jul 1994—Nicholson assigned to the CIA's training facility as an instructor

Dec 1994—Hanssen is reassigned to FBI headquarters, in the office of the assistant director for the national security division

Jan 1995—Pitts is moved to the behavioral sciences unit at Quantico

10 Jan 1995—Woolsey resigns

12 Feb 1995—Hanssen is detailed to serve as the FBI's senior representative to the Office of Foreign Missions at the State Department. He functions as the head of an interagency CI group, and as FBI's liaison to State's Bureau of Intelligence and Research

May 1995—Jack Downing becomes DDO, replacing Price

10 May 1995—John Deutch becomes DCI, replacing Woolsey

Aug 1995—FBI launches a sting, reactivating Pitts

28 Feb 1996—Lonetree released from prison

Jul 1996—Nicholson assigned to the counterterrorism center

16 Nov 1996—Nicholson arrested for espionage

15 Dec 1996—Deutch resigns

18 Dec 1996—Pitts arrested for espionage

1997—David Cohen becomes DDO, replacing Downing

28 Feb 1997—Pitts pleads guilty

5 Jun 1997—Nicholson sentenced to twenty-three years and seven months

ca. 22 Jun 1997—Pitts sentenced to twenty-seven years

11 Jul 1997—George Tenet becomes DCI, replacing Deutch

1999—James Pavitt becomes DDO, replacing Cohen

Jul 1999—Hanssen resumes contact with the SVR (formerly the KGB)

Nov 2000—Hanssen's last successful dead-drop exchange with the SVR

13 Jan 2001—Hanssen reassigned to FBI headquarters as part of the investigation of his activities

18 Feb 2001—Hanssen arrested

6 Jul 2001—Hanssen pleads guilty

10 May 2002—Hanssen sentenced to life imprisonment

12 July 2002—death of Howard in Moscow

NOTES

Chapter 1. Jeanne's Story

1. For one participant's account of events after Golitsyn arrived in the United States, see Fulton, *Reflections on a Life: From California to China*, 32–35.

2. For the story of Kisevalter's adventurous life, see Ashley, *CIA Spymaster*.

Chapter 3. Overview of SE Operations

1. Perhaps the best account of the Monster Plot is contained in Tom Mangold's *Cold Warrior: James Jesus Angleton: The CIA's Master Spy Hunter*. *Molehunt: The Secret Search for Traitors That Shattered the CIA* by David Wise is also worth reading. For extensive biographical information on Angleton himself, see Winks, *Cloak and Gown: Scholars in the Secret War, 1939–1961*.

2. The Yurchenko case and his connection with Ames is discussed separately in Chapter 17.

3. For the Cherepanov story, see, among others, Andrew and Mitrokhin, *The Sword and the Shield: The Mitrokhin Archive and the Secret History of the KGB*, 185, and Mangold, *Cold Warrior*, 213, 253.

Chapter 4. The Polyakov Case—The Beginnings

1. No book has yet been written about the Polyakov case, although he richly deserves one. The best summary is perhaps Elaine Shannon's "Death of the Perfect Spy," which appeared in *Time* on 8 August 1994.

2. A different version of Polyakov's approach appears in David Wise's book *Nightmover: How Aldrich Ames Sold the CIA to the KGB for $4.6 Million*. In this version, related to Wise by John Mabey, Polyakov asked

General O'Neil if he could be put in touch with the *CIA representative* in New York, not with a *member of American intelligence* as the FBI later reported to the CIA. Accordingly, Mabey posed as a CIA officer, a fact also not mentioned in the FBI memoranda.

Chapter 5. The Polyakov Case—The Middle

1. The Russian rank translates literally as major general, but it is the equivalent of a brigadier general, that is, a one-star general in the West.

Chapter 6. The Polyakov Case—The End

1. The empty bottle of Three Stars cognac was given in the late 1990s to H. Keith Melton, author and world-renowned expert on spy equipment, for display in his private collection housed in the Spy Museum in Boca Raton, Florida.

Chapter 7. Early Major Cases

1. Ranelagh, *The Agency: The Rise and Fall of the CIA*, 638.

2. Ibid.

3. Turner, *Secrecy and Democracy: The CIA in Transition*, 141–142.

4. Ibid., 51–52.

5. Epstein, *Legend: The Secret World of Lee Harvey Oswald*, 20, 263, 273.

6. Tom Mangold in *Cold Warrior*, 340–344, details some of the most important of these GRU agents and Kalaris' efforts to rectify the damage done to Western governments by Angleton's deliberate inaction.

7. For the record, Poleshchuk is the correct U.S. Board of Geographic Names transliteration of his surname. Earley has it as Poleschuk in *Confessions of a Spy: The Real Story of Aldrich Ames*, and Bearden has it as Polyshchuk in *The Main Enemy: The Inside Story of the CIA's Final Showdown with the KGB*.

8. Krasilnikov, *Prizraki s Ulitsy Chaykovskogo*, 127–130 of the English translation.

9. Cherkashin, *Spy Handler: Memoir of a KGB Officer*, 191–192. Ames, of course, freely admits that he betrayed Poleshchuk to the KGB.

10. One of Barnett's handlers was former KGB general Oleg Kalugin, who tells the story in his book. See Kalugin, *The First Directorate: My 32 Years in Intelligence and Espionage Against the West*, 159–162.

11. The following account draws heavily on an article by Barry Royden, entitled "Tolkachev, a Worthy Successor to Penkovsky," which appeared in the CIA publication *Studies in Intelligence* in 2003. Those who wish to delve more deeply should consult this narrative, which is based on still-classified file holdings.

12. For details on Fulton's tour in Moscow, including a description of his role in the Tolkachev case, see Fulton, *Reflections on a Life*, 59–82.

13. For Sheymov's own account of his relationship with the CIA, see Sheymov, *Tower of Secrets: A Real Life Spy Thriller*.

14. Ibid., 381. Sheymov was right on both counts. In this instance, as well as several others, he demonstrated that he and his family were partners in the ultimate success of the operation.

Chapter 8. Later Major Cases

1. The most authoritative source on this case is *Carnets intimes de la DST: 30 ans au coeur du contre-espionnage francais* (Intimate notebooks of the DST: Thirty years at the heart of French counter-espionage). This book is based on interviews with Raymond Nart, former DST deputy chief, who was responsible for running the Farewell operation. Descriptions of the case in English include Gordon Brook-Shepherd's *The Storm Birds: Soviet Post-War Defectors*, 253–265, and Gus Weiss' "The Farewell Dossier," which appeared in *Studies in Intelligence* in 1996.

2. One book, however, treats this case in detail. This is *Traitors Among Us: Inside the Spy Catcher's World* by Stuart A. Herrington, which devotes more than half of its pages to Conrad and his ring.

3. This is not the way Milt Bearden tells the story. See page 107 of *The Main Enemy*. Nevertheless, early in the investigation of what had gone wrong in 1985 Jeanne read Smetanin's file with care. She believes that her memory of the event is correct.

4. Cherkashin, *Spy Handler*, 218–219.

5. Ibid., 219–224.

6. Ibid., 223.

7. Ibid., 210.

Chapter 9. Things Begin to Go Wrong

1. For Howard's own highly unbelievable account of his relationship with the KGB, see *Safe House: The Compelling Memoirs of the Only CIA Spy to Seek Asylum in Russia*. David Wise has a more balanced version in *The Spy Who Got Away: The Inside Story of Edward Lee Howard, the CIA Agent Who Betrayed His Country's Secrets and Escaped to Moscow*.

2. For an insider's account of this operation, see Olson, *Fair Play: The Moral Dilemmas of Spying*, 9–11.

3. For a detailed description of the Walker spy ring, see Earley, *Family of Spies: Inside the John Walker Spy Ring*.

Chapter 10. First Attempts

1. This case is described in Oleg Kalugin's book *The First Directorate*. See pages 46–47.

2. Two books have been written about this case. The broader and more objective one is Rodney Barker's *Dancing with the Devil*; the other is *The Court-Martial of Clayton Lonetree* by Lake Headley, a member of Lonetree's defense team.

Chapter 11. CIC Formation

1. Oddly, Milt Bearden, who is central to this fiasco and must be held responsible for it, describes it as having begun in May 1987. See Bearden, *The Main Enemy*, 297.

Chapter 12. Beginning of the Focus on Ames

1. As it turned out, this last theory was correct. The Czechs did indeed share Koecher's reporting with the KGB. See Kalugin, *The First Directorate*, 186–188. Kalugin does not provide names, but it is clear that Koecher is the person he is talking about.

Chapter 13. The Investigation Gets New Life

1. The review appeared in 2004 in *Studies in Intelligence*, published by the CIA's Center for the Study of Intelligence.

Chapter 15. The FBI Takes Over

1. Maas, *Killer Spy: The Inside Story of the FBI's Pursuit and Capture of Aldrich Ames, America's Deadliest Spy*, 129.

Chapter 16. Reactions to the Arrest of Ames

1. See I. C. Smith, *Inside: A Top G-Man Exposes Spies, Lies, and Bureaucratic Bungling Inside the FBI*, 131.

2. See HPSCI, *Report of Investigation: The Aldrich Ames Espionage Case*, and SSCI, *An Assessment of the Aldrich H. Ames Espionage Case and Its Implications for U.S. Intelligence.*

3. For an overview, see the unclassified abstract *The Aldrich H. Ames Case: An Assessment of CIA's Role in Identifying Ames as an Intelligence Penetration of the Agency.*

4. In his recent book, Cherkashin says that he met Ames on three separate occasions. See *Spy Handler*, 24.

5. Pages 151–157 of Maas' *Killer Spy* contain information from the FBI's technical coverage of the Ames residence and telephones from which the special agents drew their conclusions, and pages 222–223 outline what was found in the post-arrest search of the residence. She had sixty purses, some of them still in wrapping paper, more than five hundred pairs of shoes, dozens of ensembles, some of them still with the price tags attached, and one hundred and sixty-five pairs of unopened panty hose.

Chapter 17. Ames the Person, Ames the Spy

1. Clarridge, *A Spy For All Seasons: My Life in the CIA*, 121.

2. See Shevchenko's autobiography, *Breaking with Moscow: The Highest Ranking Soviet Official Ever to Defect.*

3. Cherkashin, *Spy Handler.*

4. Ibid., 179.

SELECTED BIBLIOGRAPHY

Adams, James. *Sellout: Aldrich Ames and the Corruption of the CIA*. New York: Penguin Books, 1995.

Andrew, Christopher, and Oleg Gordievsky. *KGB: The Inside Story of Its Foreign Operations from Lenin to Gorbachev*. New York: HarperPerennial, 1991.

Andrew, Christopher, and Vasili Mitrokhin. *The Sword and the Shield: The Mitrokhin Archive and the Secret History of the KGB*. New York: Basic Books, 1999.

Ashley, Clarence. *CIA Spymaster*. Foreword by Leonard McCoy. Gretna, LA: Pelican Publishing Company, 2004.

Barker, Rodney. *Dancing With the Devil: Sex, Espionage and the US Marines— The Clayton Lonetree Story*. New York: Simon and Schuster, 1996.

Barron, John. *Breaking the Ring: The Bizarre Case of the Walker Family Spy Ring*. Boston: Houghton Mifflin, 1987.

———. *KGB: The Secret Work of Soviet Secret Agents*. New York: Reader's Digest Press, 1974.

Bearden, Milt, and James Risen. *The Main Enemy: The Inside Story of the CIA's Final Showdown with the KGB*. New York: Random House, 2003.

Brook-Shepherd, Gordon. *The Storm Birds: Soviet Post-War Defectors*. London: Weidenfeld and Nicolson, 1988.

Cherkashin, Victor. *Spy Handler: Memoir of a KGB Officer*. New York: Basic Books, 2005.

Clarridge, Duane. *A Spy For All Seasons: My Life in the CIA*. New York: Scribner, 1997.

Earley, Pete. *Confessions of a Spy: The Real Story of Aldrich Ames*. New York: G. P. Putnam's Sons, 1997.

———. *Family of Spies: Inside the John Walker Spy Ring*. New York: Bantam Books, 1988.

Epstein, Edward Jay. *Legend: The Secret World of Lee Harvey Oswald*. New York: Reader's Digest Press, 1978.

Fulton, Bob. *Reflections on a Life: From California to China*. Bloomington, IN: AuthorHouse, 2008.

Galayko, Vladimir. "Major General Dmitriy Polyakov." *Novoye Russkoye Slovo* (New Russian Word) (10 November 1998).

Gates, Robert M. *From the Shadows: The Ultimate Insider's Story of Five Presidents and How They Won the Cold War*. New York: Simon and Schuster, 1996.

Havill, Adrian. *The Spy Who Stayed Out in the Cold: The Secret Life of FBI Double Agent Robert Hanssen*. New York: St. Martin's Press, 2001.

Headley, Lake, and William Hoffman. *The Court-Martial of Clayton Lonetree*. Introduction by William Kunstler. New York: Henry Holt and Company, 1989.

Herrington, Stuart A. *Traitors Among Us: Inside the Spy Catcher's World*. Novato, CA: Presidio, 1999.

Howard, Edward Lee. *Safe House: The Compelling Memoirs of the Only CIA Spy to Seek Asylum in Russia*. Bethesda, MD: National Press Books (An Enigma Book), 1995.

Kalugin, Oleg. *The First Directorate: My 32 Years in Intelligence and Espionage Against the West*. With Fen Montaigne. New York: St. Martin's Press, 1994.

Kessler, Ronald. *Escape from the CIA: How the CIA Won and Lost the Most Important KGB Spy Ever to Defect to the U.S.* New York: Pocket Books, 1991.

———. *Moscow Station: How the KGB Penetrated the American Embassy*. New York: Charles Scribner's Sons, 1989.

Krasilnikov, Rem Sergeyevich. *Prizraki s Ulitsy Chaykovskogo: Shpionskyye Aktsii TsRU SShA Sovetskom Soyuze Rossiyskoy Federatsii 1979–1992.* (The Spies from Tchaikovsky Street: Espionage Actions of the CIA in the Soviet Union and Russian Federation 1979–1992.) Moscow: Geya Iterum, 1999. U.S. Defense Intelligence Agency translation, 2003.

Maas, Peter. *Killer Spy: The Inside Story of the FBI's Pursuit and Capture of Aldrich Ames, America's Deadliest Spy.* New York: Warner Books, 1995.

Mangold, Tom. *Cold Warrior: James Jesus Angleton: The CIA's Master Spy Hunter.* New York: Simon and Schuster, 1991.

Martin, David C. *Wilderness of Mirrors.* New York: Harper & Row, 1980.

Merlen, Eric, and Frederic Ploquin. *Carnets intimes de la DST: 30 ans au coeur de contre-espionnage francais.* (Intimate notebooks of the DST: Thirty years at the heart of French counter-espionage). Paris: Librairie Artheme Fayard, 2003.

Olson, James M. *Fair Play: The Moral Dilemmas of Spying.* Washington, D.C.: Potomac Books, 2006.

Ranelagh, John. *The Agency: The Rise and Fall of the CIA.* New York: Simon and Schuster, 1986.

Redmond, Paul J. Book review of *The Sword and the Shield: The Mitrokhin Archive and the Secret History of the KGB,* by Christopher Andrew and Vasili Mitrokhin. *Studies in Intelligence* 11 (Fall–Winter 2001).

Royden, Barry G. "Tolkachev, a Worthy Successor to Penkovsky." *Studies in Intelligence* 47, no. 3 (2003).

Schiller, Lawrence. *Into the Mirror: The Life of Master Spy Robert P. Hanssen.* New York: HarperCollins, 2002.

Shannon, Elaine. "Death of the Perfect Spy." *Time* 144, no. 6 (8 August 1994): 32–34.

Shannon, Elaine, and Ann Blackman. *The Spy Next Door: The Extraordinary Secret Life of Robert Philip Hanssen, the Most Damaging FBI Agent in U.S. History.* Boston: Little, Brown and Company, 2002.

Shevchenko, Arkady N. *Breaking with Moscow: The Highest Ranking Soviet Official Ever to Defect.* New York: Alfred A. Knopf, 1985.

Sheymov, Victor. *Tower of Secrets: A Real Life Spy Thriller.* Annapolis, MD: Naval Institute Press, 1993.

Shvets, Yuriy B. *Washington Station: My Life as a KGB Spy in America.* New York: Simon and Schuster, 1994.

Smith, I. C. *Inside: A Top G-Man Exposes Spies, Lies, and Bureaucratic Bungling Inside the FBI.* Nashville, TN: Nelson Current, 2004.

Sterling, Claire. *The Terror Network: The Secret War of International Terrorism.* New York: Holt, Rinehart and Winston, 1981.

Turner, Stansfield. *Secrecy and Democracy: The CIA in Transition.* Boston: Houghton Mifflin, 1985.

U.S. Central Intelligence Agency. *Statement of the Director of Central Intelligence on the Clandestine Services and the Damage Caused by Aldrich Ames,* 7 December 1995.

———. *Statement of Frederick P. Hitz, Inspector General, Central Intelligence Agency, Before the Select Committee on Intelligence, United States Senate,* 27 November 1995.

U.S. Central Intelligence Agency. Office of the Inspector General. *Unclassified Abstract of the CIA Inspector General's Report on the Aldrich H. Ames Case.* Washington, D.C.: Central Intelligence Agency, 21 October 1994.

U.S. Department of Justice. *A Review of FBI Security Programs: Commission for Review of FBI Security Programs.* March 2002.

U.S. Department of Justice. Federal Bureau of Investigation. *Special Agent, Earl Edwin Pitts, Arrested for Espionage,* 18 December 1996.

U.S. Department of Justice. Office of the Inspector General. *A Review of the FBI's Performance in Deterring, Detecting, and Investigating the Espionage Activities of Robert Philip Hanssen.* Washington, D.C., 14 August 2003.

———. *A Review of the FBI's Performance in Uncovering the Espionage Activities of Aldrich Hazen Ames: Unclassified Executive Summary.* Washington, D.C., 21 April 1997.

U.S. District Court, Eastern District of Virginia. *United States of America v. Aldrich Hazen Ames and Maria Del Rosario Casas Ames: Criminal Complaint, Warrant and Affidavit.* Alexandria, VA, 1 February 1994.

———. *United States of America v. Robert Philip Hanssen: Affidavit in Support of Criminal Complaint, Arrest Warrant and Search Warrants.* Alexandria, VA, February 2001.

U.S. Federal Bureau of Investigation. *Robert Philip Hanssen—Alleged KGB "Mole" Within the FBI.* Laguna Hills, CA: Aegean Park Press, 2001.

U.S. Federal Bureau of Investigation and U.S. Central Intelligence Agency. *United States v. Harold J. Nicholson*. 18 November 1996.

U.S. House of Representatives. Permanent Select Committee on Intelligence. *Report of Investigation: The Aldrich Ames Espionage Case.* Washington, D.C.: U.S. Government Printing Office, 30 November 1994.

U.S. Senate. Select Committee on Intelligence. *An Assessment of the Aldrich H. Ames Espionage Case and Its Implications for U.S. Intelligence: A Report of the U.S. Senate Select Committee on Intelligence.* Washington, D.C.: U.S. Government Printing Office, 1 November 1994.

Vertefeuille, Jeanne. "Myths and Misconceptions: Jeanne Vertefeuille's Address at CIRA Luncheon, 5 May 97." *CIRA Newsletter* 22, no. 2 (Summer 1997): 3–5.

Vise, David A. *The Bureau and the Mole: The Unmasking of Robert Philip Hanssen, the Most Dangerous Double Agent in FBI History.* New York: Atlantic Monthly Press, 2002.

Wallace, Robert, and H. Keith Melton. *Spycraft: The Secret History of the CIA's Spytechs from Communism to Al-Qaeda.* New York: Dutton, 2008.

Weiner, Tim, David Johnston, and Neil A. Lewis. *Betrayal: The Story of Aldrich Ames, an American Spy.* New York: Random House, 1995.

Weiss, Gus W. "The Farewell Dossier." *Studies in Intelligence* 39, no. 5 (1996).

Winks, Robin W. *Cloak and Gown: Scholars in the Secret War, 1939–1961.* New Haven, CT: Yale University Press, 1996.

Wise, David. *Molehunt: The Secret Search for Traitors That Shattered the CIA.* New York: Random House, 1992.

———. *Nightmover: How Aldrich Ames Sold the CIA to the KGB for $4.6 Million.* New York: HarperCollins, 1995.

———. *Spy: The Inside Story of How the FBI's Robert Hanssen Betrayed America.* New York: Random House, 2002.

———. *The Spy Who Got Away: The Inside Story of Edward Lee Howard, the CIA Agent Who Betrayed His Country's Secrets and Escaped to Moscow.* New York: Random House, 1988.

———. "The Spy Who Sold the Farm." *GQ* (March 1998): 294–301.

———. "Our Man in Moscow." *George* (October 1997): 118–121.

Wolton, Thierry. *Le KGB en France.* Paris: Bernard Grasset, 1986.

Woodward, Bob. *Veil: The Secret Wars of the CIA 1981–1987.* New York: Simon and Schuster, 1987.

INDEX

ABOUT THE AUTHORS

Sandra Grimes is a twenty-six-year veteran of the CIA's clandestine service who spent the majority of her career working against the former Soviet Union and Eastern Europe. Born in New York State, she spent her childhood and formative years in Colorado. She joined the CIA in July 1967, shortly after graduating from the University of Washington with a degree in Russian. A mother of two daughters and grandmother of four, she lives in Great Falls, Virginia, with her husband of forty-three years.

Jeanne Vertefeuille was a CIA officer from 1954 to 1992, specializing in the Soviet target during the Cold War, particularly in the counterintelligence area. Born in Connecticut, she holds a BA in history from the University of Connecticut and an MA from George Mason University. A veteran of five overseas tours, she led the small task force that resulted in the 1994 arrest of Soviet mole Aldrich Ames. She has served on contract as an analyst since 1993.

CPSIA information can be obtained
at www.ICGtesting.com
Printed in the USA
FSOW01n1344270218
45091FS